A Research Agenda for East Asian Social Policy

Elgar Research Agendas outline the future of research in a given area. Leading scholars are given the space to explore their subject in provocative ways, and map out the potential directions of travel. They are relevant but also visionary.

Forward-looking and innovative, Elgar Research Agendas are an essential resource for PhD students, scholars and anybody who wants to be at the forefront of research.

Titles in the series include:

A Research Agenda for East Asian Social Policy

Edited by

MISA IZUHARA

Professor of Social Policy, University of Bristol, UK

Elgar Research Agendas

Edward Elgar
PUBLISHING

Cheltenham, UK • Northampton, MA, USA

Published by
Edward Elgar Publishing Limited
The Lypiatts
15 Lansdown Road
Cheltenham
Glos GL50 2JA
UK

Edward Elgar Publishing, Inc.
William Pratt House
9 Dewey Court
Northampton
Massachusetts 01060
USA

A catalogue record for this book
is available from the British Library

Library of Congress Control Number: 2023931365

This book is available electronically in the **Elgar**online
Sociology, Social Policy and Education subject collection
http://dx.doi.org/10.4337/9781800376113

ISBN 978 1 80037 610 6 (cased)
ISBN 978 1 80037 611 3 (eBook)

Printed and bound in Great Britain by
TJ Books Limited, Padstow, Cornwall

Contents

Figures

Tables

Contributors

Aya Abe is Professor of Social Policy at the Tokyo Metropolitan University, Japan. She is also Director of the Centre for Research on Child and Adolescent Poverty at the University. She has participated in and led many research projects on poverty and inequality in Japan and has published numerous books and articles on poverty issues, especially child poverty in Japan. Her 2008 book entitled *Child Poverty: Re-examining Japan's Inequality* is widely acclaimed as be the first book in Japan which focuses on child poverty in the country. She serves on numerous committees of national and local government on poverty and social assistance issues.

Young Jun Choi is Professor at the Department of Public Administration and Director of the Institute for Welfare State Research, Yonsei University, South Korea. He has advised governmental ministries and committees including the Presidential Committee on Policy Planning in South Korea. He also serves as Chair of the East Asian Social Policy Research Network (2021–2023). His research interests include ageing and public policy, social investment policy, innovation and social policy and East Asian welfare states. He was co-editor of *Welfare Reform and Social Investment Policy in Europe and East Asia* (2021). He has extensively published his studies in international journals including the *Journal of European Social Policy, Policy and Society, Policy and Politics, Ageing and Society, International Journal of Social Welfare* and *Risk Analysis*.

Ye Eun Ha is a DPhil student in social policy at the University of Oxford, UK. Her research focuses on policy ideas and the development of universal health coverage in Indonesia. She obtained a master's in public policy at Seoul National University and worked as an assistant researcher at the Global Development Institute for Public Affairs. She is co-author of 'Policy analysis of Korea's development cooperation with Sub-Saharan Africa: A focus on fragile states' (*International Development Planning Review*, 2022).

Ijin Hong is Associate Professor at the School of Government, Sun Yat-sen University, Guangzhou, China. She got her MA in sociology and political institutions at La Sapienza University in Rome, Italy, and completed her PhD at the

Social Welfare Department in Yonsei University in Seoul, South Korea. Her research covers welfare state development, social care markets, public opinion and labour market policies with a focus on East Asia (South Korea and China in particular) and Southern Europe. Among her recent publications, she guest edited a special issue for *Social Policy and Administration* about welfare development in China with Kinglun Ngok (2022); she also contributed chapters to *The World Politics of Social Investment* (2022) and *De Gruyter Handbook of the Contemporary Welfare States* (2022). Since 2023, she is a co-editor of the *Journal of International and Comparative Social Policy*.

Misa Izuhara is Professor of Social Policy at the School for Policy Studies, University of Bristol, UK. She has been undertaking research extensively, both nationally and internationally, in the areas of housing and social change, ageing and intergenerational relations, and comparative policy analysis between the East and West as well as within East Asia. Her current research includes 'Collaborative Housing Communities and Innovative Care Practice' funded by the National Institute for Health and Care Research. She is co-author of *Housing in the Post-Growth Society* (2018) and editor of *The Handbook on East Asian Social Policy* (2013). Misa is also a former co-editor of the *Journal of Social Policy*. She is Fellow of the Academy of Social Sciences.

Stefan Kühner is Associate Professor in the Department of Sociology and Social Policy, Lingnan University, Hong Kong. His academic interests centre on comparative and international political economy, emphasising the policies and politics of welfare state change from a historical perspective. In Hong Kong, he recently examined the social gradient in multi-dimensional child well-being, the experiences of young people with changing school-to-work transitions, the effect of working family support on gendered labour market outcomes and the stigma attached to welfare benefit receipt among older adults. He is co-editor of the book series, Research in Comparative and Global Social Policy, launched together with Policy Press/Bristol University Press. He is also co-editor of the *Journal of International and Comparative Social Policy*. His research was published in the *Journal of Social Policy*, *European Journal of Social Policy*, *Policy and Society*, *Social Policy and Administration* and *Social Policy and Society*, among others.

Tommy Chung Yin Kwan is Lecturer with the Department of Asian and Policy Studies at the Education University of Hong Kong. He is a PhD candidate at SOAS, University of London, focusing on the relationship between political parties and social movements in Taiwan. He also received his MSc in politics of China from SOAS. Tommy is also a writer and broadcasting presenter in Hong Kong. He comments on Hong Kong and Taiwan's political and cultural scenes. His books *Learnings from Solitude* and *Old World in a New Day* are anthologies of essays.

Huck-Ju Kwon is Professor at the Graduate School of Public Administration and the Global Development Institute for Public Affairs, Seoul National University, South Korea. He was a Fulbright-Democracy Senior Visiting Fellow of the Ash Center, Harvard Kennedy School (2021–2022). He served as co-editor for *Global Social Policy*. His publications include *International Development Cooperation of Japan and South Korea* (2021), *The Korean Government and Public Policy in a Development Nexus* (2017), 'Policy analysis of Korea's development cooperation with sub-Saharan Africa: a focus on fragile states' (*International Development Planning Review*, 2022).

Seongyeon Park is a research assistant at the Global Development Institute for Public Affairs, pursuing a master's programme at the Graduate School of Public Administration, Seoul National University, South Korea. After three years of fieldwork as a project manager in African countries, she studies social policy and international development cooperation.

Shih-Jiunn Shi is Professor of Social Policy in the Graduate Institute of National Development, National Taiwan University, Taiwan. His fields of research include comparative social policy with a particular regional focus on mainland China and Taiwan and East Asian social policy. He has conducted research projects on the development of social policy in Greater China; and is collaborating with other scholars in the research on social investment reforms in East Asian social policy. Specific topics covered include population ageing and old-age security, federalism and welfare states, ideas and social policy and social policy response to the pandemic crisis. He has published research work in numerous journals, including the *Journal of Social Policy, Social Policy and Administration, Policy and Politics, Policy and Society, International Journal of Social Welfare, Ageing and Society* and *Public Management Review*.

Naoko Soma is Professor at International Graduate School of Social Sciences, Yokohama National University, Japan. Her research interests are comparative care and family policy in East Asia, multi-responsibilities of social care and statistics of social care and caring democracy. She has published papers and books in Japanese, English and Korean on childcare, double care (multi-responsibilities of care) and family policy in Japan and South Korea. She co-authored *Gendered Pandemic In Japan: Childcare, Parents' Employment, and Housework during Covid-19 through Survey in Yokohama* (2022) and *Hitori de Yaranai Ikuji Kaigo no Daburu Kea* (Don't Manage It Alone: Dual Care of Childcare and Elderly Care) (2020).

Junko Yamashita is Senior Lecturer at the School of Sociology, Politics and International Studies, University of Bristol, UK. She is known for her work on social and policy analysis of welfare, care, families, intergenerational relations, inequalities and gender with a specific focus on care and care work. Yamashita co-edited *The Routledge Handbook of East Asian Gender Studies* (2020) and co-authored *Hitori de Yaranai Ikuji Kaigo no Daburu Kea* (Don't Manage It Alone: Dual Care of Childcare and Elderly Care) (2020). Her recent research projects include an international collaborative research project on 'Dual Responsibility of Care in East Asia'. She also co-led 'Experiments in Collective Care', collaborating with a local artist, bringing together art, archival research and public engagement through a public exhibition on collective care.

Kyungchul Yang is a researcher at Korea Institute of Public Administration. He studied public administration at Seoul National University and Kyunghee University, South Korea.

Chung-Yang Yeh is Associate Professor in Department of Sociology, Soochow University, Taipei, Taiwan. He received his PhD from the Division of Sociology, Social Policy and Criminology at the University of Southampton, UK. His main research interests include comparative East Asian welfare states, welfare attitudes and pension policy. He published some journal articles and books chapters focusing on pension policies, social investment policies and in-work poverty in East Asia.

Bongjo Yi is a PhD graduate in policy studies at the University of Bristol, UK. He has conducted research projects on housing poverty, including homelessness, housing deprivations and generation-related housing inequality. His current research interests are urban housing issues associated with the financialisation and commodification of housing. Bongjo focuses on housing studies in relation to East Asian contexts as well as global experiences.

Sodam Yi is a graduate student at the Graduate School of Public Administration and an assistant researcher at the Global Development Institute for Public Affairs, Seoul National University, South Korea.

Wenjing Zhang is Research Fellow at the Centre for Health Services Studies, University of Kent, UK. Her research interests focus on long-term care, ageing and international social policy. She has worked on a diverse range of policy- and practice-oriented research projects related to long-term care. Straddling the fields of social gerontology and public policy implementation, Wenjing especially focuses to adapt and extend concepts developed in a Western context to the study of East Asian policy implementation.

1 Introduction to the *Research Agenda for East Asian Social Policy*

Misa Izuhara

East Asian social policy is at a critical juncture. Since the turn of the millennium, significant social, economic, political and technological transformations have brought policy issues to prominence in East Asian societies as part of the globalisation process. Both internal and external pressures, which constantly demand policy responses, are part of the driving forces shifting the contemporary research agenda in the respective fields of social policy in East Asia.

The impact of globalisation and post-industrialisation are external factors, which have raised questions about the sustainability of previous patterns of welfare provision based on stable families and labour market participation. A series of regional and global financial crises exacerbated the dualism that existed in the labour markets. The rise of labour market flexibility and the casualisation of the workforce are the products of post-industrialisation, generating new social risks not previously covered for individuals and households in the standard industrial life-course (see Bonoli, 2006; Taylor-Gooby, 2004). While some East Asian societies are still addressing old social risks of retirement pensions, healthcare and employment protection, emerging social risks from changing families and work patterns have a profound impact on new risk groups such as children, young adults, women and low-skilled workers. Child poverty is on the rise with the increase in low-income households, while a significant delay has been observed in youth transitions to financial and residential independence. Extending working life beyond the nominal retirement age has become a trend not only for the pursuit of active ageing but also out of financial necessity.

Shared internal challenges in the region constitute demographic change, including the phenomenal speed of societal ageing, ultra-low fertility and changing patterns of household formation and their functions while traditional family values remain relatively strong (see Sung and Pascall, 2014). This is also in line with the global trend among developed nations, but the phenomenal speed of demographic change has produced distinctive policy challenges in East Asia. Although old age is no longer a synonym of dependency and decline, 'who will provide and finance long-term care for older people' has become an even more pressing question in super-aged societies like Japan where 28.9 per cent of its population has already reached age 65 and older (Cabinet Office, Japan, 2022).

Culture and traditional family-centred values have provided a foundation for the development of post-war social policy in East Asia, especially in the fields of social protection and care provision. Women's rights and agency are increasingly debated in this context of familial welfare approaches. At the same time, the institution of marriage is no longer universal in the region. A substantial increase in late/no marriage and late singlehood have been impacting on the region's fertility rates since marriage and childbirth are still strongly connected; and this will also have long-term implications for future demographic change in the region (Esteve et al., 2020; Jones, 2019). Ultra-low fertility is the product of the decline of marriage and is intertwined with women's increased agency and social participation. The urgent need to address the fertility crisis by various work–life reconciliation policies has so far met with little success. In China, where the state-led family planning has shifted from controlling fertility under the 'One-Child Policy' in the 1980s to encouraging women of reproductive age to have two to three children, it may take a generation to reverse women's attitudes and behaviours in the current competitive economic and education context. This shift challenges the 'family and welfare' nexus drawing family obligations and responsibilities to care. Policy analysis in relation to demographic change is indeed one of the major research agendas as the distinctiveness of East Asian welfare systems underpinned by strong families diminishes.

Beyond the East Asian welfare model/s

This volume takes a regional, international and comparative approach in social policy analysis. There exists a diverse range of societies in East Asia in terms of size, stages of socio-economic development, political systems, types of institutions, history and culture, which make the comparative analysis dynamic but complex (Izuhara and Zhang, 2022). The region includes both the small city states such as Singapore and Hong Kong Special Administrative Region and the world's most populated country, the People's Republic of China. There are complex relationships among the 'Chinese societies', including the 'one-country, two systems' since the transfer of sovereignty over Hong Kong from the United Kingdom to China in 1997. The political economy of the nations in the region differs from the increasingly democratised capitalism of Japan, South Korea and Taiwan to 'soft-authoritarian' Singapore, to the transitional economy of China, ambiguously known as 'market socialism' or 'state capitalism'. For policy analysis, boundaries defining the region are fluid and sometimes include wider developing Southeast Asian countries such as Indonesia, Malaysia, Thailand and the Philippines, some of which also have different political economies and colonial histories with a less developed nature of social policy programmes.

Distinctive and shared characteristics of the welfare systems and approaches in East Asia, compared to Europe and Anglo-Saxon models, have stimulated the development of comparative social policy analysis and theorising of potential regional model/s of welfare capitalism and its validity since the 1990s (see, for example, Goodman et al., 1998; Holliday, 2000; Izuhara, 2013; Ku and Finer, 2007; Kwon, 2005). The early analysis of social policy in the region was dominated by Japan and the four 'tiger economies' of Hong Kong, Singapore, South Korea and Taiwan. Developmentalism argued, for example, for the strong and distinctive role of the state facilitating and regulating welfare provision. Small states in terms of low public expenditure especially on social security are indeed one of the shared political and institutional characteristics in the East Asian welfare regimes (see Yang, 2020). As many countries in the region are increasingly democratised through globalisation and post-crises austerity prevails, there has been a shift away from the developmental state-focused approaches in discourse and policy making, instead looking into other sectors such as civil society, enterprises and innovation for shaping future social policy development and reforms. Examining bottom-up approaches thus forms part of a new research agenda in the field of East Asian social policy (see Chapters 3 and 4 in this volume).

The four tiger economies mentioned are dispersed geographically in the region but provided a comparative cluster for analysis and contributed to the development and critique of welfare regime theories from East Asian perspectives, more recently examining the recovery paths from the Asian Financial Crisis (Holliday, 2005; Hwang, 2011; Kim, 2015). Paying particular attention to the relationship between economy and social policy development, theories of productivist welfare capitalism identified the dominance of the state in coordinating socio-economic institutions and the subordinance of social policy to economic growth (Gough, 2004; Holliday, 2000). The post-crisis recovery processes, however, witnessed the divergence of this productivist approach in the region (Choi, 2013; Hudson et al., 2014), which provided further food for thought on analysing differentiated policy trajectories among East Asian societies in the post-Global Financial Crisis as well as in the more recent post-COVID-19 pandemic landscape (see Chapters 2 and 10 of this volume).

As we moved into the new millennium, a new body of literature started challenging the conventional approaches based on small states, strong economy (thus secure employment) and traditional families of developmentalism and productivism to understand and theorise East Asian welfare systems (Estévez-Abe, 2008; Kim, 2015). The rise of social citizenship is a notable trend in many East Asian societies which have expanded social policy introducing more universal programmes in the range of healthcare, pensions, unemployment protection, childcare and long-term care for older people. As Fleckenstein and Lee (2017) argue, democratisation and post-industrialisation are important drivers to shift the developmental and productivist characteristics in countries like Taiwan and South Korea into more social investment approaches in response to labour market flexibility. In this vein, the distinctiveness of an employment-based East Asian welfare model using employment as access to welfare has started to be replaced by more inclusive approaches protecting the rising 'non-productive' population in the economic and system transitions (Choi et al., 2020, 2021). The safety net and social protection are thus debated differently in the post-industrial, knowledge-based economies, as presented in Chapters 3 and 6 of this volume.

Then there has been the rise of the People's Republic of China since the 1990s to the centre stage of the global economy through its market-orientated reforms. For the last two decades, a growing body of literature on China has added further dynamism in the existing comparative analysis and the volume has started to dominate social policy research in East Asia (see Lei and Chan, 2018; Ngan and Chan, 2013; Ngok and Chan, 2018). Its remarkable transition from a planned economy with universal but low-level welfare provisions through work units to a privatised and marketised model has produced substantial social policy measures and research (see, for example, Mok et al., 2021; Ngok and Chan, 2018; Saunders and He, 2019). The introduction of a market approach for employment, social security and housing meant dismantling the socialist welfare state, instead expecting citizens to secure their own welfare in the private market. This process has opened up opportunities for individuals and households but at the same time has produced significant new social risks. Consequently, we observed the dilemma of the marketisation of public services and uneven outcomes of the reforms between households, generations as well as urban/rural regions in China (Mok et al., 2009, 2021; see also Chapter 8 of this volume). Furthermore, the 1997/98 Asian Financial Crisis coincided with the return of Hong Kong from British governance to mainland China.

The 2019 anti-government protests in Hong Kong, however, mean that the 'one-country, two-system' model is under severe scrutiny as autonomy and governance are important elements of social policy making and implementation (Mok and Forrest, 2009). The influence of China on Hong Kong in terms of integration and policy making has indeed become a contemporary research agenda in the region (see Chapter 5 in this volume).

In contrast to the remarkable upward development trajectory of China, for the same period Japan as the most mature welfare state in the region (as social policy development started in the early phase of the post-Second World War period and introduced the universal pension and healthcare systems in the early 1960s) has started exhibiting significant post-growth characteristics in its demography and economy (Chiavacci and Hommerich, 2016; Hirayama and Izuhara, 2018). The growth-centric approach is no longer sustainable in the region, and this shift has led to a search for alternative approaches. Secure employment and strong family-based welfare systems no longer endure the new social risks in super-aged, ultra-low fertility Japan, while a more liberal-market approach is replacing the state-led developmental approach on welfare provision and has resulted in widening social inequalities across generations and across households. Social policy debates and an agenda built around economic growth as the national priority have increasingly shifted to sustainability, basic incomes, livelihood and the wellbeing of individuals. Maximising individual and community capability may still be identified as important resources to cope with post-crisis austerity.

Furthermore, the recent COVID-19 pandemic has exposed the vulnerability of nation states, the existing welfare systems and thus the importance of global governance in delivering public health interventions. The public health crisis brought up equity issues in terms of social protection across different sections of society (An and Tang, 2020) and taught lessons on the importance of institutional infrastructures to effectively respond, as discussed in Chapter 10 of this volume.

In this broader context, the aims of the volume include examining recent converging and diverging shifts of social policy reforms across East Asian societies and exploring under-researched policy fields to challenge common assumptions and highlight areas for urgent policy initiatives. The volume will also contribute to new conceptualisations and theorisations of social policy and practice in East Asia in the post-financial crises and post-pandemic landscape to take the research agenda forward.

The structure of the volume

The volume has nine substantive chapters, each exploring different areas of the contemporary social policy research agenda in East Asia. The majority of the chapters take a regional and comparative approach in analysis, while some such as Chapter 6 on child poverty policy in Japan examine distinctive national cases. Many chapters include the authors' original and some longstanding empirical research. To move social policy debates forward, selected contemporary and innovative research agendas will be presented in the following chapters.

In Chapter 2, Kühner and Shi present our first research agenda on the politics and policies of social investment from the East Asian perspective. Social investment as a new social policy approach has emerged, emphasising human capital accumulation over income maintenance. Using case studies from Hong Kong and Taiwan, this chapter demonstrates widening institutional diversity in social investment initiatives responding to new social risks in the region. Despite shared challenges, however, such diverging reform trajectories are considered to be an adjustment of the existing 'productivist' features instead of a radical shift towards a new form of post-productivist welfare capitalism. The chapter argues that a more nuanced perspective sensitive to institutional complementarities between social investment, labour market flexibilisation and social protection is required to capture and theorise the policy shifts in the post-crisis and post-pandemic East Asian context.

Innovation is a key driver of contemporary socio-economic development, yet innovation and social policy development are often mutually exclusive in the developmental context. Generous state welfare provision supported by high taxation, for example, may discourage entrepreneurship and companies' motivation for innovation. In Chapter 3, Choi will explore the relationship between social policy and innovation with particular attention to the case of South Korea, and also using the European innovation elite of Sweden as a sounding board. South Korea represents an ideal case in the East Asian context due to the dominance of *chaebol* (large conglomerate)-led innovation and a significant productivity gap between large and small/medium-sized enterprises. The chapter considers why more inclusive innovation alongside robust social policy is required to tackle widening social inequalities and associated issues. As civil society and enterprises can play a significant role in addressing fundamental social challenges, the chapter presents the current state and future possibilities of non-state actors.

In Chapter 4, in order to better understand the politics and current welfare reforms, Yeh and Hong argue that more attention needs to be paid to the role of public opinion and civil society. Public opinion is the source of welfare state legitimacy (Taylor-Gooby and Leruth, 2018) and part of the policy process. Public opinion plays a greater role in new democracies in East Asia, where interest groups such as labour unions are still underdeveloped, but its influence in social policy making has been marginal compared to the triangular power of the state, bureaucrats and businesses. In this context, the chapter will examine the role of public opinion in shaping social policy development and what reform strategies can be adopted to manage welfare politics, drawing evidence from relatively liberal electoral competitions (of Japan, South Korea and Taiwan) and less democratic regimes (of Singapore, Hong Kong and China). This chapter moves forward the debates around the opinion–policy linkage in the era of permanent austerity when the politics of welfare retrenchment are often conflicting.

Chapter 5 engages with governance and policy-making autonomy with a special focus on climate policy. Kwan explores the increasing Chinese influence on social and public policy processes in Hong Kong which undermine the policy-making autonomy promised under the framework of 'one-country, two-systems'. This is in the context of the profound shifts of the Hong Kong government in terms of its political discourse and rhetoric especially since 2019. The influence of China on Hong Kong's climate policy has been prominent since the accelerated political integration in 2019. To understand the change in discourse, the chapter reviews the application of the 'mainland frame' (the style of governance in the government's political communication), comparing two government documents on climate policy published before and after 2019. The emergence of the 'mainland frame' can be clearly observed in the *Climate Action Plan 2050* published in 2021, which represents a change in political discourse by the Hong Kong government and climate governance.

The volume then moves on to discuss one of the most pressing contemporary social policy issues – child poverty – in the post-Global Financial Crisis context of Japan. Despite the common perception of Japan being a wealthy egalitarian society, poverty has started to pose a threat to the wellbeing of children as Japan ranks among the worst-performing developed nations in terms of tackling child poverty, as discussed in Chapter 6 by Abe. The chapter evaluates policy development in poverty alleviation and support for low-income households with children in the context of the shifting familial welfare model in Japan. It is evident that the government takes a 'productivist' welfare approach in order to tackle child poverty by investing in higher education (and thus improving the future productivity of children) rather than through income maintenance such as cash-based public assistance for poor households. This approach in policy development is underpinned by the traditional role of families as welfare producers and ignores the rights of children. The chapter argues for the persistence of the familial welfare model in this field of social policy in Japan.

Chapter 7 by Izuhara and Yi also focuses on the impact of globalisation and the financial crises but this time on the contemporary phenomenon of stagnated youth transitions from the housing perspectives of Japan and South Korea. The consequences of the recent economic and labour market transformations mean that young adults no longer benefit from the features of post-war welfare development such as job security and access to home ownership compared to their parents' generation and, thus, they experience a delay in upward housing trajectories such as movement from the parental home to independent living, and from private rental to home ownership. The chapter examines what successful and sustainable residential transitions entail for young adults following the non-conventional life-course in the Japanese and Korean markets, and what is the role of the state, market and families in assisting or hindering such processes. The conflictive yet inter-related concepts of autonomy and dependence of young adults in the post-growth social contexts will be also examined.

The marketisation of public services is a shared trend in many East Asian societies. It is significant in the field of social care as new markets have been created to respond to the growing care needs of the rapidly ageing population in East Asia. Chapter 8 by Zhang examines the emerging role of the market in the mixed economy of care, focusing on long-term care for older people. It discusses how market mechanisms such as contracting out to private providers, care vouchers and the direct purchasing of services by older people and their families can be applied to the long-term care systems in the region. Such approaches differ across East Asian societies: for example, while the Chinese model of marketisation has a strong steer from the state who can or cannot provide services, the Japanese social insurance-based model expanded services and non-profit/for-profit providers. The impact of the marketisation strategies on the care markets and care participants will also be examined. The analysis pushes the theoretical debates around different marketisation models in contemporary East Asia.

The trend of late childbirth has created a cross-over period for some women providing care for both their children and ageing parents(-in-law). Such multi-generational care, going beyond dyadic caring relationships, is a contemporary but under-researched demographic phenomenon. By connecting childcare and elderly care, Yamashita and Soma provide a holistic approach to investigating caring practices and relationships beyond dyadic family relations in Chapter

9. Drawing on contrasting evidence from Hong Kong, Japan, South Korea and Taiwan, this chapter examines the impact of recent policy reforms on women's responsibility of caregiving in East Asia and provides an insight into why the expansion of the state role in financing and organising care provision has not reduced the responsibility of women. The concept of defamilialisation will be used as a theoretical framework to understand the contradictions and limitations of the policy reforms on the gendered division of care.

The volume concludes with a policy analysis from Indonesia and the Philippines. The COVID-19 pandemic hit these developing nations hard. Both Indonesia and the Philippines have an established universal public healthcare system, but the approaches taken to protect their population against new social risks have been selective and fragmented. Chapter 10 by Kwon, Ha, Yang, Park and Yi examines the contrasting policy responses to the healthcare crisis caused by the COVID-19 pandemic. A perspective of crisis management with cognition, coordination and capacity as core components is used to consider the public healthcare system as a part of the wider governance structure. Although universal in coverage, the existing public systems in these countries are under-resourced in terms of both facilities and human resources and thus have not brought about real changes in the welfare system. The pandemic placed the healthcare systems under severe scrutiny and exposed the lack of capacity in times of crisis.

References

An, B.Y. and Tang, S.-Y. (2020) 'Lessons from COVID-19 responses in East Asia: Institutional infrastructure and enduring policy instruments', *American Review of Public Administration*, 50(6–7): 790–800.

Bonoli, J. (2006) 'New social risks and the politics of post-industrial social policies', in K. Armingeon and J. Bonoli (Eds) *The Politics of Post-Industrial Welfare States*, London: Routledge: 3–26.

Cabinet Office, Japan. (2022) *Annual Report on the Ageing Society*, Tokyo.

Chiavacci, D. and Hommerich, C. (Eds) (2016) *Social Inequality in Post-Growth Japan: Transformation during Economic and Demographic Stagnation*, London: Routledge.

Choi, Y.J. (2013) 'Developmentalism and productivism in East Asian welfare regimes', in M. Izuhara (Ed.) *Handbook on East Asian Social Policy*, Cheltenham, UK and Northampton, MA, USA: Edward Elgar Publishing: 207–25.

Choi, Y.J., Huber, E., Kim, W.S., Kwon, H.-y. and Shi, S.-j. (2020) 'Social investment in the knowledge-based economy: New politics and policies', *Policy and Society*, 39(2): 147–170.

Choi, Y.J., Fleckenstein, T. and Lee, S.-h.C. (Eds) (2021) *Welfare Reform and Social Investment Policy in Europe and East Asia: International Lessons and Policy Implications*, Bristol: Policy Press.

Esteve, A., Kashyap, R., Roman, J.G., Cheng, Y.-h. A., Fukuda, S., Nie, W. and Lee, H.-o. (2020) 'Demographic change and increasing late singlehood in East Asia, 2010–2050', *Demographic Research*, 43: 1367–1398.

Estévez-Abe, M. (2008) *Welfare and Capitalism in Postwar Japan*, Cambridge: Cambridge University Press.

Fleckenstein, T. and Lee, S.C. (2017) 'Democratization, post-industrialization, and East Asian welfare capitalism: The politics of welfare state reform in Japan, South Korea, and Taiwan', *Journal of International and Comparative Social Policy*, 33(1): 36–54.

Goodman, R., White, G. and Kwon, H.-j. (1998) *The East Asian Welfare Model: Welfare Orientalism and the State*, London: Routledge.

Gough, I. (2004) 'Welfare regimes in development contexts: A global and regional analysis', in I. Gough, G. Wood, A. Barrientos, P. Bevan, P. Davis and G. Room (Eds) *Insecurity and Welfare Regimes in Asia, Africa and Latin America: Social Policy in Development Contexts*, Cambridge: Cambridge University Press: 15–48.

Hirayama, Y. and Izuhara, M. (2018) *Housing in Post-Growth Society: Japan on the Edge of Social Transition*, London: Routledge.

Holliday, I. (2000) 'Productivist welfare capitalism: Social policy in East Asia', *Political Studies*, 48(4): 706–723.

Holliday, I. (2005) 'East Asian social policy in the wake of the financial crisis: Farewell to productivism?', *Policy and Politics*, 33(1): 145–162.

Hudson, J., Kühner, S. and Yang, N. (2014) 'Productive welfare, the East Asian "model" and beyond: Placing welfare types in greater China into context', *Social Policy and Society*, 13(20): 301–315.

Hwang, G.-J. (2011) *New Welfare States in East Asia: Global Challenges and Restructuring*, Cheltenham, UK and Northampton, MA, USA: Edward Elgar Publishing.

Izuhara, M. (Ed.) (2013) *Handbook on East Asian Social Policy*, Cheltenham, UK and Northampton, MA, USA: Edward Elgar Publishing.

Izuhara, M. and Zhang, W. (2022) 'Social policy in East Asia', in P. Alcock, T. Haux, V. McCall and M. May (Eds) *The Student's Companion to Social Policy*, 6th Edition, Chichester: Wiley-Blackwell: 462–468.

Jones, G.W. (2019) 'Ultra-low fertility in East Asia: Policy responses and challenges', *Asian Population Studies*, 15(2): 131–149.

Kim, M.M.S. (2015) *Comparative Welfare Capitalism in East Asia: Productivist Models of Social Policy*, Basingstoke: Palgrave Macmillan.

Ku, Y.W. and Finer, C.J. (2007) 'Developments in East Asian welfare studies', *Social Policy and Administration*, 41(2): 115–131.

Kwon, H.-j. (Ed.) (2005) *Transforming the Developmental Welfare State in East Asia*, Basingstoke: Palgrave Macmillan.

Lei, J. and Chan, C.K. (Eds) (2018) *China's Social Welfare Revolution: Contracting Out Social Services*, London: Routledge.

Mok, K.H. and Forrest, R. (Eds) (2009) *Changing Governance and Public Policy in East Asia*, London: Routledge.

Mok, K.H., Wong, Y.C. and Zhang, X. (2009) 'When marketisation and privatisation clash with socialist ideals: Educational inequality in urban China', *International Journal of Educational Development*, 29: 505–512.

Mok, K.H., Chan, C.K. and Wen, Z. (2021) 'Searching for new welfare governance in China: Contracting out social service and impact on government–NGOs relationship', *Journal of Asian Public Policy*, 14(1): 63–80.

Ngan, L.L.-S. and Chan, K.-W. (2013) 'An outsider is always an outsider: Migration, social policy and social exclusion in East Asia', *Journal of Comparative Asian Development*, 12(2): 316–350.

Ngok, K. and Chan, C.K. (Eds) (2018) *China's Social Policy: Transformations and Challenges*, London: Routledge.

Saunders, P. and He, A.J. (Eds) (2019) *Social Protection in East Asian Chinese Societies: Challenges, Responses and Impacts*, London: Routledge.

Sung, S. and Pascall, G. (Eds) (2014) *Gender and Welfare State in East Asia: Confucianism or Gendered Equality?*, Basingstoke: Palgrave Macmillan.

Taylor-Gooby, P. (Ed.) (2004) *New Risks, New Welfare: The Transformation of the European Welfare State*, Oxford: Oxford University Press.

Taylor-Gooby, P. and Leruth, B. (2018) 'New challenges for the welfare state and new ways to study them, in P. Taylor-Gooby and B. Leruth (Eds) *Attitudes, Aspirations and Welfare: Social Policy Directions in Uncertain Times*, Basingstoke: Palgrave: 1–28.

Yang, J.-J. (Ed.) (2020) *The Small Welfare State: Rethinking Welfare in the US, Japan and South Korea*, Cheltenham, UK and Northampton, MA, USA: Edward Elgar Publishing.

2 Diversity of institutional change in East Asian social investment policy: the cases of Hong Kong and Taiwan

Stefan Kühner and Shih-Jiunn Shi

Introduction

Research on East Asian social policy has gained significance since the 1990s. Inspired by the typology approach distinguishing welfare regimes (Esping-Andersen, 1990), East Asian social policy scholars wondered where the newly industrialised countries and territories stood relative to their Western counterparts. As a result, research on East Asian welfare state development has advanced several theoretical explanations ranging from the cultural account of Confucianism (Jones, 1990; Rieger and Leibfried, 2003) to the emphasis on past institutional legacy (Hwang, 2006; Tang, 2000), advocacy coalitions in politics (Kim, 2008), international diffusion of welfare ideas and discourse (Kim and Shi, 2013), and the political economy of productivism and developmentalism (Holliday, 2000, 2005; Kwon, 2005). Despite their various approaches, these accounts share an interest in ideal over real types and attempt to distinguish the defining attributes of East Asia as a distinct welfare geography.

However, the 'welfare modelling business' of East Asian social policy analysis has gradually reached an impasse. While accounts of the historical development of East Asian welfare policy catch various essential characteristics, they tend to assume the latter's institutional homogeneity that can be summarised with generic terms. The strength of holistic conceptualisation lies in its analytical parsimony to capture complex phenomena with succinct notions. Still, it is prone to encounter difficulties in explanatory power when confronted with the variation and deviation of institutional change over time. As Ku and Finer (2007: 123) point out, one problem has been that 'those studies which follow Esping-Andersen in their efforts to identify an East Asian welfare regime to contrast with his three other types of regimes are based more upon conceptual construction than empirical data analysis'. As a result, the current state of East Asian welfare studies continues to present an abundance of theoretical conceptualisation and scarcity in the empirical investigation (Choi et al., 2021; Nam, 2020).

Given the variation amongst East Asian countries and territories regarding their economic and social development, seeking a holistic understanding of a single East Asian 'welfare regime' – whether that is productivist or developmental[1] – has stumbled upon limitations. For a region characterised by constant institutional transformations, attempts to identify a unique East Asian model have struggled to produce compelling insights. One classic example is the categorisation of cases such as Japan, South Korea (henceforth: Korea) and Taiwan as having 'inclusive social insurance' in contrast to 'individualistic social protection', which is held to characterise the Hong Kong Special Administrative Region (henceforth: Hong Kong), Singapore and the People's Republic of China (henceforth: China) (Holliday, 2000; Peng and Wong, 2010). Whilst Hong Kong and Singapore both have a clear individualistic bent in social protection, China has been subject to re-examination given its recent redirection towards statist orientation and the growing awareness of variation at the regional level (Mok et al., 2017; Shi, 2012, 2017). Equally controversial is the conflation of Taiwan with Korea and Japan since the latter two cases demonstrate a more extensive involvement in occupational welfare, which the former lacks (Hudson and Kühner, 2011).

The difficulty of pinpointing the characteristics of a unique East Asian welfare model is further aggravated since East Asian countries and territories tread divergent paths of social investment reforms. Unlike Korea and Japan, which have widely been regarded as forerunners of the East Asian social investment turn, Taiwan has taken a more lukewarm stance towards the social investment idea even though declining fertility rates have been haunting policymakers. Only recently did the Taiwanese government explicitly embrace this notion, but the implementation of relevant reform measures has remained sluggish, fragmented and predominantly localised (An and Peng, 2016; Huang, 2012; Wang, 2014). Meanwhile, in Hong Kong, little structural change has taken place concerning the critical productive and protective social policy measures

---

[1]   For argumentative concision, 'productivism' and 'developmentalism' are used here as analogous concepts, although some nuanced distinction holds. While developmentalism denotes the collective pursuit of fully fledged national modernisation under the state's lead, productivism's major concern is narrower, focusing primarily on economic development. For further discussion, see Choi (2013).

(Yang and Kühner, 2020) despite noticeable government activity to address a range of social problems, including the persistent care burden for working families, rapid societal ageing, the looming long-term care crisis and the various pressures on the well-being of children and young people.

This chapter looks at social policy development in Taiwan and Hong Kong, and asks how and why the two societies began to diverge in their reform endeavour towards social investment despite common challenges. Taiwan and Hong Kong are chosen as 'meaningful' cases since they present different social policy trajectories before and, as we argue in this chapter, during their respective social investment turns. The chapter also considers how, collectively, the policy changes in Taiwan and Hong Kong can be characterised and what these trajectories signify conceptually for the study of social investment across East Asia. The chapter is structured as follows: first, we briefly introduce the rise of the social investment paradigm in European welfare states and compare it to the specific features of East Asian social policy as discussed in the mainstream literature. Second, we examine the recent social investment initiatives in Taiwan and Hong Kong in more detail, and third, we discuss the key reasons behind emerging institutional diversity in these two East Asian societies. Finally, we summarise the findings and reflect on their theoretical significance in light of the COVID-19 pandemic and future scholarship on social investment in East Asia.

Towards the social investment turn in East Asia?

Social investment has arisen as the mainstream idea in Western welfare state research since the late 1990s. It addresses the insufficiency of the institutional arrangement of the conventional Keynesian welfare state and is conceived as an alternative to the neoliberal, free-market response for coping with the transformation to the post-industrial society. More precisely, the social investment perspective emphasises resource reallocation from income maintenance into human capital accumulation, attaches importance to employment policies that increase labour market fluidity and stresses work–family reconciliation. Collectively, social investment policies cater more effectively for 'new social risk' groups, including young people, women and those with low-level or obsolete skills, via investments into healthcare and education, labour market activation and defamilisation (Morel et al., 2012).

The social investment state has been portrayed as an effective response to economic crises (Hemerijck and Vandenbroucke, 2012) and as being specifically geared towards meeting the demands of the global knowledge-based economy, which operates in the context of deindustrialisation and rapid ageing (Choi et al., 2020; Hudson and Kühner, 2009). Moreover, the social investment perspective contains a notion of the state's responsibility to cater to working families, particularly vulnerable groups inside and outside the labour market, following a normative focus on equality of opportunity. Indeed, empirical examinations have linked social investment initiatives to various social indicators, including social inclusion, quality employment, and capabilities enhancement (Jenson, 2013). At the same time, empirical evidence suggests a positive effect of public early education and child and elderly care services on employment rates (Nelson and Stephens, 2012) but less so on inequality (Vaalavuo, 2013) and poverty dynamics (Van Vliet and Wang, 2015).

Social investment *in practice* may combine generous social protection with more preventative and inclusive social investment (Ronchi, 2018) and become part of deliberate strategies to complement increasingly fluid labour markets and labour relations with enhanced social security (Burroni and Keune, 2011). It may also combine short- and long-term strategies. For instance, the social investment state has been conceptualised as combining a future-oriented child-centred approach, including investment in early cognitive development and high-quality after-school programmes, with more immediate improvements in working conditions of working mothers; at the same time, scholars have called for the promotion of longer-term life-long learning and active ageing strategies together with the short-term expansion of zero pillar pensions as part of a new social contract for older people (Esping-Andersen et al., 2002).

In East Asia, the quest for catch-up modernisation has historically shaped the common mindset of policymakers. Even after East Asian societies have become advanced economies, pursuing industrial upgrading and further economic development has remained top of their political agenda. An early argument gaining traction was that East Asian nations emphasised economic growth over social policy. Heavily influenced by Johnson's (1999) notion of the East Asian developmental state, Midgley (1986) first considered 'reluctant welfarism' as a vital ingredient of the East Asian political economy. Tang (2000) described social development in East Asia as subscribing to a 'production first' approach, which primarily utilised social policies to promote state legitimacy, pacify strategically significant parts of the labour force and guarantee investment in the education and health of the workforce.

Low public social expenditure, labour market flexibility and limited universalism and egalitarianism became key to the understanding of 'productivist'

East Asian welfare types (Holliday, 2000, 2005; Kwon, 2005). Countries or territories that fell into the 'productivist welfare' category included Japan, Korea, Taiwan and Hong Kong. Indeed, these East Asian cases eschewed primary responsibilities, particularly for social protection, and left them to civil society, individuals and families. As a result, social security systems were highly stratified alongside various occupational groups. Moreover, labour rights remained underdeveloped as the state wielded control over worker movements and trade unions.

However, the East Asian landscape changed after political democratisation forged ahead in the region in the late 1980s. For instance, the transition from authoritarianism to democracy in Korea and Taiwan generated the political imperative for successive governments to revamp the existing social security systems to broaden their coverage and increase benefits for the vulnerable groups (Haggard and Kaufman, 2008). Moreover, the Asian Financial Crisis (1997–1998) caused profound challenges for social policy in East Asian societies and arguably motivated a tentative move beyond the productivist welfare paradigm (Tang and Midgley, 2002). As a result, there has been a slow but steady increase in social expenditures, which indicates the sustained expansion of social policy in this region (Figure 2.1).

East Asian states have faced interlinked socio-economic challenges on several fronts. The sharp decline of fertility rates and the associated population ageing have eroded institutional sustainability, especially those welfare systems with social insurance as the backbone. Behind the demographic transformation lie the changing roles of women in society, from homemakers to career planners, who aspire to strike a work–family balance. Furthermore, economic globalisation has led to the structural transformation of labour markets, greater labour market pprox.ionion and increased wage inequality, all of which had profound implications on the East Asian economy of care (Peng, 2012). The rise of the knowledge economy is widening the gap between the low-skilled workers in the traditional manufacturing sectors and their high-skilled colleagues in the new industrial sectors (Choi et al., 2020; Fleckenstein and Lee, 2017). Social mobility across East Asia has declined as more young people face increasingly extended, non-linear, precarious school-to-work transitions (Mok and Jiang, 2018), and the valorisation of higher education credentials, particularly short-cycle tertiary degrees, has come increasingly under scrutiny (Kühner et al., 2021). Consequently, the momentum of welfare expansion since the 1990s has given way to efforts to recalibrate the institutional frameworks of the East Asian welfare geography.

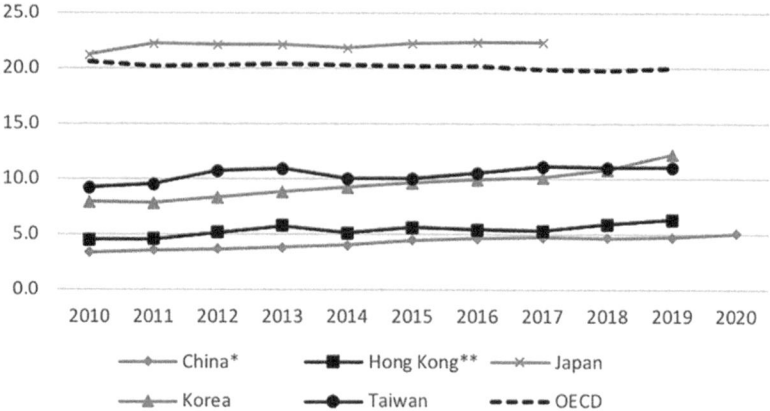

Note: * China: public expenditure on social security, employment and health; **
Hong Kong: public spending on health and social welfare.
Source: China: National Bureau of Statistics, 2021 (https://data.stats.gov.cn/
easyquery.htm?cn=C01) and Ministry of Finance, PRC, 2021 (http://gks.mof.gov.cn/
tongjishuju/index_2.htm); Hong Kong: Census and Statistics Department, 2021 (www
.censtatd.gov.hk/en/); Japan, Korea and OECD: OECD Social Expenditure Database,
2021 (www.oecd.org/social/expenditure.htm); Taiwan: Directorate-General of
Budget, Accounting and Statistics, Executive Yuan, ROC, 2021 (www.dgbas.gov.tw/ct
.asp?xItem=46677&ctNode=5624&mp=1).

Figure 2.1   Social expenditure (in percentage of gross domestic product)
in China, Hong Kong, Japan, Korea and Taiwan, compared
to OECD average, 2010–2020

Recent social policy reforms in two East Asian cases

As the productivist welfare state prototypes, Taiwan and Hong Kong attached
importance to the contributory role of social policy to economic development.
To catch up with advanced industrialised countries, successive governments
adopted a market-conform approach that restrained public responsibility for
social provision. The primary goal of social policy was less 'decommodification' than 'commodification' of labour in line with the demand for a skilled
workforce in labour markets (Kwon, 2005; Rudra, 2008). Taiwan and Hong
Kong concentrated the available resources on policies conducive to economic
development and avoided expenditure in other areas. Consequently, productive welfare (e.g. healthcare and education) outweighed protective or consum-
erist welfare (e.g. pensions) (Hudson and Kühner, 2011). However, economic
globalisation and the emergence of phenomena such as rising inequality and

the working poor, low fertility and the resultant population ageing have posed challenges to the existing institutional arrangements in Taiwan and Hong Kong. Together these phenomena required recalibration of social policy mechanisms and goals, which the following sections will consider in more detail.

Taiwan

The end of the Second World War brought about a change of political regime on this island when Japan returned Taiwan to the then Republic of China. The ensuing outbreak of the civil war between the authoritarian Kuomintang (KMT) regime and the communist rebels led to the former's collapse in mainland China. After it retreated to Taiwan, the KMT consolidated its political rule over the island. In social welfare, the government successively established social insurance programmes for specific groups who pledged loyalty: military service members, civil servants and teachers (elementary schools and junior high schools) (Ku, 1997; Lin, 2006; Wong, 2004: 43–61). The government also addressed labour welfare by introducing the Labour Insurance (LI) in March 1950 to cover ordinary workers of enterprises with at least 20 employees. By 1953, the LI programme extended its coverage to small firms with over ten employees and fishers and those working in even smaller firms voluntarily. The LI provided benefits for work injury, old age, medical care, disability, death and maternity. In the same year, the Military Servicemen Insurance Programme came into force, together with the introduction of the Government Employee Insurance Programme in 1958.[2] Apart from the social insurance programmes for different occupational groups, the government virtually forwent its welfare responsibility for a large swathe of the population (such as peasants, the inactive workforce and unemployed persons).

The landscape changed after democratisation in the 1990s, propelling the government to heed the people's need for social security. This set in motion a considerable institutional expansion to broaden coverage and raise benefit levels in the existing social safety net, along with the advent of new social programmes exemplified by the milestone National Health Insurance in 1995 (Haggard and Kaufman, 2008; Wong, 2004). Pension reforms followed suit and led to the introduction of the Old Peasant Allowances (1995), Labour Pension Act (2004) and National Pension Insurance (2009) (Chen and Shi, 2021). In addition, the civic engagement of non-governmental organisations to advocate for human rights has played a critical role in contributing to the

---

2   These two social insurance schemes also covered major risks, albeit with much more lavish benefit levels than the LI.

universalisation of the Taiwanese welfare state. This momentum continued in the new millennium.

Meanwhile, the democratic drive for welfare growth reached its impasse. Structural factors such as the pprox.ionion of labour markets out of economic globalisation together with population ageing resulting from the transformation of gender roles have constrained the dynamics of welfare expansion (Choi et al., 2021; Fleckenstein and Lee, 2017; Lue, 2014). The rising unemployment after the 1997–1998 Asian Financial Crisis motivated the government to incorporate unemployment benefits into the existing LI in 1999, with coverage extended to more unemployed workers in 2001. These endeavours crystallised in the promulgation of a separate Employment Insurance Act in 2003 (Kim and Shi, 2020; Lee, 2010; Lin, 2006). Following the workfare doctrine, this act made access to unemployment benefits conditional on the beneficiaries' readiness to participate in programmes arranged by the public employment service agencies. Under the rubric of 'three in one employment services' (*sanheyi jiuye fuwu*), the overall policy framework combined passive unemployment benefits with the active provision of occupational training opportunities and support in finding jobs. The statutory regulation aimed to monitor job search behaviours and emphasised the responsibilities of job seekers to return to labour markets. Each case management bundled employment counselling and vocational training together, tailored to the individual situations of the unemployed workers.

These reforms envisaged a clear direction towards labour activation but failed to address the growing informal employment and related in-work poverty (Fleckenstein and Lee, 2017; Ko and Chang, 2014).[3] The transition to the knowledge economy took its toll on the labour markets, evident in the constant increase of precarious employment such as dispatched workers, fixed-term labour contracts, and part-time employment. The government tried to revamp the existing Labour Standards Act promulgated in 1984. However, reform efforts have seen mediocre progress owing to the discord amongst the responsible ministries, labour rights non-governmental organisations and experts involved. Moreover, the elusive nature of irregular employment made any attempt at specific statutory regulation extremely difficult. A common practice by the regulatory authority was to employ the standard set by the existing law universally in cases of labour disputes, with conceivable regulative loopholes

---

[3]   According to the Annual Manpower Employment Survey 2020, Taiwan registered nearly 799,000 workers active in informal employment in 2020, about 6.97 per cent of the total workforce. Accessed 25 July 2021 at National Statistics ROC (Taiwan): www.stat.gov.tw/ct.asp?xItem=46590&ctNode=3579&mp=4.

(Lee, 2010; Lin, 2006). In 2011, to address the issue of the working poor, the government reformed the existing social assistance programme by loosening the definition of the poverty line (uplifting the median disposable income per capita from 50 to 60 per cent – albeit subject to local variety) to help more families that were struggling to make ends meet (Goishi, 2011).

Labour market policy cannot work alone without the corresponding policy supporting families, particularly when Taiwan is witnessing declining fertility and the advent of an aged society. Yet, whilst the importance of family policy has gained wide recognition amongst academics and practitioners, its development has been fragmented over the past decades (An and Peng, 2016). Significant efforts began with cash subsidies of monthly 3000NTD (pprox.. £80) to families in need of childcare in 2008, followed by the initiation of child allowances the following year (monthly 2500NTD (pprox.. £66)). As these measures showed little effect, policies shifted attention to strengthening childcare support thanks to the call of women's rights groups for public care provision (TFSA, 2014). However, in the absence of central integration, various approaches to local pilot programmes prevailed – ranging from fully public provision to public subsidies of private childcare. Local variation exists not only in the subsidy amount but also in the substance of the childcare services. As a result, family policy is on the move but lacks an integral nationwide framework with effective coordination, which countervails positive policy results. In 2014, the government voluntarily adopted the Convention on the Rights of the Child as a benchmark against which future progress in facilitating an environment conducive to children's physical and mental well-being can be assessed.

Another policy field that was less noted but equally related to the labour markets concerned the welfare of persons with disabilities. In the early 1990s, the government faced pressure from advocacy associations for disability welfare to enact law amendments and policy changes (Chang, 2007; Lin, 2006). Major improvement revolved around increasing cash benefits for persons with disabilities and measures to promote their labour market participation. In 2014, the government voluntarily declared its willingness to implement the United Nations Convention on the Rights of Persons with Disabilities at the national level. This commitment has elevated public responsibility for ensuring the equal participation of persons with disabilities in all spheres of society. Policy reforms in recent years addressed primarily the elimination of barriers for persons with disabilities in their access to labour markets, coupled with enablement measures. Employability enhancement features employment quota regulation, vocational rehabilitation and the establishment of shelter factories.

The picture emerging from the above Illustration of the Taiwan case is that welfare reforms here involve restructuring (even retrenching) existing social programmes (such as pensions) and expanding the new ones (such as family support and children's rights). Pension policy features this trend clearly: although the government brought new pension insurance programmes into force, it also revamped existing ones in terms of recalibrating parameters (benefit cuts and retirement postponements); e.g. the reform of Pension Insurance for Civil Servants and Public School Teachers in 2016. The same plan is under discussion about reforming the LI, which will soon deplete its funding reserves given the ongoing population ageing (Chen and Shi, 2021). However, one should not overlook the institutional backbone of the Taiwanese welfare state that relies heavily on public social insurance for risk aversion and income maintenance. Whist social insurance is susceptible to the looming financial burden resulting from population ageing, the momentum of democratic politics is likely to generate enormous pressure on politicians to keep it above water. This means that the 'maintenance cost' of social insurance will consume a significant proportion of the public purse and constrain its fiscal capacity.

Hong Kong

Under the post-war British administration (1945–1997), Hong Kong pursued a welfare model that intended to reduce the moral hazard of welfare dependence and reduce the fiscal burden on the government (Chui and Ko, 2011). Initially, the system was designed to ensure that benefits were not overly generous or disincentivised work (Chan, 2006). However, throughout much of the second half of the twentieth century, Hong Kong's booming economy further disincentivised the development of a robust welfare system. Economic growth meant that the unemployment rate was low and jobs were secure, which dampened public demand for social welfare.

By the 1970s, however, there was a recognition that some form of social welfare was needed, especially to respond to the large-scale riots against the British Hong Kong government in Hong Kong between 1967 and 1969. As a result, the British administration established Hong Kong's first social welfare programme designed to provide financial support to needy individuals and their families, the Public Assistance (PA) scheme, in 1971. This non-contributory, means-tested scheme consisted of a basic allowance, a rent allowance and other cash payments for recipients in exceptional circumstances and saw a swift increase in caseloads and expenditures during the 1970s. In addition to the PA, replaced in 1992 by the Comprehensive Social Security Assistance (CSSA) scheme, Hong Kong began to develop comprehensive healthcare, education and public housing programmes, which contrasted this global city with other liberal welfare regime types. As policies promoted a developmental welfare role, their primary purpose was to ensure that workers (as opposed to citizens) were educated and healthy and that they would facilitate ongoing real estate development.

The number of welfare beneficiaries increased further during the 1980s and 1990s due to economic restructuring that resulted in the loss of local manufacturing jobs and a rise in casual labour (Chan and Chan, 2013). As a result, Hong Kong saw rising unemployment and a rise in the working poor, especially amongst vulnerable groups who suffered due to low education and low skills. Whilst these groups began to draw upon the CSSA, concerns about welfare dependency and threats to fiscal sustainability were equally on the rise. These fears were further aggravated by the publication of an official report on the CSSA in 1998 that presented welfare fraud cases as though they were widespread, thus further turning public perception against welfare beneficiaries (Wong and Lou, 2010).

The 1997 Asian Financial Crisis and the 2003 SARS outbreak led to further increases in the number of welfare beneficiaries and governmental concerns about the need to encourage them to return to work to prevent dependence. These initiatives also included the launch of specific activation measures for persons with disabilities. For instance, the 'On the Job Training Programme for People with Disabilities' programme, implemented in 2001, provided individual counselling, job matching, job attachment and post-placement service to persons with disabilities. In addition, the Work Orientation and Placement Scheme, implemented in 2005, aimed to further enhance the employability of persons with disabilities through offering bespoke pre-employment training and work placements.

In 2014, the then chief executive C.Y. Leung introduced the so-called Low-Income Working Family Allowance, renamed Working Family Allowance (WFA) in 2018, designed to facilitate self-reliance through employment. More precisely, eligibility for tiered allowances is determined by meeting specific working hour requirements and income and asset limits for low-income individuals and households not receiving CSSA. Additional child allowances exist under the WFA scheme, and most applications have been approved in conjunction with these child allowances. As a result, the total number of approved WFA applications more than doubled from 52,354 in 2016–2017 to 124,167 in the 2020–2021 fiscal year.

Other innovations in welfare policy have primarily been focused on alleviating poverty amongst current and future generations of Hong Kong older adults. In 2000, the Hong Kong government first addressed the economic hardship of Hong Kong's older adults by introducing the Mandatory Provident Fund, a privately managed, employment-based, defined contribution scheme. In 2013, the Old Age Living Allowance (OALA), a tax-funded, means-tested social pension programme for those aged 65 and older, was introduced alongside the existing old-age CSSA and the non-means-tested Old Age Allowance. A higher tier of assistance was introduced under OALA in April 2018, with a higher monthly allowance and stricter asset limits. Rather than a radical shift, these expansions of social rights in old-age income protection have been classified as path consistent (Yang and Kühner, 2020) and marked by a careful process of institutional layering (Kühner and Chou, 2019). In other words, Hong Kong continues to emphasise a residualist welfare type in which means-tested benefits predominate. Consequently, the government takes a minimal role in providing social security to citizens.

In 2021, 19 per cent of Hong Kong's 7.5 million population was aged 65 or above, a majority of which lived with their spouse or children. According to official government projections, the share of older Hong Kong adults will approach 30 per cent by mid-2036. Despite this rapid ageing trend, the number of elderly residential respite places has been outpaced by demand, leading to long waiting lists for subsidised residential care places. Since June 2014, the Hong Kong government has provided care allowances under the Community Care Fund on a pilot basis to support low-income carers' financial burden ('Pilot Scheme on Living Allowance for Carers of Elderly Persons from Low-income Families'). Under this scheme, a carer who provides at least 80 hours of care per month for an older Hong Kong adult waiting for subsidised care services may qualify for a means-tested monthly allowance. At the same time, efforts to develop Hong Kong into an 'age-friendly city' have included the Hong Kong Housing Society's 'Ageing in Place Scheme', which promotes older adults' well-being by enabling them to remain with their families (Lam and Fong, 2020).

In the meantime, care services for young children under the age of three continue to be provided by non-governmental Child Care Centres and the Neighbourhood Support Child Care Project, both subsidised by the Social Welfare Department. However, similar to subsidised residential care places for older people, the supply of care services for children falls far short of demand (Yu et al., 2019). Children in Hong Kong usually start receiving free education at the age of five, suggesting a considerable gap between the end of statutory maternity leave, access to limited care services for young children and the beginning of compulsory early education. The female labour participation rate for those aged 25–29 was as high as 84.3 per cent in 2018 (Census and Statistics Department, 2017). Still, the rate of women's employment decreased steadily after the age of 30, and close to 500,000 total women of working age were economically inactive (Census and Statistics Department, 2017). More specifically, labour market participation of younger mothers has decreased in recent years, whilst most analysts see a direct link between the challenges of the maternal workforce and the lack of adequate childcare services (Legislative Council Secretariat Research Office, 2019). Women have faced rigid working hours and implicit discrimination (the 'motherhood penalty') in the workplace.

Finally, the Hong Kong government also emphasised youth development by investing significant resources into various initiatives specifically geared towards young people. In the Long-Term Social Welfare Planning in Hong Kong Consultation Paper, which was published by the Social Welfare Advisory Committee in April 2010, it was stated that young people are 'the future pillars of Hong Kong' and that the 'Hong Kong SAR government and the community as a whole attach great importance to nurturing and developing them into our "capital"' (p. 8). Launched as a special initiative by the Labour Department in 2018, the 'Career Let's Go' programme for young people aged 15 to 24 with educational attainment at or below sub-degree level, i.e. associate degrees and higher diplomas, includes a series of pre-employment training and employment services to provide relevant employment information and help young people develop a firm career plan. In addition, the Labour Department launched the 'Youth Employment and Training Programme' to provide one-stop comprehensive pre-employment and on-the-job training for the same target group of young people. Nevertheless, education and English proficiency have remained strongly related to occupational status. Limited upward social mobility has been prevalent amongst young Hongkongers, particularly those with a working-class background.

Explaining institutional diversity in Taiwan and Hong Kong

The social investment perspective emphasises the positive role of human capital investment as part of a recasting of the traditional welfare state in favour of economic development and job creation, whereas 'productivist' East Asian governments, including Taiwan and Hong Kong, have long emphasised healthcare and education – two major boosters of human capital accumulation – in the overall allocation of social spending (Kühner, 2015). However, when it comes to social security, East Asian welfare policy has remained much closer to the residualist or neoliberal types of social investment (Jenson, 2013; Morel et al., 2012). Consumptive social policies such as pensions and unemployment benefits have traditionally played a minor role, although some East Asian cases historically boasted significant levels of employment protection (Hudson and Kühner, 2011). Even when they were introduced, the benefit levels of social security were kept modest and were often conditional on the recipients' active labour market participation.

Moreover, whilst East Asian governments have seemingly followed the call of social investment proponents for early childhood education, parental leave and other support for women's employment (Fleckenstein and Lee, 2017; Lee, 2011), the rationale for these policy shifts has largely remained economic, i.e. retaining female skills and maximising female labour force participation, or less frequently natalist, i.e. alleviating the economic and social costs of rapidly ageing societies. Traditional Confucian ideals of filial piety and the role of the family within the care mix have taken longer to adjust, and not all East Asian welfare states have kept the same pace in taking responsibility for dealing with familisation risks and recognising concerns of gender equality (Nam, 2020; Yeh and Ku, 2017; Yeh et al., 2020).

In short, what appears in East Asia as a social investment policy may remain 'productivist' *in essence*, as reflected in the policy discourses and concrete approaches adopted by the state bureaucrats and experts involved. Therefore, any attempt to maintain the East Asian social policy turn to a social investment paradigm should be practised with caution.

The previous sections have shown that social policy initiatives in Taiwan and Hong Kong featured more significant concerns in supporting new social risk groups through various social investment initiatives (see Table 2.1). However, the active labour market policy in Hong Kong has typically been characterised as *workfarist* in nature, and pro-market policies have continued to predominate (Chan, 2011; Chan and Chan, 2013). The Hong Kong government consulted the public concerning supporting working families to increase women's labour participation rate in 2014, and the chief executive pledged efforts by the Hong Kong government to unleash women's working potential in her 2017 Policy Address. These policy ideas seemed to favour a move beyond the market-focused adult worker model, but overall, the supported adult worker model in Hong Kong has been judged as 'truncated' (Yu et al., 2019). By contrast, Hong Kong continues to emphasise the public sector's minimal role in providing social services, especially for children and young people. These services have often been conceived as part of a push towards advancing social innovation and entrepreneurship in close partnership between government

Table 2.1   Selected social policy initiatives in Taiwan and Hong Kong

Policy area	Beneficiaries	Taiwan	Hong Kong
Active labour market policy	Unemployed and working poor	Employment Insurance Act, 1999 and 2003 Adjustment of the national poverty line in Social Assistance, 2011	Low-Income Working Family Allowance, 2014
	Young people	Youth Employment Flagship Programme, 2016 Employment Assistance Programme, 2020	Career Let's Go Programme, 2018 Youth Employment and Training Programme, 2019
	Persons with disabilities	Implementation of the Convention on the Rights of Persons with Disabilities, 2014	On the Job Training Programme for People with Disabilities, 2001 Work Orientation and Placement Scheme, 2005
Family support	Working families and children	Cash subsidies for families in need of childcare, 2008 Local government initiatives of childcare provision since 2011 Implementation of the Convention on the Rights of the Child, 2014	Ageing in Place Scheme, 2012 Pilot Scheme on Living Allowance for Carers of Elderly Persons from Low-Income Families, 2014
Retirement income	Older adults	Labour Pension Act, 2004 National Pension Insurance, 2009 Pension Reform for Civil Servants and Public School Teachers, 2016	Mandatory Provident Fund, 2000 Old Age Living Allowance, 2013 Higher Tier of Old Age Living Allowance, 2018

departments, welfare organisations, healthcare service providers and other stakeholders (Choi et al., 2022).

In Taiwan, new social programmes such as active labour market policy and family support have also not entirely corresponded to the social investment doctrine. Instead, policy reforms are best understood as recalibration within the productivist paradigm. As such, the emphasis on human capital accumulation and its contribution to the economy remains inscribed in the genes of the Taiwanese welfare state. Social investment initiatives have risen to political importance, but a closer look reveals that private service provision remains dominant. This was the legacy when the state eschewed responsibility, and families in need had to turn to the individual network (primarily grandparents) or private care markets for resources. Even now, when the government recognises the significance of public care provision, policy design can barely ignore the predominance of providers in care markets. Thus, regulating private care providers to support family policy goals will become essential in future development.

As a heuristic device, empirical studies of social policy development have drawn a conceptual distinction between new, post-industrial, preventative, inclusive welfare policies on the one hand and old, industrial, compensatory, exclusive welfare policy approaches on the other (Kuitto, 2011). However, a question has been raised about whether such a distinction of policy areas is conceptually useful (Nolan, 2013). For instance, generous unemployment and sickness benefit schemes have long been argued to support aggregate consumer demand in the local economy by improving affected individuals' household incomes and enabling young people to search for jobs commensurate with their attained skills (Clasen, 1999). Similarly, work pay measures, such as the minimum wage policy, make paid employment financially more attractive for young women than remaining on benefits or depending on a male breadwinner (Annesley, 2007). Moreover, by giving young female workers additional financial resources through paid maternity leave and job-related retirement programmes, governments may assist women in taking full advantage of their attained skills and qualifications and helping them achieve a reasonable independent standard of living over the life course (Yu et al., 2019).

In Taiwan and Hong Kong, social investment initiatives have been implemented alongside attempts to provide better social protection for certain groups of beneficiaries, particularly older adults. Taiwan's welfare recalibration generally allowed more room for extending social security for older adults by passing landmark social insurance legislation from the mid-1990s (Yang and Kühner, 2020). However, efforts specifically for informal employment bore little fruit despite ongoing policy debates about including these precarious workers in the existing labour protection system. By comparison, the Hong Kong government has generally remained much more reluctant to expand social rights in any meaningful way. What welfare is provided has remained strictly targeted and selective, stressing engagement with the labour market and the deservingness aspect of welfare (Chan, 2006). The welfare system in Hong Kong has held steadfast in its avoidance of any profligacy whilst ensuring that welfare subsidies are fiscally sustainable and do not disincentivise work.

The social investment policies in Taiwan and Hong Kong have been diverse, but how can we explain this diversity? First, the social politics in East Asia has changed since the 1990s. Although democratisation has provided vulnerable population groups with an avenue to vent their voice, the pluralistic and contested policymaking processes render the government officials, legislators and civil society groups not only chances of policy breakthrough but also risks of political backlash, mainly depending on the contingent junctures of policy networks and advocacy coalitions (Sabatier and Jenkins-Smith, 1993). Democratic politics does not always head towards welfare expansion, as actor constellations turn versatile, complicating policymaking processes. The partisan competition also invites diverse proposals from the major parties that may constrain the state's administrative capacity to strengthen social protection.

Furthermore, industrial structures or production regimes matter. There is a wide variety amongst East Asian countries in this regard, particularly when it comes to firm size in the organisational composition of the economic sector. Japan and Korea are well known for their reliance on industrial conglomerates (*keiretsu* and *chaebol*, respectively) as the heavyweight of the national economy. Employees of these economic giants generally enjoy job security and lavish fringe benefits compared to their colleagues of other small- and middle-sized enterprises (SMEs). In other words, labour markets here feature pronouncedpprox.ionn in employment protection and income security. By contrast, Taiwan has historically developed an industrial structure with SMEs as the major player, absorbing most of the labour force. Hong Kong, as a global city that acts as a hub that concentrates key industrial sectors into a small number of large metropolitan agglomerations, has grown into a strategic conduit 'connecting global capital and China' that thrives in the role of China's 'offshore financial centre' (Lai, 2012: 1275; Taylor et al., 2014). As a result, transnational elites working in APS firms have increasingly become the dominant force in economically dominated global cities, such as Hong Kong, which have transformed to cater to the specific lifestyles and occupational needs of its wealth creators, including ensuring low tax rates and the availability of world-class education systems, healthcare facilities, policing and informational infrastructure (Florida, 2014).

In addition to the political economy, institutional arrangements of social security can shape how ideas and interests posed by actors find their expression leading to institutional continuity and change (Bonoli and Natali, 2012; Streeck and Thelen, 2005). A critical lesson in pension policy is that countries with pay-as-you-go pension insurance programmes often find it hard to switch to fully funded schemes at one stroke but rather seek to incorporate partially funded pensions into overall old-age security systems (Ebbinghaus, 2011). The East Asian welfare states feature rather diverse configurations of their social security systems – in contrast between those with social insurance programmes and public provision as the centrepiece (such as Korea and Taiwan) and others with social assistance and private provision as the prime welfare (such as Hong Kong and Singapore) (Kim, 2015; Peng and Wong, 2010). The variety of social security systems can facilitate or constrain the policy repertoire available to the political and social actors involved in policy processes.

Finally, this raises questions about the prospect of social investment policy in East Asia. The realisation of 'smart' social investment policies in East Asia, including Taiwan and Hong Kong, may depend on the deliberate combination of social investment and social protection policies to increase their functionality mutually. To achieve such institutional complementarity is, of course, extremely difficult. It has been argued, for instance, that many historical 'good practice' constellations were not deliberately designed by policymakers but rather resulted from singular moments of serendipity (Streeck and Yamamura, 2001). 'Good practice' constellations are challenging to achieve because they present a moving target (Crouch et al., 2005) and rely on path-dependent fundamental first policy settlements (Mahoney and Thelen, 2010). Moreover, institutional complementarity has been shown to depend on effective synergies with the private sector and other stakeholders (Lange and Rueschemeyer, 2005) and are subject to negotiated political processes, which may considerably slow down the 'response time' of governments.

Conclusion

In reviewing the evidence of the politics and policies of social investment, this chapter argued that Taiwan and Hong Kong, despite sharing many commonalities in terms of the contemporary social pressures they face, began to diverge in their reform endeavour towards social investment. So far, these initiatives are best understood as part of an adjustment of productivist features rather than a radical shift towards an East Asian post-productivist settlement to a social investment state. Nevertheless, the analysis points to important implications for understanding the current development of East Asian social policy, namely the increasing heterogeneity in institutional building and restructuring.

This chapter also drew on the various factors that account for diverging social investment policy in Taiwan and Hong Kong, including political advocacy coalitions that favour or discourage policy change, production regimes that shape the public–private mix of social provision and existing social security systems that place constraints on the political and social actors involved. Given the increasing heterogeneity in institutional building and restructuring, the broad concept of social investment fails to fully capture the essence of a quickly changing East Asian policy landscape. We concluded by suggesting that a search for a deliberate strategy to complement social investment and social security policy promises to be the best way for East Asian policymakers to promote new social risk groups via fostering human capital accumulation and more efficient labour markets.

So far, a shift towards such an institutional complementarity has not been discernible even when considering the immediate crisis responses to the global COVID-19 pandemic in the two East Asian societies. After suffering disproportionately during the SARS pandemic, Taiwan and Hong Kong successfully limited the number of confirmed cases with their public health and community responses to the global COVID-19 pandemic (Choi et al., 2022; Lei and Klopack, 2020; Soon et al., 2021). Furthermore, to protect the labour market from mass dismissal, the governments in Taiwan and Hong Kong strengthened corporate cash subsidies and wage subsidies paid directly to employees. Social assistance recipients in Taiwan and Hong Kong received additional one-off support for a certain period to mitigate the financial pressure on vulnerable groups. The issuance of time-limited stimulus vouchers to be redeemed for retailers' purchase of consumer goods was designed to revitalise the domestic economy.

The introduction and expansion of labour market programmes and cash benefits responding to the pandemic were costly. As a result, governments in Taiwan and Hong Kong resorted to extraordinary supplementary budgets for resources. In 2020, Taiwan's related additional government spending reached over 2.2 per cent of its gross domestic product (GDP). As the COVID-19 cases in Taiwan soared in June 2021, the government handed out an additional 260 billion yuan relief package (about 1.3 per cent of the 2019 GDP). The initial economic response by the Hong Kong government centred on a HK$25 billion stimulus package pprox.x. £2.4 billion). In March 2020, retailers and factory tenants were granted rent concessions, followed by additional subsidies for the aviation industry and ancillary services worth HK$1 billion pprox.x. £97 million). The final phase of the stimulus response was announced on 8 April 2020 with an additional HK$138 billion pprox.x. £13.4 billion, about 0.5 per cent of GDP), which included an enhanced SME financing scheme, transportation fare discounts and student loan repayment deferrals.

Despite these various short-term responses to the pandemic, institutional continuity of social policy was reflected within the policy discourses that framed the crisis as merely temporary. In Taiwan, expanding the existing social security programmes with extraordinary budgets was considered sufficient to help people weather the storm. During the new pandemic waves in mid-2021 and early 2022, the opposition party vented the idea of a basic income for all but has so far received little resonance in the public policy discussion. The Taiwanese government stuck to the original idea and insisted on its course of selective programmes. As for Hong Kong, the focus on emergency relief and stimulus measures is perhaps of little surprise given the staunch residualist value inherent in Hong Kong's social security system. Throughout the local COVID-19 outbreak, the Hong Kong government was reluctant to commit to any long-term structural expansion of social rights, instead firmly pointing to concerns about government profligacy and the long-term sustainability of social security.

Overall, recent policy reforms in Hong Kong and Taiwan may indicate signs of the social investment turn but its substance remains vague. A firm push against the institutional legacies in Hong Kong and Taiwan may still be on the horizon. Whilst the global COVID-19 pandemic was not the trigger that some commentators had expected, the social investment paradigm may still play a major role to alleviate the ensuing deterioration in physical and mental health via increasing individuals' sense of economic security and ability to engage in rational self-actualisation – 'entrepreneurially' motivated or otherwise.

References

An, M. Y., and Peng, I. (2016). 'Diverging paths? A comparative look at childcare policies in Japan, South Korea and Taiwan'. *Social Policy and Administration*, 50(5): 540–558.

Annesley, C. (2007). 'Women's political agency and welfare reform: Engendering the adult worker model'. *Parliamentary Affairs*, 60(3): 452–466.

Bonoli, G., and Natali, D. (eds) (2012). *The politics of the new welfare state*. Oxford: Oxford University Press.

Burroni, L., and Keune, M. (2011). 'Flexicurity: A conceptual critique'. *European Journal of Industrial Relations*, 17(1): 75–91.

Census and Statistics Department (2017). Feature article on Hong Kong Labour Force Projections for 2017 to 2066. www.statistics.gov.hk/pub/B71710FB2017XXXXB0100.pdf

Chan, C. K. (2011). 'Hong Kong: Workfare in the world's freest economy'. *International Journal of Social Welfare*, 20(1): 22–32.

Chan, R. K. H. (2006). 'Risk and its management in post-financial crisis Hong Kong'. *Social Policy and Administration*, 409(2): 215–229.

Chan, R. K. H., and Chan, C. K. C. (2013). 'The shifting boundary between work and welfare: A review of active labour market policies in Hong Kong'. *Journal of Asian Public Policy*, 6: 26–41.

Chang, H.-H. (2007). 'Social change and the disability rights movement in Taiwan'. *Review of Disability Studies: An International Journal*, 3(1–2): 1–17.

Chen, H.-H., and Shi, S.-J. (2021). 'Changing dynamics of social policy in democracy: Comparing pension and health reforms in Taiwan'. *Journal of Asian Public Policy*, 14(1): 30–44.

Choi, Y. J. (2013). 'Developmentalism and productivism in East Asian welfare regimes', in M. Izuhara (ed.), *Handbook on East Asian social policy*, Cheltenham, UK and Northampton, MA, USA: Edward Elgar Publishing, pp. 207–225.

Choi, Y. J., Huber, E., Kim, W.-S., Kwon, H.-Y., and Shi, S.-J. (2020). 'Social investment in the knowledge-based economy: New politics and policies'. *Policy and Society*, 39(2): 147–170.

Choi, Y. J., Fleckenstein, T., and Lee, S.-H. C. (eds) (2021). *Welfare reform and social investment policy in Europe and East Asia: International lessons and policy implications*. Bristol: Policy Press.

Choi, Y. J., Kühner, S., and Shi, S. J. (2022). 'From "new social risks" to "COVID social risks": The challenges for inclusive society in South Korea, Hong Kong, and Taiwan amid the pandemic'. *Policy and Society*, 41(2): 260–274.

Chui, E., and Ko, L. (2011). 'New wine or old? From colony to SAR – elderly welfare in Hong Kong'. *China Journal of Social Work*, 4(1): 5–22.

Clasen, J. (1999). 'Beyond social security: The economic value of giving money to unemployed people'. *European Journal of Social Security*, 1(2): 151–179.

Crouch, C., Streeck, W., Boyer, R., Amable, B., Hall, P. A., and Jackson, G. (2005). 'Dialogue on institutional complementarity and political economy'. *Socio-Economic Review*, 3(2): 359–382.

Ebbinghaus, B. (ed.) (2011). *The varieties of pension governance: Pension privatisation in Europe*. Oxford: Oxford University Press.

Esping-Andersen, G. (1990). The Three Worlds of Welfare Capitalism. Princeton, New Jersey: Princeton University Press.

Esping-Andersen, G., Gallie, D., Hemerijck, A., and Myles, J. (2002). *Why we need a new welfare state*. Oxford: Oxford University Press.

Fleckenstein, T., and Lee, S.-H. C. (2017). 'Democratisation, post-industrialisation, and East Asian welfare capitalism: The politics of welfare state reform in Japan, South Korea, and Taiwan'. *Journal of International and Comparative Social Policy*, 33(1): 36–54.

Florida, R. (2014). *The rise of the creative class – revisited: Revised and expanded*. New York: Basic Books.

Goishi, N. (2011). 'Social safety net for the working poor in Japan, Korea and Taiwan', in G. J. Hwang (ed.), *New welfare states in East Asia: Global challenges and restructuring*. Cheltenham, UK and Northampton, MA, USA: Edward Elgar Publishing, pp. 108–124.

Haggard, S., and Kaufman, R. R. (2008). *Development, democracy, and welfare states: Latin America, East Asia, and East Europe*. Princeton, NJ: Princeton University Press.

Hemerijck, A., and Vandenbroucke, F. (2012). 'Social investment and the Euro crisis: The necessity of a unifying social policy concept'. *Intereconomics*, 47(4): 200–206.

Holliday, I. (2000). 'Productivist welfare capitalism'. *Political Studies*, 48: 706–723.

Holliday, I. (2005). 'East Asian social policy in the wake of the financial crisis: Farewell to productivism?'. *Policy and Politics*, 33(1): 145–162.

Huang, C.-L. (2012). 'Integrating breadwinning and childcare in the family policy formation in Taiwan'. *Journal of Social Sciences and Philosophy*, 24(3): 331–366 (in Chinese).

Hudson, J., and Kühner, S. (2009). 'Towards productive welfare? A comparative analysis of 23 OECD countries'. *Journal of European Social Policy*, 19(1): 34–46.

Hudson, J., and Kühner, S. (2011). 'Analysing the productive dimensions of welfare: Looking beyond East Asia', in G.-J. Hwang (ed.), *New welfare states in East Asia: Global challenges and restructuring*. Cheltenham, UK and Northampton, MA, USA: Edward Elgar Publishing, pp. 35–60.

Hwang, G.-J. (2006). *Pathways to state welfare in Korea: Interests, ideas and institutions*. Aldershot: Ashgate.

Jenson, J. (2013). 'Changing perspectives on social citizenship: A cross-time comparison', in A. Evers and A.-M. Guillemard (eds), *Social policy and citizenship: The changing landscape*. Oxford: Oxford University Press, pp. 57–79.

Johnson, C. (1999). 'The developmental state: Odyssey of a concept', in M. Woo-Cumi (ed.), *The developmental state*. Ithaca, NY: Cornell University Press, pp. 32–60.

Jones, C. (1990). 'Hong Kong, Singapore, South Korea and Taiwan: Economic welfare states'. *Government and Opposition*, 25(4): 447–462.

Kim, M. M. S. (2015). *Comparative welfare capitalism in East Asia: Productivist models of social policy*. Basingstoke: Palgrave.

Kim, W. S., and Shi, S.-J. (2013). 'Emergence of new welfare states in East Asia? Domestic social changes and the impact of "welfare internationalism" in South Korea and Taiwan (1945–2012)'. *International Journal of Social Quality*, 3(2): 106–124.

Kim, W. S., and Shi, S.-J. (2020). 'East Asian approaches of activation: The politics of labor market policies in South Korea and Taiwan'. *Policy and Society*, 39(2): 226–246

Kim, Y.-M. (2008). Beyond East Asian Welfare Productivism in South Korea. Policy and Politics, 36(1): 109–125.

Ko, J.-J., and Chang, P.-C. (2014). 'Segmented labor markets? An investigation of job mobility and wage differences between standard and nonstandard workers in Taiwan'. *Taiwanese Journal of Sociology*, 55: 127–177 (in Chinese).

Ku, Y.-W. (1997). *Welfare capitalism in Taiwan: State, economy and social policy*. Basingstoke: Macmillan.

Ku, Y. W., and Finer, C. J. (2007). 'Developments in East Asian welfare studies'. *Social Policy and Administration*, 41(2): 115–131.

Kühner, S. (2015). 'The productive and protective dimensions of welfare in Asia and the Pacific: Pathways towards human development and income equality?'. *Journal of International and Comparative Social Policy*, 31(2), 151–173.

Kühner, S., and Chou, K. L. (2019). 'Poverty alleviation, coverage and fiscal sustainability: Investigating the effect of a new social pension in Hong Kong'. *International Journal of Social Welfare*, 28(1): 89–99.

Kühner, S., Jiang, J., Lau, M., and Wen, Z. (2021). 'Labour market experience, educational attainment, and self-reported happiness: Crowding-out among young people in Hong Kong?'. *Journal of Education and Work*, 34(3): 275–291.

Kuitto, K. (2011). 'More than just money: Patterns of disaggregated welfare expenditure in the enlarged Europe'. *Journal of European Social Policy*, 21(4): 348–364.

Kwon, H. J. (ed.) (2005). *Transforming the developmental welfare state in East Asia*. Basingstoke: Palgrave Macmillan.

Lai, K. (2012). 'Differentiated markets: Shanghai, Beijing and Hong Kong in China's financial centre network'. *Urban Studies*, 49(6): 1275–1296.

Lam, C., and Fong, B. (2020). *'Ageing in place': Social and health implications in Hong Kong*. Hong Kong: Hong Kong Polytechnic University.

Lange, M., and Rueschemeyer, D. (2005). *States and development: Historical antecedents of stagnation and advance*. Cham: Springer.

Lee, C. H. (2010). 'The practical dilemma of employment insurance's unemployment benefit institutions in the mode of activation governance'. *Taiwan Democracy Quarterly*, 7(2): 125–176 (in Chinese).

Lee, S.-Y. (2011). 'Labour market risks in de-industrializing East Asian economies: The cases of Korea, Japan and Taiwan', in G. J. Hwang (ed.), *New welfare states in East Asia: Global challenges and restructuring*. Cheltenham, UK and Northampton, MA, USA: Edward Elgar Publishing, pp. 61–89.

Legislative Council Secretariat Research Office (2019). 'Opportunities and challenges facing maternal workforce in Hong Kong'. www.legco.gov.hk/research-publications/english/ 1819rb02 -opportunities -and -challenges -facing -maternal -workforce -in -hong-kong-20190716-e.pdf

Lei, M. K., and Klopack, E. T. (2020). 'Social and psychological consequences of the COVID-19 outbreak: The experiences of Taiwan and Hong Kong'. *Psychological Trauma: Theory, Research, Practice, and Policy*, 12(S1): S35.

Lin, W. I. (2006). *Taiwanese social welfare: Historical experiences and institutional analysis*. Taipei: Wunan Publishing Company (in Chinese).

Lue, J.-D. (2014). 'Globalisation, democratisation and the institutional transformation of Taiwan's welfare regime'. *Social Policy and Society*, 13(2): 275–284.

Mahoney, J., and Thelen, K. (2010). *Explaining institutional change: Ambiguity, agency and power*. Cambridge: Cambridge University Press.

Midgley, J. (1986). 'Industrialisation and welfare: The case of the four little tigers'. *Social Policy and Administration*, 20(3): 225–238.

Mok, K. H., and Jiang, J. (2018). 'Massification of higher education and challenges for graduate employment and social mobility: East Asian experiences and sociological reflections'. *International Journal of Educational Development*, 63: 44–51.

Mok, K. H., Kühner, S., and Huang, G. (2017). 'The productivist construction of selective welfare pragmatism in China'. *Social Policy and Administration*, 51(6): 876–897.

Morel, N., Palier, B., and Palme, J. (2012). *Towards a social investment state? Ideas, policies and challenges*. Bristol: Policy Press.

Nam, Y. (2020). 'The divergent evolution of East Asian welfare states: Japan, South Korea, Taiwan, and Singapore'. *Asian Politics and Policy*, 12(4): 559–574.

Nelson, M., and Stephens, J. D. (2012). 'Do social investment policies produce more and better jobs?', in N. Morel, B. Palier and J. Palme (eds), *Towards a social investment state? Ideas, policies and challenges*. Bristol: Policy Press, pp. 205–234.

Nolan, B. (2013). 'What use is social investment?'. *Journal of European Social Policy*, 23(5): 459–468.

Peng, I. (2012). 'The social and political economy of care in Japan and South Korea'. *International Journal of Sociology and Social Policy*, 32: 11/12.

Peng, I., and Wong, J. (2010). 'East Asia', in F. G. Castles, S. Leibfried, J. Lewis, H. Obinger and C. Pierson (eds), *The Oxford handbook of the welfare state*. Oxford: Oxford University Press, pp. 656–670.

Rieger, E., and Leibfried, S. (2003). *Limits to globalisation: Welfare states and the world economy*. Cambridge: Polity Press.

Ronchi, S. (2018). 'Which roads (if any) to social investment? The recalibration of EU welfare states at the crisis crossroads (2000–2014)'. *Journal of Social Policy*, 47(3): 459–478.

Rudra, N. (2008). *Globalization and the race to the bottom in developing countries: Who really gets hurt?* Cambridge: Cambridge University Press.

Sabatier, P. A., and Jenkins-Smith, H. C. (eds) (1993). *Policy change and learning: An advocacy coalition approach*. Boulder, CO: Westview Press.

Shi, S.-J. (2012). 'Towards inclusive social citizenship? Rethinking China's social security in the trend towards urban–rural harmonisation'. *Journal of Social Policy*, 41(4): 789–810.

Shi, S.-J. (2017). 'Social decentralization: Exploring the competitive solidarity of regional social protection in China'. *Journal of Asian Public Policy*, 10(1): 74–89.

Social Welfare Advisory Committee (2010). 'Long-term social welfare planning in Hong Kong'. Consultation paper. www.legco.gov.hk/yr09-10/english/panels/ws/papers/ws0605cb2-1649-1-e.pdf

Soon, S., Chou, C. C., and Shi, S.-J. (2021). 'Withstanding the plague: Institutional resilience of the East Asian welfare state'. *Social Policy and Administration*, 55(2): 374–387.

Streeck, W., and Thelen, K. (eds) (2005). *Beyond continuity: Institutional change in advanced political economies*. Oxford: Oxford University Press.

Streeck, W., and Yamamura, K. (eds) (2001). *The origins of non-liberal capitalism: Germany and Japan in comparison*. Ithaca, NY: Cornell University Press.

Tang, K. L. (2000). *Social welfare development in East Asia*. Basingstoke: Palgrave.

Tang, K. L., and Midgley, J. (2002). 'Social policy after the East Asian financial crisis: Forging a normative basis for welfare'. *Journal of Comparative Asian Development*, 1(2): 301–318.

Taylor, P. J., Derudder, B., Faulconbridge, J., Hoyler, M., and Ni, P. (2014). 'Advanced producer service firms as strategic networks, global cities as strategic places'. *Economic Geography*, 90(3): 267–291.

TFSA (Taiwanese Feminist Scholars Association) (2014). *White paper of women's situations in Taiwan*. Taipei: Fembooks Publish House (in Chinese).

Vaalavuo, M. (2013). 'The redistributive impact of "old" and "new" social spending'. *Journal of Social Policy*, 42(3): 513–539.

Van Vliet, O., and Wang, C. (2015). 'Social investment and poverty reduction: A comparative analysis across fifteen European countries'. *Journal of Social Policy*, 44(3): 611–638.

Wang, S.-Y. (2014). 'The analysis of infant care policies and debates in Taiwan'. *Taiwan: A Radical Quarterly in Social Studies*, 96: 49–93 (in Chinese).

Wong, C.-K., and Lou, V. W.-Q. (2010). '"I wish to be self-reliant": Aspiration for self-reliance, need and life satisfaction, and exit dilemma of welfare recipients in Hong Kong'. *Social Indicators Research*, 95: 519–534.

Wong, J. (2004). *Healthy democracies: Welfare politics in Taiwan and South Korea*. Ithaca, NY: Cornell University Press.

Yang, N., and Kühner, S. (2020). 'Beyond the limits of the productivist regime: Capturing three decades of East Asian welfare development with fuzzy sets'. *Social Policy and Society*, 19(4): 613–627.

Yeh, C.-Y., and Ku, Y.-W. (2017). 'From productivist welfare states to social investment welfare state: Comparing Taiwan and Korea'. *Social Policy and Social Work*, 21(1): 97–147 (in Chinese).

Yeh, C.-Y., Cheng, H. W., and Shi, S.-J. (2020). 'Public–private pension mixes in East Asia: Institutional diversity and policy implications for old-age security'. *Ageing and Society*, 40(3): 604–625.

Yu, S., Chau, R., and Kühner, S. (2019). 'Defamilisation and familisation risks, adult worker models, and pro-employment/decommodification measures for women: The case of Hong Kong'. *Journal of International and Comparative Social Policy*, 35(2): 194–210.

3   Exploring the relationship between social policy and innovation in South Korea

Young Jun Choi

Introduction

Innovation has been a key component of and driver behind social and economic development in contemporary capitalism. Schumpeter (1934), who first introduced the concept of innovation, defined it as new combinations of new or existing knowledge, resources, equipment, and other factors and equated it with 'creative destruction'. In a recent attempt, after reviewing various key definitions of innovation, Dwyer (2021) defined it as the process of creating *value* by applying *novel solutions* to meaningful problems. It has different dimensions, including both radical/product and incremental/process innovation. Romer (1986) drew attention for noting that innovation contributes to productivity growth by creating a variety of new products. Later, Aghion and Howitt (1992) added the incremental aspect of innovation, suggesting that the creative destruction discussed earlier by Schumpeter is possible even through quality improvement involving the refining of existing products. Both product and process innovations influence the level of national productivity (Crespi and Pianta, 2008).

Traditional innovation has been discussed only at the economic and commercial levels, but recently, the social aspect has been simultaneously emphasised. Drucker (1985) noted that innovation is a specific instrument of entrepreneurship and expanded the scope of innovation by stating that its concept is not limited to technological development or business but is a broad one that occurs within a social system. The Organisation for Economic Co-operation and Development (OECD, 2010) and Gault (2018) stated that innovation not only promotes growth but also helps to solve social problems. The subjects of innovation can be actors at various levels such as individuals, corporations, civil society, and the state. Their innovative activities include not only for-profit activities but also non-profit ones. Therefore, recent discussion of innovation is not limited to business innovation but is applied to social innovation as well.

In the age of climate change, the pandemic, and digitalisation, innovation is more essential than ever. In recent years, however, as national productivity has been staggering (Zukunft, 2018), many countries are finding a way to improve and facilitate innovative activities, for example by providing more investment in research and development. Interestingly enough, since inequality has been the most critical obstacle to growth and innovation (OECD, 2016; IMF, 2017; Gordon, 2018), the role of social policy has been put in the spotlight. Indeed, Nordic countries are the frontrunners in terms of innovation and inclusive social policy (*The Economist*, 2013). Social inequality in this region is among the lowest in the world. However, very few studies have explored the relationship between innovation and social policy. In particular, scholars barely focus on the role of social policy when discussing innovation and entrepreneurship in East Asia where strong developmentalist legacies exist.

In this context, this chapter has two objectives. It aims to examine how social policy and innovation can reinforce each other and explore the causal mechanism between them. Then it critically reviews the Korean case in terms of social policy and innovation and the Swedish case as an example. This chapter is based on qualitative interviews with Korean and Swedish academics, policymakers, and entrepreneurs in 2019 and 2020. South Korea (hereafter Korea) is one of the most studied East Asian welfare states from comparative perspectives. In Korea, innovation and economic growth, instead of social welfare, have always been the top national goals, but they suffer from elite/*chaebol*-led innovation and a tremendous productivity gap between large and small to medium-sized enterprises (SMEs), which also affects its high rate of inequality (OECD, 2018). Thus, Korea presents a good case by which to discuss this issue. In the end, I will argue that to tackle increasingly distressing socio-economic problems, inclusive innovation along with robust social policy is required in Korea and other East Asian countries.

Innovation and welfare state in crisis?

The most common perception of innovation and social policy is that they are inversely related. This traditional view of innovation and welfare states is that innovation is more likely to occur in unequal societies, and innovation inevitably leads to inequality. Some studies predict that generous welfare benefits and a heavy tax burden will reduce entrepreneurship and the motivation for innovation (Henrekson and Rosenberg, 2001).

However, recent studies and empirical evidence suggest that welfare state institutions can instead become the basis for innovation and growth. Social policy, not only education but also unemployment benefits, helps individuals accumulate stable human capital, reinforcing innovation by bolstering risk-taking motivations and behaviours rather than avoiding them (Mkandawire, 2007; Filippetti and Guy, 2016; Bell et al., 2017). At the same time, the inclusion formed by the welfare state increases the sense of solidarity with social capital, thereby strengthening participation and autonomy and enhancing social innovation. In fact, according to the European Union in 2018, the generous welfare states of Sweden, Denmark, Finland, and the Netherlands have the highest innovation rankings (European Union, 2018). This evidence also means that innovation and welfare states are compatible.

While this debate has not yet been settled, welfare states, including Korea, are experiencing several challenges regarding innovation and welfare. First, the trend of various productivity indicators shows that productivity is decreasing rather than increasing despite recent technological developments (OECD, 2016). This is called the 'productivity paradox' at the national level (Soete, 2018). Although productivity increases periodically as seen in the 1990s, in general, the rate of increase has been steadily falling since the 1970s. Paradoxically, this phenomenon has become more prominent in recent years, with the digital revolution. As innovation is an important driver behind productivity, this could also mean there is an innovation crisis. Gordon (2012, 2014) observed this situation and argued that it would be difficult to expect a remarkable speed of growth and innovation in the near future.

The second challenge is unequal and uninclusive growth, which has deepened social polarisation. It is true that the rate of increase in productivity of some high-end multinational companies such as Apple and Samsung increased considerably even after 2000, but the problem is that the productivity of most SMEs that make up most of the economy has been stagnating or even decreasing since 2000 in many OECD countries (Andrews et al., 2015). At the enterprise level, productivity increases considerably when the workforce is reduced by introducing machines or automation. However, on a national level, the productivity rate will be affected by whether a company's human resources pushed out by automation can continue to work with high productivity in other firms or become unskilled and unemployed. Depending on whether this segment is made up of low-wage/low-productive jobs, the country's productivity may vary.

These two challenges, stagnant innovation and unequal growth, have produced poor socio-economic outcomes. On the one hand, slow growth and innovation could aggravate socio-economic conditions, including employment and state fiscal capacity. On the other hand, even if innovation continues to grow, the large productivity gap and the subsequent wage gap between large corporations and SMEs is still problematic. It reinforces income inequality without substantial efforts to redistribute across different income groups. Indeed, successful growth and innovation for the last decades have not necessarily produced desirable social outcomes in many economically advanced states.

Against these challenges, scholars and governments pay attention to the effect of inequality on growth and innovation. International organisations such as the OECD and International Monetary Fund (IMF) have consistently emphasised inclusive growth and argued that reducing inequality is a vital foundation for sustainable growth (OECD, 2016; IMF, 2017; Gordon, 2018). For example, the IMF report *Tackling Inequality*, though less specific about innovation, pointed out that inequality undermines not only social cohesion and political polarisation but also economic growth. As a policy measure, IMF emphasised fiscal redistribution, including progressivity of income taxation, universal basic income, and public spending on better education and health. In this context, the agenda of inclusive growth and innovation is of greater importance for creating high-quality jobs and strengthening SMEs. The OECD (2016) highlighted the role of inclusive innovation policies to remove the barriers faced by individuals, firms, and regions that participate in innovation activities.

These studies pay attention to the role of social policy and its positive feedback with innovation and growth. In sum, innovation is important for social inclusion. It is not feasible to overhaul the dualisation in the labour market only with social policy and redistribution. Innovative firms and quality jobs are essential for dealing with social inequality. Simultaneously, policy measures are required to reduce insecurity and inequality in individual lives, which can be the most critical obstacles to innovation. Innovation and welfare should be mutually reinforcing.

Why is innovation problematic in South Korea?

Korea has implemented a number of innovation policies as part of its efforts to revitalise the economy. As a result of these endeavours, it currently ranks 11th worldwide based on the Global Innovation Index 2019, as compared to 28th worldwide in terms of 2018 per capita gross domestic product (GDP) (World Intellectual Property Organization, 2019). China and Japan ranked 14th and 15th, respectively. Korea's innovation index is at a much higher level compared to its economic level. Indeed, innovation has been a forefront keyword over the last two decades, particularly since the Kim Dae-Jung government took office in 1997. The common point of these policies is to break away from a paradigm based on factor-driven growth and pursue innovation-based economic growth with high value-added products and services.

Social innovation also began to take off, inducing progress in the social economy as the government rapidly expanded institutional support in the 2000s. Since the enactment of the Social Enterprise Promotion Act in 2007, support for various social economy-related policies such as cooperatives, self-supporting enterprises, and village enterprises has been introduced. As a result of these efforts, Korea ranked 12th in the 2016 International Evaluation of Social Innovation published by *The Economist* Intelligence Unit (2016). Despite these achievements, innovation in Korea has exposed serious defects in the following aspects.

Elite-oriented innovation

For innovation to occur sustainably and become inclusive, it must occur everywhere by anyone. The first and most crucial problem with Korea's innovation is that the foundation for innovation is not broad, and innovation is carried out by a small number of people and firms. This elite-oriented innovation leads to the polarisation of wages and productivity, leading in turn to the polarisation of the labour market. In addition, when the excessive influence of large corporations and exploitative structures in terms of business to business and regular versus non-regular workers are combined, the productivity gap between large corporations and SMEs in Korea is significant. According to the OECD (2014a), while the productivity of large enterprises with 250 or more employees was rated 100, the productivity of small workplaces with one to nine employees was only about 30. However, not all countries have a significant gap in productivity between large and small enterprises. In countries with more inclusive policies and politics, such as the Netherlands, Denmark, Finland, France, and Sweden, the rate was 70–80 per cent.

This productivity gap also leads to a wage gap. According to a study by Roh (2018), when the wages of large companies with 500 or more workers in Korea were 100, the wages of firms with five to nine workers were 48, and only 33 for workers at firms with one to four workers. However, in the case of the United States, the wage level of workplaces with one to four people was 79 compared to that of large corporations. Japan was 66 and France was 59. In other words, the difference in the productivity gap significantly affects the wage level, and it also implies that the difference in the productivity gap deepens the labour market's dualisation.

According to the Global Entrepreneurship Monitor (2015), the proportion of those engaged in innovation activities within the company was quite low at 2.4 per cent, one of the lowest in OECD countries (author's calculation). This number is surprising because most of the innovation in Korea comes from in-house innovators of companies rather than through entrepreneurship innovators. However, there are still very few employees taking part in innovation. Although there are in-house innovation activities centred on large companies, most workers are less inclined to work with creativity and autonomy in a hierarchical corporate structure. If many people do simple tasks or perform according to instructions, it is difficult to engage in innovation activities. Also, among OECD countries, Korea had the lowest proportion of women among in-house innovators (Global Entrepreneurship Monitor, 2015), reflecting high gender inequality and a male-dominated culture in the Korean labour market.

Low utilisation rate and mismatch of human capital

The university entrance rate in Korea has steadily risen, reaching almost 70 per cent. The problem is that the rise in the college enrolment rate is not leading to productivity in industry. As mentioned earlier, SMEs, which account for 99 per cent of enterprises and more than 80 per cent of employment, have significantly lower productivity than large enterprises. On the other hand, large corporations account for only about 20 per cent of employment but produce about 80 per cent of GDP. In other words, 70 per cent of Koreans go to college, but they are unlikely to get a job in a highly productive company. This appears to be a mismatch in the labour market, and from a different point of view, no condition can be fully utilised for human capital. These mismatches are currently appearing as various issues related to youth in Korean society (see also Chapter 7 by Izuhara and Yi in this volume). The NEET (not in education, employment, or training) rate of college graduates is only 13 per cent in OECD countries, whereas in Korea it is 24 per cent (OECD, 2014b). The underutilisation of human capital, as well as young people, is also occurring among women and adults. The employment rate is quite low compared to women's education level, and the gender wage gap is also the highest among OECD countries. Further, it has been shown in previous studies that the skill level rapidly declines as one gets older, compared to other advanced countries (Ban, 2016). The present state of human capital shows the need for a new social and economic system that can properly utilise human capital.

Lack of creativity

Creativity is a product of socio-economic and institutional environments (Glăveanu, 2010), which is increasingly important in the knowledge-based economy (Florida, 2006). Also, creativity has been emphasised in the era of artificial intelligence (AI) technology as it can replace human labour. Frey and Osborne (2017) predicted that computer technology would replace routinised jobs, and that level would be 47 per cent of jobs in the United States, which shocked many. However, Goos, Manning, and Salomons (2014) argued that the occupations that perform routine jobs are likely to be replaced by AI and automation technology. Those who perform creative tasks will dominate the labour market. It shows how important creativity will be in our society in the future. Creativity is essential for workers to adapt to new situations and increase their problem-solving capability quickly.

The lack of creativity in the workplace is remarkable throughout Korean society. Choi, Koo, and Yun (2018) examined whether their work is repetitive or creative through the 6th World Value Survey and simultaneously asked whether they perform work independently or subordinately (Figure 3.1). Workers in countries such as the Netherlands, Sweden, and New Zealand responded that they worked creatively and independently with considerable discretion. In contrast, in Spain and Korea, this response was quite low. Japan was slightly higher than Korea but belonged to the lower group. This lack of creativity is also seen in innovation indicators. In the most widely used Global Innovation Index, Korea ranked 11th in 2019, but the indicators related to creativity were considerably lower, such as creative goods and services (42nd) and online creativity (37th) in 2019. It seems that the hierarchical culture of workplaces and the labour market hinders creativity.

Tendency to seek excessive stability

Entrepreneurship is the ability to innovate to capture business opportunities in the marketplace and obtain high rewards (Deepa Babu and Manalel, 2016), taking appropriate risks based on a strong need for achievement. Knight (1921) defined an innovative entrepreneur as a person with the ability to calculate and sort out risk and uncertainty, and McClelland (1965) emphasised that due to a strong need for achievement, they should be able to take risks. Therefore, a country's entrepreneurial spirit represents its innovation. The key element of entrepreneurship is the risk-taking tendency. If people have a high risk-aversion tendency such as not trying new things, it is difficult for innovation to come through. In that sense, the high risk-taking propensity in

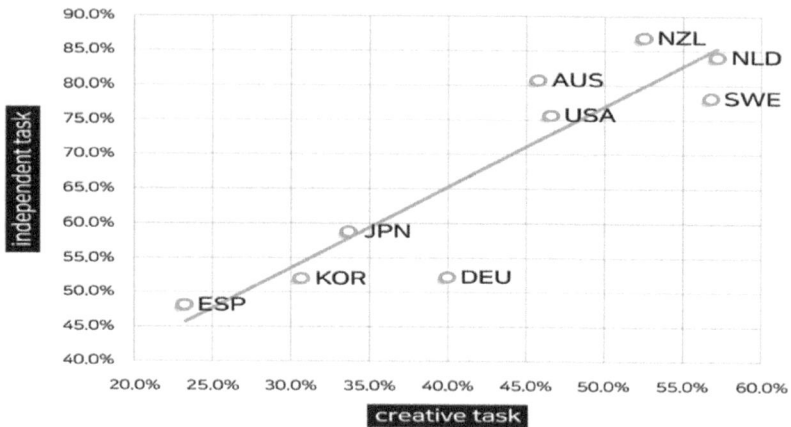

Source: 6th wave of the World Value Survey (Choi et al., 2018).

Figure 3.1   International comparison of creativity

each society can be said to be one of the significant barometers that show how active innovation would be in the future.

In particular, risk-taking tendencies in the 20s and 30s are important. According to the analysis of Bell et al. (2017), in the period when the highest patent citation index was published, most patents were sought by individuals aged from their late 30s to early 40s. In other words, this period is when many of the most creative ideas come to mind and the innovation capacity to realise them is high. However, to have a high innovation capability in these age cohorts, experience must be accumulated in the 20s and 30s. In other words, through the experience of 10 years of challenges, we can achieve outstanding results from our late 30s to early 40s.

According to the National Statistical Office of Korea (2017), young Koreans have fairly low risk-taking tendencies. The social survey shows that most young people wanted to work in government (25.4 per cent) or public enterprises (19.9 per cent). They had a higher preference for working in the public sector than in large companies (15.1 per cent), which do not guarantee life-long employment. Facing an uncertain future with increasing insecurity, young people simply desire stable jobs and pensions in the public sector rather than pursue what they want to do (Figure 3.2). In contrast, the preference for venture entrepreneurs, which means entrepreneurial innovators, was only about 3 per cent. Even internationally, the proportion of those unable to start a business because of the fear of failure was very high among the OECD countries (Global Entrepreneurship Monitor, 2015).

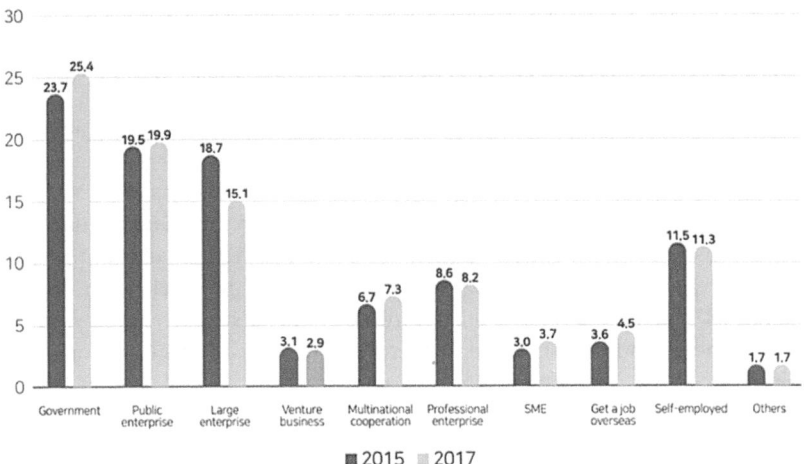

Source: National Statistical Office of Korea (2017).

Figure 3.2   Young people's future job prospects

Vulnerable self-employed people

As the importance of startups was attracting attention, many types of startup policies were implemented in Korea, leading to an increase in their number. However, rather than simply a number of startups, a quality startup maintained for a long time is the driving force of practical innovation. Although several criteria can assess their quality, one of the key dimensions to distinguish them is motivation. A necessity-type startup refers to a case in which a business provides a livelihood such as there are no other means to survive. An opportunity-type startup refers to starting a business to seize better business opportunities. The higher the opportunity-type entrepreneurship index and the lower the livelihood-type entrepreneurship index, the more positively the entrepreneurial spirit is affected.

According to *Entrepreneurship at a Glance* (OECD, 2014a), 21 per cent of domestic startups were opportunistic, and 63 per cent were the necessity type. In the case of Denmark, however, the situation was the opposite, with about 76 per cent of startups the opportunistic type and only 10 per cent the necessity type. Among OECD countries, Korea is the country with the highest portion of necessity-type startups. In sum, compared to the OECD, Korea is the country that has the lowest proportion of entrepreneurs whose motivation is enthusiasm and interest in business opportunities (OECD, 2018).

Low public acceptance of innovation

Fundamentally, innovation is the process by which new ideas become a reality, which entails substantial change. The resistance of society to these changes can cause innovation to fail to function properly in society. Innovation resistance refers to the inability to accept innovative technology or change situations, where resistance is the state of consumers who refuse to change from their current circumstances, reflecting the sense of threat they feel about change (Ram, 1987). Such high resistance to innovation means a decrease in demand for technology and industry, and furthermore, there is a risk of causing social upheaval.

As an example, we can look at the reaction to a ride-sharing service. Uber is a company that provides a service that connects drivers and passengers by using smartphone applications as a platform. Similar services have been introduced around the world, but the patterns of support and the degree of public opposition or conflict vary from country to country. Uber Korea was launched in August 2013. Since then, opposition to ride-sharing services and conflict have continued. Taxi drivers have been protesting to address the threat to their right to make a living and there have even been suicide attempts.

This fierce opposition resembles the Luddite movement in Britain in the early eighteenth century, which feared that machines would destroy jobs. Therefore, there is a perspective that sees this phenomenon itself as a neo-Luddite movement. Neo-Luddism is a modern philosophy that means fear or disbelief about changes made unavoidable by new technologies. Adherents believe that the use of technology has serious ethical, moral, and social implications. Hence, they are critical of technology and are very cautious about using it, and some accept the simple life of not using technology at all (Hunt-Bull, 2006). Interestingly, the degree of acceptance and rejection of new innovative changes seems to be influenced by social policy. Where social policies are secured, safety nets are strong, and people tend to accept changes rather than reject them because they feel threatened. The countries with high consumer acceptance for autonomous vehicles, an innovative new technology, are the Netherlands, Norway, and Sweden. On the other hand, in Korea, which has a high level of technology (7th) and infrastructure (4th), consumer acceptance is low at 19th (KPMG, 2019).

Weak foundation for social innovation

The development of new technologies such as information and communication technology and AI is expected to bring about a new change in our society as a whole (Bulut et al., 2013). However, since the 2008 economic crisis, discussions have been actively conducted on whether the results of creating added value in the economic field create positive values for society, the environment, and culture (Hubert, 2010). In particular, problems in modern society tend to be diversified and complicated, and the existing state-centred policy approach alone is too rigid or insufficient in responding to new problems (Weber and Khademian, 2008). Accordingly, the ability of citizens to resolve voluntary/ autonomous problems, innovation initiatives in non-governmental sectors such as social enterprises and non-profit sectors, and technological development are being emphasised as factors that will contribute to social innovation. In other words, this shows that social innovation and business innovation do not work independently as separate areas but are intertwined.

The importance of civil society in terms of reciprocity between social innovation and business innovation also emerges in the role of non-profit sectors in the United States and Europe. In the United States, non-profits' role in resolving social problems and preserving social potential during the economic crisis has been attracting attention (Graddy-Reed and Feldman, 2015). Friesenhahn (2016) evaluated that the non-profit sector played a role in buffering and absorbing the risk of employment decline in the private sector during the economic crisis, thereby retaining the growth potential of the subsequent economic recovery period. In Europe, the non-profit sector represents the share of employment comparable to that of the trade and manufacturing sectors. It has been identified as a major factor in solving social problems with the government (Salamon and Sokolowski, 2018). However, of these sectors, about 20 per cent and 15 per cent of those employed worked in this sector in the United States and Europe as of 2015, but in Korea's case, the employment share in the sector is around 5 per cent.

The key resources in social innovation are civil society and social innovators aware of social values and the finances supporting them. Social trust and social capital have become major resources for social innovation (Murphy et al., 2016). Social innovation is supported by individuals who, as members of society, try to make social changes on their own, or by individuals who want to participate in these changes. In this respect, it can be said that the higher the trust a member has in civil society, the more likely it is that many citizens will participate in innovation activities (Audretsch et al., 2018). However, Korea's social innovation capacity has been evaluated as lower than that of other countries. According to the World Value Survey and the European Social Survey, social trust in Korea is lower than in Western Europe or the United States. In addition, the experience of helping others, as indicated in the World Giving Index (Charity Aid Foundation, 2015), is lower than that of most Western countries, such as Belgium, Sweden, Spain, and Germany.

Social innovation is a practical strategy for social enterprises, social ventures, and private enterprises to create social value. It is actively promoted and implemented through the activities of social innovators with creativity or entrepreneurship at the private level. They tend to strive to realise their ideas or visions in solving social problems, and they become key actors who try new ways to solve problems and create new products (Robinson et al., 2012). However, the activities of social innovators in Korea have been suggested to be conducted at a lower rate than in other advanced countries. According to the Global Entrepreneurship Monitor (2015), the proportion of respondents who responded that they had recently started or were currently carrying out activities to promote social, environmental, and public interests was the lowest in the advanced industrial society group after Spain at 1.8 per cent. In addition, the proportion of women involved in innovative activities was the lowest after Taiwan at 37 per cent. Support by the government is now on the rise, and this has raised Korea's ranking by *The Economist* for social innovation. However, the foundation for social innovation is still very limited.

Finally, financing is recognised as a key resource in social innovation. Research related to social innovation has commonly emphasised the importance of financing for social value creation and social innovation (*The Economist* Intelligence Unit, 2016). Korea's social financing is carried out within the existing SME/private policy finance support system, centring on the government and public resources. However, the financial capacity of Korea's social innovation field is very low. According to the social impact investment database of the Brookings Institute, social impact investment is mostly concentrated in the United States and Europe and is low in East Asia and Africa, including Korea.[1]

---

[1]   www.brookings.edu/research/social-and-development-impact-bonds-by-the-numbers/.

Building a virtuous circle between innovation and social policy

From exclusive growth to inclusive growth

As the 'productivity paradox' suggests, it is highly likely that technological advancement will not lead to productivity and more jobs. The productivity of advanced industries and corporations has indeed exploded. The more people are replaced by machines, the more goods and services are produced and delivered with fewer people, which inevitably increases productivity. However, different conclusions can be reached by shifting the gaze from the corporate perspective to the national perspective. If we change from a system where 100 people produce 100 products to a system where 10 people produce 100 products, a company's productivity has grown remarkably. Yet, the government has no choice but to think about where the remaining 90 people are working. National productivity would increase if 90 people work in an industry or company with high productivity like the previously mentioned workplace, but if they are pushed to the low-skilled/low-wage/low-productivity sectors, the overall rate of productivity growth may be slower than before. This can be said to be the phenomenon discussed by Soete (2018), 'the snake's head goes forward, but the tail remains in its place'.

If a few industries or firms record high productivity, but most do not, this is exclusive growth due to exclusive innovation. This would directly influence the dualisation of the labour market. Conversely, with an overall increase in productivity across all companies and industries, it can be said that inclusive growth and inclusive innovation are taking place. If exclusive growth occurs, it will be difficult to create an inclusive society with only the welfare state or social security system. Since deindustrialisation and globalisation have strengthened the duality of the labour market, a new inclusive growth strategy is needed to strengthen the middle class and create higher-quality jobs. At the core of this inclusive growth strategy, inclusive innovation should be established where everyone participates in innovation and shares its fruits.

As noted, the overall decline in productivity growth is a common phenomenon across OECD countries, but not all countries show the same pattern. According to the OECD (2016), since 2000, in some countries such as Finland, productivity had steadily increased in all levels of companies, while in other countries, such as Italy, productivity has decreased in all company types. In Finland, companies with a record of low productivity have increased their productivity faster than those with a record of high productivity. In contrast, in Sweden, advanced companies do better, and the productivity of companies with low productivity records has barely increased. What these examples show is that deindustrialisation, technological change, and population change are being experienced by all countries, but in the end, depending on the country's institutional strategies, completely different outcomes can be achieved.

The socialisation of entrepreneurial failure costs

Innovation can be said to be 'a flower that blooms on the grave of failure'. There are very few existing and widely used technologies, apps, and research achievements at universities that anyone has developed from start to finish. Most success, including innovation, comes from luck rather than individual effort (Frank, 2016). Many try to marketise a product or a new service by accumulating and developing knowledge, but few are successful. However, one can exceed a certain threshold based on accumulated knowledge and failure, recognised as 'innovation' in the market, and economic success is achieved. Commonly, the successful innovator monopolises economic wealth, but the success is due to the failure of many predecessors.

For inclusive and sustained innovation to occur in a society, anyone should be able to challenge without fear of failure, and failure must be tolerated. In some economies, failures provide a basis for innovation and rechallenge, and in other economies, failure ends in situations in which it is difficult for individuals to recover. In the former case, more people will take on the challenge, and risk taking will likely be very high. On the other hand, in the case of the latter, rather than taking a risk, they will seek stability and, unless the idea is very certain, will not take up the challenge. Thus, it is important to create an environment where all individuals can challenge themselves without relying on the family. Solid startup and venture funds can play an important role. However, it is crucial to have social policies that both provide stability to individuals and strengthen their capabilities, so they do not have to worry about their financial burden. Not only success but also the failure of entrepreneurs can thus remain essential assets to society and the economy.

The virtuous circle between innovation and social policy

This chapter argues that a welfare state with an inclusive social policy can reinforce inclusive innovation, creating a virtuous circle. Figure 3.3 illustrates the virtuous circle. First, inclusive social policy targeting individuals' freedom and stability promotes people's trust and happiness. Second, as it stabilises livelihood, it induces effective human capital formation. People with security and freedom are more likely to be more active in risk taking. Finally, if people feel secure about their life, their attitude towards technological innovation or new types of services can be more favourable, which leads to increasing the accept-ance of new products and services. The results of these inclusive social policies serve as the basis for individual creativity, self-realisation, and active activities in local communities, creating social and economic innovation. Social inno-vation becomes the basis for solving severe social problems in society, and through this process, individual capacities are enhanced and social capital is accumulated. Economic innovation creates economic growth. Growth leads to increased employment and taxation, an important foundation for promoting universal and inclusive social policies.

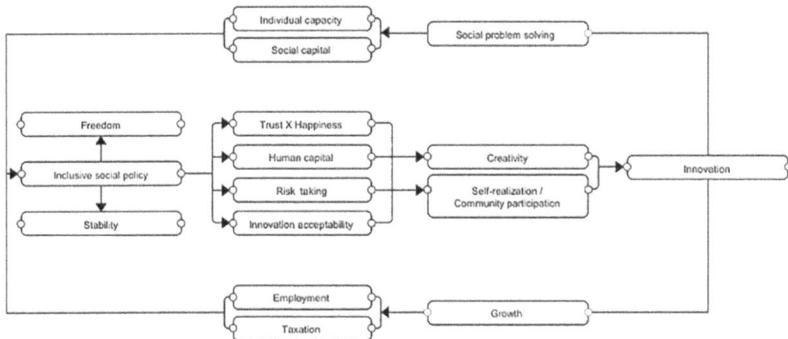

Figure 3.3   The virtuous circle between innovation and social policy

Existing studies support this circle. The main policy goal of the welfare state is to improve the happiness and quality of life of citizens. Previous studies have shown that decommodification, which represents both the level of security and the level of liberating citizens from the labour market, has a positive correla-tion with happiness (Pacek and Radcliff, 2008; Anderson and Hecht, 2015). Also, it has been shown that workers' level of work commitment increases if active labour market policy, parental leave, and childcare services are univer-sally provided (Esser, 2009; Van der Wel and Halvorsen, 2015). High work commitment and motivation raise workers' levels of discretionary learning, which is the basis for their innovative behaviour (Lorenz, 2015). Van der Wel and Halvorsen (2015) confirmed the positive correlation between the generos-ity of social policy and work commitment from various aspects.

Positive psychological assets, such as citizens' happiness and trust in others, indirectly affect creativity and innovation in society. This is because people with positive psychological assets tend to use a variety of perspectives to solve problems around them (MacLeod, 1973). In other words, the welfare state raises the level of positive psychological assets of citizens, increasing their cognitive diversity (Page, 2007). Recent studies also state that happiness and satisfaction with life are closely correlated with creativity and innovation (Cohen et al., 2009).

According to a study by Lorenz and Lundvall (2010), creative work shows a high correlation between the universal education system and the flexible and stable welfare system. Also, an atmosphere in which anyone can express their opinions freely and equally must be formed to be creative. According to self-determination theory, individuals who perform their duties autonomously have a sense of self-determination because they feel free from external controls or restrictions, which leads to a higher level of creativity (Deci et al., 1989; Gagne and Deci, 2005). High job autonomy and security promotes creativity by allowing individuals to take risks and immerse themselves in exploring alternatives (Amabile, 1988; Oldham and Cummings, 1996). These factors are at the heart of entrepreneurship. According to the World Happiness Report (Helliwell et al., 2019), the degree of freedom in Northern Europe is highest, whereas Korea ranked 144th in degree of freedom and 54th on the happiness index. With such a low degree of freedom, it is more difficult for creativity to emerge, and therefore less innovation occurs.

Social capital, represented by generalised trust in others, is a variable that promotes innovation (Akçomak and Ter Weel, 2009; Barczak et al., 2010). The higher the level of trust in others, the higher the level of tolerance for risk, which increases the likelihood of cooperating with others in innovative activities. In addition, general trust increases the possibility of people's creative cooperation with social and professional groups completely different from themselves (Miettinen, 2013). Sharing various ideas through cooperation can strengthen cognitive diversity and increase the possibility of innovation. The high level of general trust in social democratic countries, which are universal welfare states, will serve as another basis for explaining that they are leading innovation.

An example of the virtuous circle: Sweden

If one picks a country that they think has the most active startups and innovation, people think of the United States with Silicon Valley. However, recent media and academia are paying more attention to Sweden. For example, according to the Global Innovation Index in 2019, which is the most widely used worldwide in terms of innovation ranking, Switzerland has the highest innovation index, Sweden is second, and the United States is third (World Intellectual Property Organization, 2019). According to the World Economic

Forum, when looking at the number of Patent Cooperation Treaty information and communication technology patent applications per million people, Sweden ranks first at 153 and the United States ranks sixth at 69.8. In a study by Heyman et al. (2019), comparing recent startups in the United States and Sweden, the United States showed a considerable decline in startups over the past 20 years, but Sweden showed that its economic revival through startups was more rapid.

Until now, as the United States has been known as a representative example country for innovation, it has been a general logical conclusion that startups and innovations are more likely to occur in countries with less redistribution and low taxation and regulation (Henrekson and Rosenberg, 2001). However, Sweden is the largest redistributive country, known as an inclusive and universal welfare state. In particular, since the 1990s, new innovative firms have grown rapidly through various social and economic reforms. These changes were not unique to Sweden in Northern Europe but were also common in other social democratic countries, such as Denmark and Finland. In fact, according to the European Innovation Scoreboard (European Union, 2018), Sweden is the most innovative country, Denmark is second, and the largest welfare countries such as Finland and the Netherlands were top innovation leaders (see Figure 3.4).

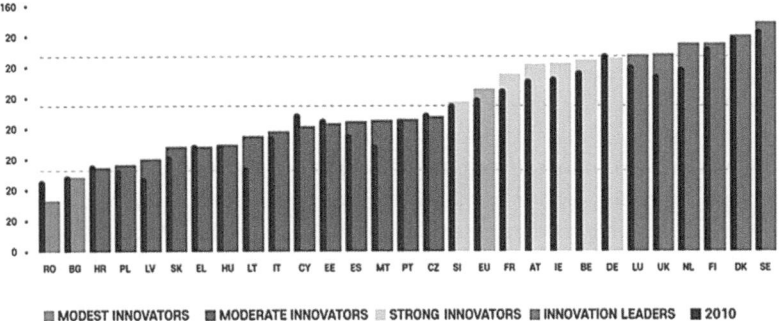

Source: European Union (2018).

Figure 3.4   European Innovation Scoreboard

How, then, can Northern Europe, including Sweden, make a generous welfare state, redistribution, and innovative economy compatible? Sweden is said to graft the flexibility of a free market economy and stability onto a coordinated market economy in a Nordic way. The Swedish state provides a strong social protection system in which each individual is not afraid of failure, and simultaneously, a social investment system from childcare services to university education almost free of charge so that there are no people who do not have the opportunity to acquire knowledge or who are unable to take on the challenge because they are not healthy.

Lorenz (2015) found the success of Swedish innovation lay in a flexible security model. According to his work, Sweden has a traditional coordinated market economy and has developed its economy centring on process innovation rather than product innovation. The economy centred on process innovation, which values tacit knowledge rather than new ideas, but began a new phase when the free labour market was combined after the 1990s. Innovation occurred as individuals with tacit knowledge/skilled individuals who had free movement in the labour market entered the industry, or individuals with completely new tacit knowledge. This freedom of movement was possible because solid social security was its basis; this was known as a flexible security model.

According to my interview (January 2020) with David Sonnek, the chief executive officer of a venture capital company named Indusfonen, as the profit rates of large corporations have fallen since the 1970s, the Swedish government tried to pursue productivity innovation in large corporations by creating companies like Indusfonen. However, these policies were not effectively implemented. Rather, the government attempted to maintain the competitiveness of conglomerates with the devaluation of the Swedish currency. Eventually, it was revealed that this direction was not sustainable due to the economic crisis and pressure of globalisation in the 1980s and early 1990s, and it became an opportunity for the direction of investment to turn to small businesses and startups. Along with a turn in investment direction, Sweden promoted entrepreneurial innovation through labour market deregulation, tax and economic reforms, and rationalisation to overcome the economic crisis of the 1990s.

Regulatory and tax reforms have indeed played essential roles in promoting innovation. However, experts in Sweden assessed that regulation and tax reform in the 1990s was an attempt to restructure and reorganise the route rather than a break away from the Swedish social and economic system. The elements of innovation that are still central to this pragmatic change are the welfare state and the free and equal Swedish organisational culture. Claire Ingram Bogusz, one of Sweden's leading scholars of entrepreneurship research, found a Swedish organisational culture where innovation and entrepreneurship easily occur in the system of 'flat hierarchy' and 'flat wage' (interview, January 2020). A culture without hierarchies makes it easier to communicate with people with high and low positions in the organisation. It allows more ideas to be communicated without going through bureaucratic stages. The flat wage also contributes to innovative activities. It may not make sense to say that an equal pay system is conducive to innovation. According to Bogusz, however, because of the 'flat wage', even if entrepreneurs fail in business, there is nothing to lose, so people can pursue their interests instead of being dependent. According to the experts, entrepreneurs who innovate in Sweden are characterised by their passion, interest, and desire to use their time autonomously rather than to make a fortune.

These experts have commonly pointed out the significance of Swedish social policy. First, the inclusive social policies that promote innovation include the parental leave system. While the parental leave system has been introduced in most OECD countries, the entrepreneurship/academic leave system (leave of absence) is a unique system introduced by the Swedish labour management agreement. It is a policy that supports six months of vacation to start a business or study. This long vacation creates an environment where employees can experience more creative thinking and autonomy. Many Swedish youths change their careers from employee to entrepreneur while actively developing their ideas using parental or entrepreneurial vacations. Second, the social investment system provides an opportunity to choose an autonomous life in the long term while maintaining individual skill and competency levels. Finally, a comprehensive and inclusive social policy, including a free medical system, long-term sustainable social insurance, and pension policy, plays a key role in enhancing risk-taking behaviours and stable human capital formation. This view is gaining importance through the media, economic organisations, and Mikael Damberg, Sweden's minister for enterprise and innovation. The following speak of the importance of social security and social safety nets in Sweden:

> I think if you want to be an innovative country, you have to give people security, so they dare to take risks. Birk Nilson, for instance, knew that if his company fell apart, he'd still have health coverage; he also didn't have any student-loan debt to pay off. Even if you fail, even if you file for bankruptcy, Sweden has a well-known and ambitious safety net. So, I do think that taking on risk is not as daunting in Sweden as it is in the US. (Mikael Damberg)[2]

Sweden is a risk-friendly place. 'Sweden has a lot of safety nets from an income perspective, which reduces the risk of starting your own company,' says Mattias

---

[2]   Why does Sweden have so many start-ups? *The Atlantic* (www.theatlantic .com/business/archive/2017/09/sweden-startups/541413/?fbclid=IwAR2hv _aTzcPNVrq_CbheOHVCrSfHLYASIguSY6BG9MIk72LUGV2GMh8WBC0).

Ward at Swedish startup Innometrics, who thinks that potential employees are also less wary of working for a startup. 'With cheap or free higher education, students from Sweden's excellent universities also do not have crippling levels of debt before they even start.'[3]

In sum, if you want to create an innovative country, you must first identify the high-risk characteristics of innovation. The foundation for successful innovation is a sound social safety net, which is essential to protect against innovation failures. Stable health and social security systems, a quality education system, workplace culture, and vacation systems enabling family balance all encourage entrepreneurship. Along with life-long educational systems, these are the fundamentals leading Sweden's innovative economy.

Conclusions: lessons for South Korea and East Asia

The implications of the Swedish and Northern European examples are clear. First, there is more than one way to an innovative economy. Innovative and entrepreneurial economies are possible without a 'winner-takes-all' economy that allows successful people to take all the financial benefits. Second, inclusive social policy is fully compatible with inclusive innovation, creating inclusive growth. Inclusive growth has been the most important current topic discussed by the OECD (2016) and the IMF (2017). Increasing inequality has been pointed out as an essential factor that hinders sustainable growth and innovation beyond the impoverishment of individuals' lives (Gordon, 2016). Therefore, inclusive social policy reducing social inequality could contribute to economic growth.

Unlike their Nordic counterparts, Korea and East Asian countries face serious challenges in innovation and inclusion. Although their international rankings for innovation are high, the foundation for innovation is weak and narrow. The results of innovation are also concentrated among a few rather than benefiting all societies and people. Korea is one of the countries with the greatest productivity gap between large and small enterprises in the OECD, resulting in high inequality. In fact, income inequality levels in Korea and Japan ranked 28th and 26th among OECD countries in 2018.[4] Other East Asian economies

---

3   The reasons why Sweden is a hotbed for digital innovation, Techradar.pro (www
     .techradar.com/news/world-of-tech/the-reasons-why-sweden-is-a-hotbed-for
     -digital-innovation-1292681).
4   https://data.oecd.org/inequality/income-inequality.htm.

have higher income inequality rates. However, social spending in Korea such as the percentage of GDP was the lowest of all OECD countries in 2018.[5] Social spending in Japan is more than the average of OECD countries, but a large portion goes to the elderly. As a result, it is more likely to lead to an unequal labour market and society.

There are more reasons why inclusive and intensive innovation is essential for Korea and East Asian societies. The first reason is rapid ageing. A high productivity economy with intensive innovation is particularly required in Korea and East Asian economies to maintain sustainable development in the age of rapid ageing and low fertility. The speed of population ageing is most conspicuous in Korea as its fertility rate in 2020 was around 0.9. As fewer working-age people support a more elderly population, widespread innovation is key if the country is not receiving a massive influx of immigrants. Second, East Asian economies must transform themselves to become greener and eco-friendlier. Currently, they are 'villains' in terms of climate change. According to the Union of Concerned Scientists,[6] China ranked as the top emitter of annual carbon dioxide in 2018; Japan ranked 5th and Korea 8th in 2018. While their economic development has been remarkable, these countries will greatly contribute to climate disasters unless there is dramatic success in reducing carbon emissions.

Last but not least, social innovation is as important as business innovation. State-centric problem solving has been dominant in most East Asian countries, but social problems are more pressing than ever. Yet, social trust and solidarity have been much weaker than in their European counterparts. Social innovation can contribute to solving these issues by providing new solutions and building social trust across societies.

It is evident that policymakers and media commentators emphasise the importance of innovation in Korea. Their role model is normally confined to Silicon Valley and is based on neoliberal approaches, including deregulation of the labour market and the financial sector and reduction of government intervention. This chapter, however, argued that a virtuous cycle of inclusive social policy and innovation is necessary and possible to overcome the current unstable welfare state. An inclusive social policy can give individuals freedom and stability, increase risk-taking propensity, enhance human capital accumulation, and increase receptivity to innovation while at the same time increasing

---

5   https://stats.oecd.org/Index.aspx?DataSetCode=SOCX_AGG.
6   www.ucsusa.org/resources/each-countrys-share-co2-emissions.

social trust. When there are more people with creative entrepreneurship, social and economic innovations actively occur. These innovations again lay the foundation for employment and finances, which can be the foundation for maintaining the welfare state while solving social problems. Beyond an explosive increase in the productivity of a few companies, inclusive policies could increase overall national productivity, as anyone can contribute to numerous small innovations in business and society along with scientific and technological innovation.

Surely, social policies are not the only way to reduce inequality and achieve inclusiveness. Reorganisation of an economic structure centred on large enterprises or correcting labour market injustice and discrimination is the most basic starting point. Direct policies to support and nurture innovators are essential, as in the case of Sweden. In this process, innovation needs to be implemented in a social problem-solving and inclusive way so that innovation does not become another means of wage reduction or firing workers. However, social policy and the role of the welfare state are still crucial in creating an environment in which individuals can fully utilise their abilities. Success will again contribute to solving the difficulties of the faltering welfare state.

If inclusive social policy and an inclusive growth policy are carried out simultaneously, it would be possible to reduce inequality and at the same time increase the productivity of SMEs through a startup economy and various innovative activities. However, the transition to an innovative and inclusive nation is not possible with rhetoric alone. Bold investment in inclusive social policies and policy reform should be implemented. The level of social spending in Korea is 10 per cent of GDP, while the OECD average is 20 per cent, and in countries such as France and Finland it is 30 per cent. Large-scale investment in social policy is necessary. At the same time, creativity and entrepreneurship will be promoted only when, rather than rigid and conditional welfare, investments are made that allow individual freedom and capabilities to be fully displayed. Politics should find a way to encourage actual freedom through inclusive social policies rather than market liberalism.

References

Aghion, P. and Howitt, P. (1992) 'A model of growth through creative destruction', *Econometrica*, 60, 323–351.

Akçomak, I. S. and Ter Weel, B. (2009) 'Social capital, innovation and growth: Evidence from Europe', *European Economic Review*, 53(5), 544–567.

Amabile, T. M. (1988) 'A model of creativity and innovation in organizations', *Research in Organizational Behavior*, 10(1), 123–167.

Anderson, C. J. and Hecht, J. D. (2015) 'Happiness and the welfare state: Decommodification and the political economy of subjective well-being', in P. Beramendi, S. Häusermann, H. Kitschelt and H. Kriesi (eds), *The Politics of Advanced Capitalism*, New York: Cambridge University Press, 357–380.

Andrews, D., Criscuolo, C. and Gal, P. N. (2015) *Frontier Firms, Technology Diffusion and Public Policy: Micro Evidence from OECD Countries*, Paris: OECD.

Audretsch, D. B., Seitz, N. and Rouch, K. M. (2018) 'Tolerance and innovation: The role of institutional and social trust', *Eurasian Business Review*, 8(1), 71–92.

Ban, G. (2016) 'Skill mismatch in Korea in comparative perspectives', *The HRD Review*, 19(2), 6–18 (in Korean).

Barczak, G., Lassk, F. and Mulki, J. (2010) 'Antecedents of team creativity: An examination of team emotional intelligence, team trust and collaborative culture', *Creativity and Innovation Management*, 19(4), 332–345.

Bell, A. M., Chetty, R., Jaravel, X., Petkova, N. and Van Reenen, J. (2017) *Who Becomes an Inventor in America? The Importance of Exposure to Innovation* (No. w24062). National Bureau of Economic Research.

Bulut, C., Eren, H. and Halac, D. S. (2013) 'Which one triggers the other? Technological or social innovation', *Creativity Research Journal*, 25(4), 436–445.

Charity Aid Foundation (2015) *World Giving Index 2015*.

Choi, Y., Koo, J. and Yun, S. (2018) 'An exploratory study on welfare states and innovation', *Social Security Research*, 34(4), 229–258 (in Korean).

Cohen, M. A., Fredrickson, B. L., Brown, S. L., Mikels, J. A. and Conway, A. M. (2009) 'Happiness unpacked: Positive emotions increase life satisfaction by building resilience', *Emotion*, 9(3), 361–368.

Crespi, F. and Pianta, M. (2008) 'Diversity in innovation and productivity in Europe', *Journal of Evolutionary Economics*, 18(3), 529–545.

Deci, E. L., Connell, J. P. and Ryan, R. M. (1989) 'Self-determination in a work organization', *Journal of Applied Psychology*, 74(4), 580–590.

Deepa Babu, K. G. and Manalel, J. (2016) 'Entrepreneurial orientation and firm performance: A critical examination', *IOSR Journal of Business and Management*, 18(4), 21–28.

Drucker, P. F. (1985) *Innovation and Entrepreneurship: Practice and Principles*, New York: Harper and Row.

Dwyer, J. (2021) What is innovation: Why almost everyone defines it wrong. DI. https://digintent.com/what-is-innovation/

Esser, I. (2009) 'Has welfare made us lazy? Employment commitment in different welfare states', *British Social Attitudes*, 25th Report. London: Sage.

European Union (2018) *European Innovation Scoreboard*. https:// ec .europa .eu/ growth/ content/ european -innovation -scoreboard -2018 -europe -must -deepen -its -innovation-edge_en

Filippetti, A. and Guy, F. (2016) 'Skills and social insurance: Evidence from the relative persistence of innovation during the financial crisis in Europe', *Science and Public Policy*, 43(4), 505–517.

Florida, R. (2006) 'The flight of the creative class: The new global competition for talent', *Liberal Education*, 92(3), 22–29.

Frank, R. (2016) *Success and Luck: Good Fortune and the Myth of Meritocracy*, Princeton, NJ: Princeton University Press.

Frey, C. B. and Osborne, M. A. (2017) 'The future of employment: How susceptible are jobs to computerisation?', *Technological Forecasting and Social Change*, 114, 254–280.

Friesenhahn, E. (2016) 'Nonprofits in America: New research data on employment, wages, and establishments', Monthly Labor Review, US Bureau of Labor Statistics.

Gagne, M. and Deci, E. L. (2005) 'Self-determination theory and work motivation', *Journal of Organizational Behavior*, 26(4), 331–362.

Gault, F. (2018) 'Defining and measuring innovation in all sectors of the economy', *Research Policy*, 47(3), 17–22.

Glăveanu, V. P. (2010) 'Principles for a cultural psychology of creativity', *Culture and Psychology*, 16(2), 147–163.

Global Entrepreneurship Monitor (2015) *Data*, London: Global Entrepreneurship Research Association.

Goos, M., Manning, A. and Salomons, A. (2014) 'Explaining job polarization: Routine-biased technological change and offshoring', *American Economic Review*, 104(8), 2509–2526.

Gordon, R. J. (2012) 'Is US economic growth over? Faltering innovation confronts the six headwinds' (No. w18315), National Bureau of Economic Research.

Gordon, R. J. (2014) 'The demise of US economic growth: Restatement, rebuttal, and reflections' (No. w19895), National Bureau of Economic Research.

Gordon, R. J. (2016) *The Rise and Fall of American Growth*, Princeton, NJ: Princeton University Press.

Gordon, R. J. (2018) 'Why has economic growth slowed when innovation appears to be accelerating?' (No. w24554), National Bureau of Economic Research.

Graddy-Reed, A. and Feldman, M. P. (2015) 'Stepping up: An empirical analysis of the role of social innovation in response to an economic recession', *Cambridge Journal of Regions, Economy and Society*, 8(2), 293–312.

Helliwell, J., Layard, R. and Sachs, J. (2019) *World Happiness Report 2019*, New York: Sustainable Development Solutions Network.

Henrekson, M. and Rosenberg, N. (2001) 'Designing efficient institutions for science-based entrepreneurship: Lesson from the US and Sweden', *Journal of Technology Transfer*, 26(3), 207–231.

Heyman, F., Norbäck, P. J., Persson, L. and Andersson, F. (2019) 'Has the Swedish business sector become more entrepreneurial than the US business sector?', *Research Policy*, 48(7), 1809–1822.

Hubert, A. (2010) 'Empowering people, driving change: Social innovation in the European Union', Bureau of European Policy Advisors.

Hunt-Bull, N. (2006) 'A neo-Luddite manifesto: or why I do not love robots', American Association for Artificial Intelligence.

IMF (2017) *IMF Fiscal Monitor: Tackling Inequality*, IMF.

Knight, F. (1921) *Risk Uncertainty and Profit*, Boston, MA: Houghton Mifflin.

KPMG (2019) *2019 Autonomous Vehicles Readiness Index.*

Lorenz, E. (2015) 'Work organisation, forms of employee learning and labour market structure: Accounting for international differences in workplace innovation', *Journal of the Knowledge Economy*, 6(2), 437–466.

Lorenz, E. and Lundvall, B. Á. (2010) 'Accounting for creativity in the European Union: A multi-level analysis of individual competence, labour market structure, and systems of education and training', *Cambridge Journal of Economics*, 35(2), 269–294.

MacLeod, G. A. (1973) 'Does creativity lead to happiness and more enjoyment of life?', *Journal of Creative Behavior*, 7, 227–230.

McClelland, D. C. (1965) 'N achievement and entrepreneurship: A longitudinal study', *Journal of Personality and Social Psychology*, 1(4), 389–392.

Miettinen, R. (2013) *Innovation, Human Capabilities, and Democracy: Towards an Enabling Welfare State*, Oxford: Oxford University Press.

Mkandawire, T. (2007) 'Transformative social policy and innovation in developing countries', *European Journal of Development Research*, 19(1), 13–29.

Murphy, L., Huggins, R. and Thompson, P. (2016) 'Social capital and innovation: A comparative analysis of regional policies', *Environment and Planning C: Government and Policy*, 34(6), 1025–1057.

National Statistical Office of Korea (2017) *KOSIS Social Survey, 2015, 2017*.

OECD (2010) 'Social entrepreneurship and social innovation', in *SMEs, Entrepreneurship and Innovation*, Paris: OECD Publishing. https://doi.org/10.1787/9789264080355-50-en

OECD (2014a) *Entrepreneurship at a Glance*, Paris: OECD Publishing.

OECD (2014b) *Education at a Glance*, Paris: OECD Publishing.

OECD (2016) *The Productivity-Inclusiveness Nexus: Preliminary Version*, Paris: OECD Publishing. https://doi.org/10.1787/9789264258303-en

OECD (2018) *Entrepreneurship at a Glance*, Paris: OECD Publishing.

Oldham, G. R. and Cummings, A. (1996) 'Employee creativity: Personal and contextual factors at work', *Academy of Management Journal*, 39(3), 607–634.

Pacek, A. and Radcliff, B. (2008) 'Assessing the welfare state: The politics of happiness', *Perspectives on Politics*, 6(2), 267–277.

Page, S. E. (2007) 'Making the difference: Applying a logic of diversity', *Academy of Management Perspectives*, 21(4), 6–20.

Ram, S. (1987) 'A model of innovation resistance', in M. Wallendorf and P. Anderson (eds), *Advances in Consumer Research*, Volume 14, Provo, UT: Association for Consumer Research, 208–212.

Robinson, K., Robinson, D. and Westley, F. (2012) 'Agency in social innovation: Putting the model in the model of the agent', in A. Nichollas and A. Murdock (eds), *Social Innovation*, London: Palgrave Macmillan, 162–177.

Roh, M. (2018) 'Wage gap between conglomerates and SMEs and international comparison', Wage Information Brief. 2018-09 (35), 11–16 (in Korean).

Romer, P. (1986) 'Increasing returns and long-run growth', *Journal of Political Economy*, 94(5), 1002–1037.

Salamon, L. M. and Sokolowski, W. (2018) *Beyond Nonprofits: In Search of the Third Sector*, Cham: Palgrave Macmillan.

Schumpeter, J. A. (1934) *The Theory of Economic Development*, Cambridge, MA: Harvard University Press.

Soete, L. (2018) 'Destructive creation: Explaining the productivity paradox in the digital age', in M. Neufeind, J. O'Reilly and F. Ranft (eds), *Work in the Digital Age: Challenges of the Fourth Industrial Revolution*, London: Rowman and Littlefield International, 29–46.

The Economist (2013) 'The Nordic countries: Social Innovation Index 2016', 2 February.

The Economist Intelligence Unit (2016) 'Social Innovation Index 2016'.

Van der Wel, K. A. and Halvorsen, K. (2015) 'The bigger the worse? A comparative study of the welfare state and employment commitment', *Work, Employment and Society*, 29(1), 99–118.

Weber, E. P. and Khademian, A. M. (2008) 'Wicked problems, knowledge challenges, and collaborative capacity builders in network settings', *Public Administration Review*, 68(2), 334–349.

World Intellectual Property Organization (2019) *Global Innovation Index 2019*, New York: World Intellectual Property Organization.

Zukunft, D. (2018) The productivity paradox: A survey, 2 October. www.dezernatzukunft .org/the-productivity-paradox-a-survey-2/?lang=en

4 Public opinion and social policy reforms in East Asia

Chung-Yang Yeh and Ijin Hong

Introduction

Public opinion can be defined as the aggregate of individual-level attitudes and preferences on a particular issue; it is often regarded as a crucial driving force behind policy changes and welfare reforms in democracies (Glynn et al., 2018; Busemeyer et al., 2020). Although the study of the impact of public opinion on social policy is well represented in the literature (Brooks and Manza, 2007; Breznau, 2019; Busemeyer et al., 2020), research findings mostly apply to old democracies in Europe and North America with few implications outside the Western world. For newly industrialised countries in East Asia, the early discussion of welfare state development was dominated by the idea of developmentalism, whereby welfare states subordinate social policy to an economic growth-first policy and the domination of the state in coordinating socio-economic institutions. For such states, economic catch-up was the most important national goal and the source of political legitimacy (Holliday, 2000; Gough, 2004; Lee and Ku, 2007; Choi, 2009, 2013). Hence, the importance of public opinion in social policy development in East Asian welfare states went unrecognised during the post-war period because of the absence of democratic electoral competition. Instead, developmentalist scholars have highlighted the prominence of the state, the discretionary powers of bureaucracy, business interests and their connections to the state and the banking sector, while public opinion and civil society have been treated as marginal in most institutionally oriented analyses (Johnson, 1982; Haggard, 2004; Haggard and Kaufman, 2008; Ringen et al., 2011).

Although developmentalism is still useful in explaining the underdevelopment of social policy in East Asia, it no longer suffices for understanding welfare developments in this region in light of recent social policy reforms (1990s–2010s). In particular, social policy reforms in the region have been growing increasingly diverse, such as work–family policies (An and Peng, 2016; Fleckenstein and Lee, 2017a; Hong et al., 2022) and public–private pension mix reforms (Fu and Hwang, 2018; Yeh et al., 2020). For example, Taiwan differs substantially from South Korea (hereafter, Korea) in the development of work–family policies as it places great emphasis on cash benefits. On the other hand, pension retrenchment policies have affected both societies (Taiwan in 2018 and Korea in 1999), and several alternative explanations should be tested to understand the similarities and differences arising in these two economies that are similar in terms of demographic structure, timing of democratisation and political institutions. Developmentalist explanations might not suffice for this task.

In this chapter, we argue that policy makers' choices in East Asian countries have grown more complex in recent years and that we should pay more attention to the role of public opinion to better understand the politics of welfare reform. Generally speaking, public opinion is the source of welfare state legitimacy (Chung et al., 2018; Taylor-Gooby and LeRuth, 2018), regardless of the political regime. Since the introduction of social policy reforms is premised on public support, therefore, public opinion is often considered in the process of policy making, and the resulting policies often reflect public attitudes (Burstein, 1998, 2003). This is particularly the case in new democracies. Another important point to highlight is that interest groups such as labour unions, which have been considered the most significant actor in promoting social policy development in European welfare states, have not played a significant role in welfare state development in East Asia. That is because those interest groups were intentionally repressed or disbanded by the ruling elites in the post-war period (Deyo, 1989; Caraway, 2009; Yeh, 2014; Yeh and Ku, 2021). Hence, interest groups might not be developed enough to exert influence on social policy making; instead, public opinion plays a greater role in shaping social policy development in East Asian welfare states. As there are few studies of welfare attitudes in East Asia and most of them focus on the characteristics of social policy supporters, the causal mechanism between public opinion and social policy making is often overlooked.

In this chapter, we will highlight the role of public opinion in shaping social policy in the contemporary welfare states of East Asia by providing examples based on our review of specialised literature. The chapter will present a theoretical framework that incorporates public opinion into the analysis of welfare expansion and retrenchment in the region. We focus on Japan, Korea and Taiwan as relevant cases to consider because of their relatively liberal elections, while also offering perspectives on welfare reform in the 'less democratic' regimes of Singapore, Hong Kong and mainland China. Against the background of this highly dynamic and volatile context, we aim to identify important contextual features that help in better understanding the nexus of public opinion and welfare reform. The next section will examine why studying welfare attitude is important in analysing East Asian welfare state development, as we consider not only social policy expansion but also welfare retrenchment. Two arguments will be highlighted in particular: the marginal significance of interest groups in social policy development in East Asia, and the fact that public opinion plays a significant role in newly democratic welfare states. The final section aims to develop an analytical framework for East Asian welfare state development and cross-national variations.

Welfare attitudes in East Asia

This section focuses on why welfare attitudes are important for understanding the development of welfare in East Asia since the 1990s when political competition intensified. Korea and Taiwan are the most prominent examples as these countries established democratic institutions and allowed competitive elections after 1987 (Wong, 2004; Estévez-Abe, 2008; Peng and Wong, 2008). Here, we highlight two points. First, in contrast to European welfare states, interest groups play a minor role in social policy development in East Asia because such groups were not organised during the authoritarian period. Second, office-seeking political actors prefer to respond to public opinion to maximise political support and votes, as they seek to win elections in new democracies. East Asian welfare states have also engaged in a series of welfare restructuring and retrenchment programmes over the last two decades. Such phenomena should be taken into account.

Interest groups versus public opinion

In European welfare states, especially conservative welfare states and social democratic welfare states, corporatist interest groups such as labour unions and employer associations play a significant role in social policy making (Korpi, 1983; Esping-Andersen, 1985; Swenson, 2002; Ebbinghaus and Naumann, 2018). According to power resource theory, strong labour movements and their considerable representation in governments represent a major determinant of welfare state development (Korpi, 1983; Esping-Andersen, 1985). In democratic capitalist systems, the working class and capitalists have different interests and can mobilise different power resources. According to the theory, social citizenship could be seen as the outcome of the political coalition between the working class and socialist parties. Hence, it is assumed that both labour and employers can influence social policy development in countries with strong corporatist policy-making institutions. In other words, organised interest groups such as labour unions and employer associations could mobilise different power resources to influence social policy making (Korpi, 1983; Esping-Andersen, 1985; Swenson, 2002; Ebbinghaus and Naumann, 2018).

However, compared to European welfare states with a strong corporatist tradition, the role of interest groups in social policy development is less relevant in East Asia (Deyo, 1989; Song, 2014; Yeh, 2014; Yang, 2017; Yeh and Ku, 2021). For example, the left–right politicisation of welfare issues has long been lacking in East Asia (Kwon and Hong, 2019; Kwon, 2020). In fact, the most critical task for newly industrialising countries is to reduce the external inequality between developed and developing countries, rather than the internal inequality between the rich and the poor within the country (Rudra, 2008). In addition, labour commodification and the maintenance of a healthy labour force are much more important than labour decommodification in the transformation from pre-industrial society to industrial society (Gough, 2004). In the post-war period, therefore, East Asian governments had to concentrate their financial resources on economic activities to catch up with advanced economies, and productive social policies such as education and health policies received more financial resources to promote labour commodification (Gough, 2004; Rudra, 2008).

In order to concentrate financial resources on economic growth and productive social policies, two preconditions must be fulfilled: a strong state and a weak society. According to developmentalist logic, the state had to play a significant role in economic coordination to channel financial resources to facilitate economic growth and help infant industries to compete in the international market (Johnson, 1982; Amsden, 1989; Wade, 2004). In the post-war period, Korea and Taiwan had authoritarian governments, while the Japanese government was dominated by one party (after 1955). Both governments had strong state capacity to opt for developmental strategies, and more importantly, to channel financial resources to facilitate economic growth instead of responding to social demands (Holliday, 2000; Kwon, 2005; Lee and Ku, 2007; Haggard and Kaufman, 2008).

Furthermore, civil society did not have a prominent role in policy making in the developmental state. As the state had to channel financial resources to economic activities and productive social policies, social demands were ignored or minimised under slogans such as 'growth first, redistribution later', in the words of the Korean military dictator, Chunghee Park. In the post-war period, not only authoritarian Korea and Taiwan but also democratic Japan repressed or dissolved interest groups, especially labour unions, to minimise their political influence (Deyo, 1989; Ho, 2014). Even when basic labour rights were guaranteed by law, they were often disregarded in practice (Caraway, 2009; Imai, 2011; Deyo, 2012; Miura, 2012; Ho, 2014). In Japan and Korea, for example, national-level labour unions were either legally prohibited or politically restricted and controlled, while enterprise-level labour unions tended to place more emphasis on wages, job security and company welfare than public welfare policies (Song, 2014; Lee, 2016; Yang, 2017). In Taiwan, national-level labour unions were dominated by the ruling Kuomintang (KMT) government, while enterprise-level labour unions were only kept in large state or party-owned enterprises, which were often controlled by the KMT. Other large private enterprises were often subordinated to the authoritarian KMT government (Deyo, 1989; Wang, 1993; Ho, 2014). In the post-war period, therefore, interest groups were generally negligible in East Asia, unlike European social democratic welfare states.

This institutional legacy left interest groups somewhat marginalised in social policy making even after political democratisation, when welfare expansion took place. Contrary to the predictions of the power resource theory approach (Korpi, 1983; Esping-Andersen, 1985), social policy expansion in East Asia was not caused by an increase of labour power (Wong, 2004; Hwang, 2006; Yeh, 2014; Kim, 2015; Fleckenstein and Lee, 2017a). Although labour failed to play a highly influential role in social policy reform in East Asia, civic associations started to get more room to manoeuvre.

Yeh (2014) argues that despite the significant expansion of public pensions since political democratisation in Korea and Taiwan, labour unions played a very negligible role and enterprise-level labour unions and resisted the expansion of public pensions (see also Fu and Hwang, 2018). Likewise, in studying the transformation of Japanese employment relations, Imai (2011) argues that labour did not have a significant influence on some labour market reforms, including the deregulation of working hours and dispatched workers. Hence, even in the age of democratic politics, labour is considered negligible in East Asia. Another common example is the expansion of work–family policies (Peng, 2015; An and Peng, 2016; Fleckenstein and Lee, 2017a; Hong et al., 2022). Work–family policies have attracted more attention, politically and academically, for the last couple of decades due to the rise of feminist movements and the low fertility rate (Peng, 2015; Fleckenstein and Lee, 2017a; Hong et al., 2022). Although women's groups have actively promoted the expansion of work–family policies to achieve gender equality, it is debatable whether the expansion of work–family policies resulted from those groups' advocacy or from the crisis of the ultra-low fertility rate and public demand (Fleckenstein and Lee, 2017a; Lee, 2017; Hong et al., 2022). Despite strong advocacy by women in the 1990s and the early 2000s, Taiwan did not witness significant expansion of work–family policies (Tsai, 2014). Also, both Fleckenstein and Lee (2017a) and Hong et al. (2022) have observed that public attitudes appeared relevant in explaining the expansion of work–family policies in East Asia.

Although labour movements were not directly influential in fostering welfare growth, civic associations became more involved as a result of democratisation. Peng (2004) argues that the Liberal Democratic Party's (LDP) coalition government in Japan tended to be more open to non-profit organisations, so that groups representing the interests of women and older people were more involved in the planning and implementation of the long-term care reforms of the 1990s and 2000s. Likewise, Lee (2017) observes how women's movements cooperated with the government as it devised an expansion of universal childcare policies in Korea. In the Korean case, several scholars now agree that campaigns for social awareness and the involvement of civil groups contributed to the adoption of national health insurance in 1998 and the introduction of the National Basic Livelihood Security Act in 1999, among other welfare reforms (Yi et al., 2015; Kim, 2021).

The existing studies suggest that interest groups have been partially successful in influencing social policy making following democratisation. However, it would be difficult to understand and analyse the development of East Asian welfare states, whether in terms of welfare expansion or retrenchment, if we only consider the role of those interest groups.

Public support as the source of political legitimacy

Studying public opinion matters since public support for social policy development is often a significant source of political legitimacy (Chung et al., 2018; Busemeyer et al., 2020). This is particularly significant for newly democratic welfare states in the age of permanent austerity (Pierson, 1994). In Pierson's words, 'the political health of the welfare state is dependent upon popular attitudes' (Pierson, 1996, p. 146).

We consider the three East Asian welfare systems (Japan, Korea and Taiwan), which have undergone political liberalisation since the mid-1980s. The 1980s were a time when authoritarian regimes in Korea and Taiwan faced political challenges and allowed political liberalisation (Wong, 2004). The political democratisation that ensued intensified electoral competition in those societies. As for Japan, although it allowed electoral competition after the end of the Second World War, the liberal democratic regime led by the conservative LDP did not encounter significant political challenges from opposition parties until 1994. In 1994, a grand coalition ended the conservative liberal democratic regime and introduced political reform. Since then, electoral competition has intensified (Estévez-Abe, 2008).

As in old democratic welfare states, the most prominent goal of office-seeking political actors is to win elections in newly democratic welfare states. However, the absence of social protection creates a window of opportunity for office-seeking political actors to exploit political support and votes (Wong, 2004; Peng and Wong, 2008; Ringen et al., 2011, p. 215; Yeh, 2014; Fleckenstein and Lee, 2017a, 2017b; Hong et al., 2022). Public opinion consequently plays a major role in shaping social policy making because those office-seeking political actors must endeavour to introduce social policies that can meet social demands. Although several studies have supported this argument through case studies and comparative historical analyses, not enough attention has been paid to how social policies were launched in line with public demand for redistribution. Fleckenstein and Lee (2017a) and Hong et al. (2022) are two exceptions. They both argue that the expansion of work–family policies and differences between Japan, Korea and Taiwan are the results of different levels of public support for work–family policies. In Taiwan, public opinion on work–family policies was more conservative, and the public preferred cash benefits. In contrast, Koreans preferred service-oriented childcare services, while Japan did not have consistent public demand for work–family policies. Consequently, these three East Asian welfare states developed different models of work–family policies (An and Peng, 2016).

Of course, personal preferences and orientations in the sphere of public opinion cannot be positioned in a cultural or institutional void (Pfau-Effinger, 2004). More contextual features must be considered to determine to what extent public opinion matters and how it works in new democracies and authoritarian regimes. Here, we attempt to advance the discussion in respect to three additional elements: the quality of democratic systems, the policy feedback thesis and the context of welfare retrenchment measures.

First, the quality of democratic governance must be considered, as emphasising public opinion not only helps office-seeking political actors to gain more polit- ical support but also lays the foundation for political legitimacy (Kwon, 1999). As argued by neo-Marxism, the capitalist state has two contradictory goals: capital accumulation and political legitimacy (Gough, 1979). The democratic capitalist state is often responsive to the public demand for redistribution to mitigate income inequality and economic difficulties caused by capitalist development through redistributive social policies (Burstein, 1998, 2003; Powell, 2004; Brooks and Manza, 2007; Busemeyer et al., 2020). Redistributive social policies are meant to mitigate income inequality and help people with financial difficulties to cope with economic insecurity, with the possible consequence of increasing public support and political trust to achieve democratic satisfaction (that is, political legitimacy) (Rothstein, 1998; Kumlin, 2004, 2014; Rothstein et al., 2012). In other words, the quality of democratic governance directly hinges on its ability to respond to public demands (Powell, 2004).

Some studies focusing on East Asian welfare systems, broadly defined to also include less democratic systems, have found that satisfaction with social policy and democratic governance influence public support for redistribution. For example, universal healthcare systems in Hong Kong, Korea and Taiwan deliver high-quality healthcare, resulting in higher public support for healthcare (Lee et al., 2009; Park et al., 2016; He, 2018; Yeh et al., forthcoming). By studying the determinants of public support for healthcare in Taiwan, Yeh and Lin (forthcoming) find that satisfaction with healthcare and institutional trust are two prominent factors in shaping public support for expanding healthcare. They argue that cheap and high-quality healthcare increases public willingness to support the expansion of national health insurance with an increased contribution rate. The case of Hong Kong also supports this argument (He, 2018), although the Beveridgean model in Hong Kong is different from Taiwan's National Health Insurance. He (2018) also found that satisfaction with healthcare is an important factor in determining public support for healthcare expansion. The findings of other studies are mainly consistent with this argument (Lee et al., 2009; Park et al., 2016; Yeh, Lin and Lue, 2021). This is also evident in authoritarian regimes in which electoral competition is not allowed or very limited. In an analysis of the 2010 Chinese General Social Survey dataset, Xu (2016) shows that there is a strong relationship between political trust and public demand for redistribution.

Also, and on a related point, the policy feedback thesis has been much discussed in welfare attitude studies focusing on Western welfare states. For example, Kumlin (2004, 2014) shows that the quality and institutional design of the welfare state have a great impact on political trust; when personal experiences of welfare policies are more positive, political trust and democratic satisfaction are higher. Furthermore, the quality of the welfare state and government is also a prominent determinant of public support for redistribution, as evidenced by Rothstein and his colleagues (Rothstein, 1998; Rothstein et al., 2012). In other words, the quality and institutional design of the welfare state could consolidate the foundation of political legitimacy and public support for redistribution.

In the period of permanent austerity, welfare reforms are mostly unpopular, and therefore, public opinion can play a significant role in the process of welfare state restructuring (Pierson, 1994; Campbell, 2003, 2012; Brooks and Manza, 2007). A large number of studies focusing on Western welfare states have demonstrated that welfare retrenchment is often unpopular because of policy feedback. According to those studies, political actors must pursue reform strategies that can reduce political risks and avoid political blame because, as Paul Pierson (1996, p. 176) argues, 'politicians are likely to pursue strategies that will not damage their chances for re-election' (Pierson, 1994, 1996; Campbell, 2003; Brooks and Manza, 2007; Vis and van Kersbergen, 2007; van Kersbergen and Vis, 2014; Busemeyer et al., 2020). Therefore, it is important to figure out whether public opinion can play a role, and maybe even a major role, in welfare state restructuring, as argued by Brooks and Manza (2007). In democracies, elections are the main means by which political actors and governments are held accountable; therefore, in order to win elections, political actors are forced to actively represent citizens' aggregated preferences (Soroka and Wlezien, 2010). Understanding the linkage between public opinion and policy would help political actors to consider which welfare reforms are politically risky and whether the public attitude on welfare reforms is consistent or contradictory (Burstein, 2003; Soroka and Wlezien, 2010; Busemeyer et al., 2020). When public support for welfare reform is low, political actors either hesitate to launch welfare reform or pursue reform strategies to avoid political blame. When welfare reform enjoys majority support, however, political actors tend to introduce reform in a bid for more public support, even if that means losing some votes (Vis and van Kersbergen, 2007; Lee et al., 2020).

Although previous studies have shown that public opinion plays a major role in welfare reform, welfare attitude studies in East Asia have paid scant attention to them. For example, Nagayoshi and Sato (2014) and Sumino (2014) analyse the linkage between popular attitudes towards redistribution and social trust, among other self-interest factors and social values, in Japan. Wang et al. (2013) and Wu and Chou (2017) focus on the case of Hong Kong to identify the determinants of public support for redistribution. Ng (2015), Kim and Lee (2018) and Kim et al. (2018) shed light on how the perception of income inequality affects welfare attitudes, with a focus on Singapore and other East Asian welfare states. For Taiwan, Yeh and Ku (2021) analyse how democratic satisfaction and socio-economic factors shape welfare attitudes and economic developmentalism. Although China is considered an authoritarian regime, we can find many welfare attitude studies covering such cases (Han, 2012; Yang et al., 2019; Cheng and Ngok, 2020; He et al., 2020; Dalen, 2021). Cheng and Ngok (2020) find that social values are important in shaping welfare attitudes in China. Likewise, Yang et al. (2019) find that self-interest plays a role in shaping Chinese seniors' attitudes towards social welfare, social values and especially social rights. These studies are meaningful in that they consider welfare attitude as the dependent variable and search for its determinants. However, they do not consider how public opinion (i.e. citizens' aggregated policy preferences) is formed, especially in relation to earlier policy designs and legacies. As a result, the question of how public opinion influences welfare reforms in East Asia has not yet been adequately scrutinised.

As more than two decades have passed since important welfare reforms took place in East Asia, we think that the time is ripe for public opinion to be scrutinised further in future research. Shaped by institutional legacies, interest groups (labour unions in particular), though important in power resource theory, might not be directly relevant to social policy making in East Asia (even though civic groups were more effective in mobilising public support for specific welfare issues in the relatively more inclusive case of Korea). Hence, public support for welfare reforms could lay the foundation for political legitimacy in the context of welfare state restructuring. However, the question is how public opinion can be integrated into the comparative analysis of East Asian welfare states. The next section will focus on this issue, attempting to develop a useful framework for analysing East Asian welfare state development.

An analytical framework

In this section, we endeavour to introduce a framework for 'shaping and managing welfare politics'. We take into account two important contextual features: whether public opinion is coherent or conflicting; and whether welfare is expanding or retrenching.

First, we need to understand how welfare politics is shaped by public opinion, based on the social policy responsiveness thesis. There are a large number of studies analysing the linkage between public opinion and policy making based on the idea that office-seeking political actors are expected to be responsive to public demand (for redistribution) in democratic welfare states (Burstein, 1998, 2003; Brooks and Manza, 2007; Soroka and Wlezien, 2010; Busemeyer et al., 2020), and particularly to the median voter's preferences (Meltzer and Richard, 1981; Soroka and Wlezien, 2010).

With the advent of democratisation in East Asia, national elections provide a regular opportunity for voters to evaluate political parties and candidates' ideas and policies (Brooks and Manza, 2007; Soroka and Wlezien, 2010). In contrast to old political parties of the old welfare politics in European welfare states, political parties in new democracies in East Asia are more 'catch-all parties' and prefer a strategy of broad appeal to maximise their political base. That is because political bases are not consolidated in the electorates of new democracies, and voters are less willing to stay loyal to a particular party. Therefore, elections in new democratic welfare states in East Asia often exhibit a significant degree of volatility. One typical example is the change in policy orientation of the LDP before and after the administration of the Democratic Party of Japan (2009–2012): despite being a conservative party, the LDP shifted to a more progressive position on policy to attract the support of female voters (Peng, 2015; Fleckenstein and Lee, 2017a; Yeh, 2018; Hong et al., 2022). A similar scenario could be witnessed in Taiwan and Korea. In Taiwan, the KMT and Democratic Progressive Party (DPP), the two main political parties, do not have a clear division on social policy issues (Yeh and Ku, 2021). In Korea, political parties tend to change names and slogans within the broader left–right divide, and the conservative party has kept supporting social investment policies initiated by the progressists since 2007 (Fleckenstein and Lee, 2017a; Hong et al., 2022).

However, public opinion does not directly transfer into policy, and some mechanisms are typically needed (Burstein, 2003; Soroka and Wlezien, 2010; Busemeyer et al., 2020). First, Culpepper's (2011) concept of issue salience is crucial for understanding when public opinion matters in policy making. He argues that when issues do not attract public attention (i.e. there is low issue salience), public opinion has no decisive role, and organised interest groups have a stronger lobbying capacity ('quiet politics'). Recently, the Taiwanese government introduced a new defined-contribution pension scheme for farmers. This pension reform has low political salience, and there was no public debate before its introduction. In these circumstances, public opinion is *de facto* marginalised. In contrast, public opinion is critical in the case of 'loud politics' (Culpepper, 2011; Busemeyer et al., 2020). In loud politics, welfare reform attracts public attention and, therefore, office-seeking politicians endeavour to represent the policy preferences of the majority to win elections. Public opinion is decisive in policy making, thus analysing public opinion is critical for understanding the opinion–policy linkage.

The degree of coherence of public views on certain issues is the key to understanding how public opinion influences the politics of welfare reform and policy making (Busemeyer et al., 2020). When public opinion does not send a coherent and clear signal to political actors, it can appear 'noisy' (Busemeyer et al., 2020). Public attitudes towards redistribution could be conflicting or less coherent on some policy issues, especially those welfare reform issues in which there is a clear division between winners and losers (Pierson, 1994). When it comes to welfare expansion in areas such as work–family policy and education, clear losers are not immediately visible, which can make it easier to obtain broader public support. In this case, public opinion often sends a clear and coherent signal to political actors. Office-seeking political actors thus have strong incentives to use popular social policies to appeal to a new electorate beyond their traditional constituencies. One clear example of this case is the expansion of work–family policy in East Asia. In the face of a super-low fertility rate, when public demand for work–family policy is significant and coherent, office-seeking politicians have a keen interest in introducing work–family policies to attract the support of female voters (Fleckenstein and Lee, 2017a; Hong et al., 2022). That is one reason why the conservative LDP in Japan turned its focus to women-friendly policies after losing the 2009 election (Hong et al., 2022).

By contrast, public opinion is at times incoherent and conflicting. This is particularly true in the case of welfare retrenchment. As is well known, social policy creates policy beneficiaries who defend their interests and resist welfare retrenchment (Pierson, 1994; Campbell, 2003; Brooks and Manza, 2007; Lee et al., 2020). Welfare retrenchment initiatives unavoidably create a cleavage between winners and losers. A typical example is pension reform (Naumann, 2017), which often divides public opinion on a generational basis (Lynch and Myrskylä, 2009; Edlund and Svallfors, 2012; Fernández and Jaime-Castillo, 2013; Naumann, 2017; Bay and Pedersen, 2022). In this case, office-seeking political actors evaluate which reform strategy can consolidate their traditional constituencies and even increase or attract more political support from the median voters. Of course, avoiding political blame is also a crucial consideration. When pension reform can help political actors maximise their political base, pension reform can be launched even when it is unpopular with some groups, such as the 2018 pension reform in Taiwan. By contrast, when unpopular pension reform cannot consolidate or increase political bases, it will not be implemented.

Therefore, we would like to remark that public opinion should be contextualised because context matters not only in shaping welfare politics, but also in managing welfare politics. In different contexts, office-seeking political actors have different reform strategies for increasing political support (credit claiming) or reducing political risks (blame avoidance) (Pierson, 1994; Weaver, 2010; Bonoli, 2012). In the context of social policy expansion, office-seeking political actors arguably want to introduce social policies to claim political credit. By contrast, the logic of social policy retrenchment is often blame avoidance (Weaver, 1986; Pierson, 1994; Bonoli, 2012). There are exceptions:

welfare states can still successfully introduce unpopular welfare reforms without electoral punishment (Vis and van Kersbergen, 2007; Weaver, 2010; Bonoli, 2012; Naumann, 2017; Lee et al., 2020), depending on their reform strategies (Pierson, 1994; Weaver, 2010; Bonoli, 2012).

For welfare expansion with high political salience, office-seeking politicians have to comply with the policy preferences of the majority to claim political credit. In the case of welfare retrenchment, reform strategies should focus on how to reduce or diffuse political blame when the politics of welfare reform is loud. In the case of welfare retrenchment on which the public holds a coherent view, policy makers will receive a clear signal. But when public opinion on welfare retrenchment is conflicting, reform strategies will be prominent. Policy makers can turn unpopular welfare reform into welfare reform supported by the majority through political discourse (Cox, 2001; Bonoli, 2012). Public opinion can be manoeuvred through political discourse and, therefore, welfare retrenchment can in some cases be considered a strategy of credit claiming if it is promoted as being necessary for the financial sustainability of the welfare state (Bonoli, 2012). Through political propaganda, welfare retrenchment may lay the foundation of political legitimacy. Therefore, it may be appropriate to view public opinion not as a given, but as manufactured (Herman and Chomsky, 2010). Another strategy often used to gain political legitimacy in welfare reform is 'exchange' (Bonoli, 2012; Häusermann, 2012). In order to introduce unpopular welfare reforms, politicians also introduce work–family policy or other compensatory policies to gain public support.

When considering both the degree of coherence in public opinion (coherence and conflict) and the context of welfare reform (expansion and retrenchment), we can identify four situations as indicated in Table 4.1. First, on the top-left side (cell 1, 'Credit claiming'), public opinion is highly coherent in the context of welfare expansion, hence office-seeking politicians compete to introduce social policy to consolidate and increase political support through credit claiming. The 1993–2008 pension reform in Taiwan is a good example: the KMT and DPP both endeavoured to introduce National Pension Insurance and increase the benefit levels of old-age allowance schemes and Labour Insurance (Yeh, 2014; Chen and Shi, 2020). Therefore, we can witness a significant pension expansion in the 1990s and 2000s. This kind of scenario is typical for welfare latecomers when pre-existing social policies were inadequate; health-care reform in China after 2009 represents another useful example.

Even in the case of social policy expansion, however, public opinion is sometimes conflicting (the top-right side in cell 2, 'Strengthening political constituencies'). Reform strategies are still relatively safe because they would

Table 4.1   The 'shaping and managing politics' framework

		Shaping politics: degree of coherence of public opinion	
		Coherent	Conflicting
Managing politics: reform strategies	**Welfare expansion**	*1 Credit claiming* E.g. Childcare services expansion in Korea E.g. Healthcare coverage in China	*2 Strengthening political constituencies* E.g. Expansionary pension reform in Taiwan (1993–2008) E.g. Long-term care insurance in Japan
	Welfare retrenchment	*3 Blame avoidance* (a) When public support for welfare reform is high, political actors push for reform (b) When public support for welfare reform is low, unpopular welfare reform is blocked E.g. Pension retrenchment for civil servants in Taiwan (2018)	*4 Minimising political risk* (a) Political discourse used to gain public support/ consolidate political constituencies E.g. Pension reform in Taiwan (2020) (b) Exchange: simultaneous expansion and retrenchment of social policy

Source: Revised from Busemeyer et al. (2020).

not create policy losers, and the main consideration of political actors is to consolidate their political bases or increase support beyond their traditional constituencies. In the 1990s, there was a debate in Taiwan about financing the old-age allowance for farmers through general taxation. The DPP wanted to introduce this old-age allowance scheme to disrupt the KMT's traditional constituency and increase its political base, but the KMT preferred to cover farmers with a contributory pension scheme (Yeh and Chen, 2013; Yeh, 2014). DPP's strategy was very successful as farmers usually prefer tax-based social policy (Baldwin, 1990) but it also created policy beneficiaries who would resist pension reform in the 2000s (Yeh and Chen, 2013; Chen and Shi, 2020).

On the bottom-left side, public opinion is coherent in the context of welfare retrenchment (cell 3, 'Blame avoidance'), which involves two cases. In the first case, when public support for welfare retrenchment is high, policy makers may take on the political risks of welfare reform because that would help them to gain public support. However, public support for welfare reform is low in most cases of welfare retrenchment. In that case, policy makers would not adopt welfare reform or even begin debating it because it is politically risky. In Taiwan, a new debate was initiated in 2020 about pension reform that aimed to significantly reduce the benefit levels of Labour Insurance, which covers more than 60 per cent of people between 16 and 65 years old. However, public opinion on pension reform of Labour Insurance exhibits coherent resistance to pension cutbacks. That sent a clear signal to policy makers, and the debates did not even draw public attention.

In the context of welfare retrenchment, public opinion is often conflicting. In the case of less coherent public opinion on welfare reform (cell 4, 'Minimising political risk'), political actors would not receive a clear signal and must consider which reform strategies would minimise political risk or potentially even allow credit claiming (Bonoli, 2012). Intuitively, welfare retrenchment is unpopular. However, public opinion on welfare reform is usually more conflicting because there is often a clear cleavage between losers and winners of the reform (Weaver, 2010). A prototypical case is the 2018 pension reform in Taiwan, which significantly reduced benefit levels for civil servants, public school teachers and service members. Public opinion on the 2018 pension reform was very conflicting. Civil servants, public school teachers and service members – the KMT's main constituencies – resisted the pension reform. However, private-sector workers showed a higher level of support for the pension reform because of the large gap in pension benefits between labour on the one hand and public officials and service members on the other.[1] Facing that situation, the KMT and DPP adopted different reform strategies. In 2012, the KMT government gave up pension reform because of the resistance from its main constituencies. But in 2018, the DPP government chose to introduce the pension reform, not only because opposing groups were not its main constituencies, but also as part of an effort to frame the reform in terms of making the Taiwanese welfare state more financially sustainable to consolidate its political bases (mainly, labour and farmers) and to attract more political support from the median voter (Fu and Hwang, 2018). In other words, the DPP government used political discourse to minimise political risks and adopt a strategy of credit claiming to mobilise and consolidate its political bases.

Conclusion

Drawing on previous studies and discussions covering public opinion and the linkage of public opinion and social policy reform in Western countries, we presented evidence on how and why public opinion can explain social policy development in new democratic welfare states in East Asia as an alternative

---

[1]   Source: http://talk.news.pts.org.tw/show/14300.

to classic power resource theory. In the process, we endeavoured to provide an analytic framework to examine the role of public opinion in shaping social policy development and the reform strategies that can be adopted to manage welfare politics. Due to the latecomer status of welfare states in East Asia, many social policies have an expansionary nature. However, as seen in the case of pension reform, instances of welfare retrenchment have also started to emerge, signalling the need for a more nuanced understanding of the context of reform. Public opinion is particularly critical in the era of permanent austerity when the politics of welfare retrenchment are often conflicting.

Although we used an analytical framework to illustrate the linkage of opinion and policy, understanding how public opinion shapes social policy development will require more work on identifying the inherent causal mechanisms. Empirical studies combining the quantitative method, the comparative historical method and, in particular, the use of surveys is necessary to tease out the causal mechanism of the opinion–policy linkage and to identify under what conditions people would accept welfare retrenchment (Naumann, 2017; Neimanns et al., 2018; Busemeyer et al., 2020) in new democracies and less democratic polities. Another important point of consideration is the very nature of public opinion, which in East Asia, as elsewhere, is not given, and may be manufactured. How public opinion is formed and shaped deserves deeper analysis in future studies covering East Asia and beyond, especially considering that this is a crucial factor for the legitimacy of democratic and non-democratic regimes alike (Kwon, 1999).

References

Amsden, A. H. (1989), *Asia's Next Giant: South Korea and Late Industrialization*. Oxford: Oxford University Press.

An, M. Y. and Peng, I. (2016), Diverging Paths? A Comparative Look at Childcare Policies in Japan, South Korea and Taiwan. *Social Policy and Administration*, 50(5): 540–558.

Baldwin, P. (1990), *The Politics of Social Solidarity: Class Bases of the European Welfare State 1875–1975*. Cambridge: Cambridge University Press.

Bay, A.-H. and Pedersen, A. W. (2022), The Age Profile of European Welfare States: A Source of Intergenerational Conflict?, 38–58, in: Falch-Erikson, A., Takle, M. and Slagsvold, B. (Eds), *Generational Tensions and Solidarity within Advanced Welfare States*. London: Routledge.

Bonoli, G. (2012), Blame Avoidance and Credit Claiming Revisited, 93–110, in: Bonoli, G. and Natali, D. (Eds), *The Politics of the New Welfare State*. Oxford: Oxford University Press.

Breznau, N. (2019), The Underlying Public Attitude toward Government Responsibility to Intervene in Socioeconomics: 30 Years of Evidence from the ISSP. *International Journal of Sociology*, 49(3): 182–203.

Brooks, C. and Manza, J. (2007), *Why Welfare States Persist: The Importance of Public Opinion in Democracies*. Chicago, IL: University of Chicago Press.

Burstein, P. (1998), Bringing the Public Back In: Should Sociologists Consider the Impact of Public Opinion on Public Policy? *Social Forces*, 77(1): 27–62.

Burstein, P. (2003), The Impact of Public Opinion on Public Policy: A Review and an Agenda. *JSTOR*, 56(1): 29–40.

Busemeyer, Marius, R., Garritzmann, J. L. and Neimanns, E. (2020), *A Loud but Noisy Signal: Public Opinion and Education Reform in Western Europe*. Cambridge: Cambridge University Press.

Campbell, A. L. (2003), *How Policies Make Citizens: Senior Political Activism and the American Welfare State*. Princeton, NJ: Princeton University Press.

Campbell, A. L. (2012), Policy Makes Mass Politics. *Annual Review of Political Science*, 15(1): 333–351.

Caraway, T. L. (2009), Labor Rights in East Asia: Progress or Regress? *Journal of East Asian Studies*, 9(2): 153–186.

Chen, H.-H. and Shi, S.-J. (2020), Changing Dynamics of Social Policy in Democracy: Comparing Pension and Health Reforms in Taiwan. *Journal of Asian Public Policy*: 1–15.

Cheng, Q. and Ngok, K. (2020), Welfare Attitudes towards Anti-Poverty Policies in China: Economical Individualism, Social Collectivism and Institutional Differences. *Social Indicators Research*, 150(2): 679–694.

Choi, Y. J. (2009), From Developmental Regimes to Post-Developmental Regimes: Business and Pension Reforms in Japan, South Korea and Taiwan, 206–227, in: Mok, K. H. and Forrest, R. (Eds), *Changing Governance and Public Policy in East Asia*. London: Routledge.

Choi, Y. J. (2013), Developmentalism and Productivism in East Asian Welfare Regimes, 207–225, in: Izuhara, M. (Ed.), *Handbook on East Asian Social Policy*. Cheltenham, UK and Northampton, MA, USA: Edward Elgar Publishing.

Chung, H., Taylor-Gooby, P. and Leruth, B. (2018), Political Legitimacy and Welfare State Futures: Introduction. *Social Policy and Administration*, 52(4): 835–846.

Cox, R. H. (2001), The Social Construction of an Imperative: Why Welfare Reform Happened in Denmark and the Netherlands but Not in Germany. *World Politics*, 53(3): 463–498.

Culpepper, P. D. (2011), *Quiet Politics and Business Power: Corporate Control in Europe and Japan*. Cambridge: Cambridge University Press.

Dalen, K. (2021), Changing Attitudes towards Government Responsibility for Social Welfare in China between 2004 and 2014: Evidence from Three National Surveys. *International Journal of Social Welfare*, 31(2): 248–262.

Deyo, F. C. (1989), *Beneath the Miracle: Labor Subordination in the New Asian Industrialism*. Berkeley, CA: University of California Press.

Deyo, F. C. (2012), *Reforming Asian Labor Systems: Economic Tensions and Worker Dissent*. Ithaca, NY: Cornell University Press.

Ebbinghaus, B. and Naumann, E. (2018), Introduction: Analysing Organized Interests and Public Opinion towards Welfare Reforms, 1–23, in: Ebbinghaus, B. and Naumann, E. (Eds), *Welfare State Reforms Seen from Below: Comparing Public Attitudes and Organized Interests in Britain and Germany*. Basingstoke: Palgrave.

Edlund, J. and Svallfors, S. (2012), Cohort, Class and Attitudes to Redistribution in Two Liberal Welfare States: Britain and the United States, 1996–2006, 206–224, in: Vanhuysse, P. and Goerres, A. (Eds), *Ageing Populations in Post-Industrial Democracies*. London: Routledge.

Esping-Andersen, G. (1985), *Politics against Markets: The Social Democratic Road to Power*. Princeton, NJ: Princeton University Press.

Estévez-Abe, M. (2008), *Welfare and Capitalism in Postwar Japan*. Cambridge: Cambridge University Press.

Fernández, J. J. and Jaime-Castillo, A. M. (2013), Positive or Negative Policy Feedbacks? Explaining Popular Attitudes towards Pragmatic Pension Policy Reforms. *European Sociological Review*, 29(4): 803–815.

Fleckenstein, T. and Lee, S.-H. C. (2017a), The Politics of Investing in Families: Comparing Family Policy Expansion in Japan and South Korea. *Social Politics: International Studies in Gender, State and Society*, 24(1): 1–28.

Fleckenstein, T. and Lee, S.-H. C. (2017b), Democratization, Post-Industrialization, and East Asian Welfare Capitalism: The Politics of Welfare State Reform in Japan, South Korea, and Taiwan. *Journal of International and Comparative Social Policy*, 33(1): 36–54.

Fu, T.-H. and Hwang, G.-J. (2018), Reforming Public Pensions in Democratizing Korea and Taiwan: Actors, Institutions and Policy Outcomes. *Journal of Asian Public Policy*, 11(1): 67–82.

Glynn, C. J., Herbst, S., Lindeman, M. and O'Keefe, G. J. (2018), *Public Opinion*. London: Routledge.

Gough, I. (1979), *The Political Economy of the Welfare State*. Basingstoke: Macmillan.

Gough, I. (2004), East Asia: The Limits of Productivist Regimes, 169–201, in: Gough, I. and Wood, G. (Eds), *Insecurity and Welfare Regimes in Asia, Africa and Latin America: Social Policy in Development Contexts*. Cambridge: Cambridge University Press.

Haggard, S. (2004), Institutions and Growth in East Asia. *Studies in Comparative International Development*, 38(4): 53–81.

Haggard, S. and Kaufman, R. R. (2008), *Development, Democracy, and Welfare States: Latin America, East Asia, and East Europe*. Princeton, NJ: Princeton University Press.

Han, C. (2012), Attitudes Toward Government Responsibility for Social Services: Comparing Urban and Rural China. *International Journal of Public Opinion Research*, 24(4): 472–494.

Häusermann, S. (2012), The Politics of Old and New Social Policies, 111–132, in: Bonoli, G. and Natali, D. (Eds), *The Politics of the New Welfare State*. Oxford: Oxford University Press.

He, A. J.-W. (2018), Public Satisfaction with the Health System and Popular Support for State Involvement in an East Asian Welfare Regime: Health Policy Legitimacy of Hong Kong. *Social Policy and Administration*, 52(3): 750–770.

He, A. J.-W., Qian, J. and Ratigan, K. (2020), Attitudes toward Welfare Spending in Urban China: Evidence from a Survey in Two Provinces and Social Policy Implications. *Journal of Chinese Governance*: 1–24.

Herman, E. S. and Chomsky, N. (2010), *Manufacturing Consent: The Political Economy of the Mass Media*. New York: Random House.

Ho, M.-S. (2014), *Working Class Formation in Taiwan: Fractured Solidarity in State-Owned Enterprises, 1945–2012*. Basingstoke: Palgrave.

Holliday, I. (2000), Productivist Welfare Capitalism: Social Policy in East Asia. *Political Studies*, 48(4): 706–723.

Hong, I., Yeh, C.-Y., Lee, J. and Lue, J.-D. (2022), An Increasing but Diverse Support for Social Investment: Public Opinion on Social Investment in the North East Asian Welfare Systems, 259–284, in: Garritzmann, J. L., Häusermann, S. and Palier, B. (Eds), *The World Politics of Social Investment: Political Dynamics of Reforms* (Vol. 2). Oxford: Oxford University Press.

Hwang, G.-J. (2006), *Pathways to State Welfare in Korea: Interests, Ideas and Institutions*. Aldershot: Ashgate.

Imai, J. (2011), *The Transformation of Japanese Employment Relations: Reform without Labor*. Basingstoke: Palgrave.

Johnson, C. (1982), *MITI and The Japanese Miracle: The Growth of Industrial Policy, 1925-1975*. Stanford, CA: Stanford University Press.

Kim, H. and Lee, Y. (2018), Socioeconomic Status, Perceived Inequality of Opportunity, and Attitudes toward Redistribution. *The Social Science Journal*, 55(3): 300–312.

Kim, H., Huh, S., Choi, S. and Lee, Y. (2018), Perceptions of Inequality and Attitudes towards Redistribution in Four East Asian Welfare States. *International Journal of Social Welfare*, 27(1): 28–39.

Kim, M. M. S. (2015), *Comparative Welfare Capitalism in East Asia: Productivist Models of Social Policy*. Basingstoke: Palgrave.

Kim, Y. (2021), Civic Movements and the Detour to Welfare State Building in South Korea, 78–98, in: Yang, J.-J. (Ed.), *The Small Welfare State: Rethinking Welfare in the US, Japan, and South Korea*. Cheltenham, UK and Northampton, MA, USA: Edward Elgar Publishing.

Korpi, W. (1983), *The Democratic Class Struggle*. London: Routledge and Kegan Paul.

Kumlin, S. (2004), *The Personal and the Political: How Personal Welfare States Experiences Affect Political Trust and Ideology*. Basingstoke: Palgrave.

Kumlin, S. (2014), Policy Feedback in Political Context: Unemployment Benefits, Election Campaigns, and Democratic Satisfaction, 181–197, in: Kumlin, S. and Stadelmann-Steffen, I. (Eds), *How Welfare Sates Shape the Democratic Public: Policy Feedback, Voting, and Attitudes*. Cheltenham, UK and Northampton, MA, USA: Edward Elgar Publishing.

Kwon, H. J. (1999), *The Welfare State in Korea: The Politics of Legitimation*. London: Macmillan Press.

Kwon, H. J. (2005), Transforming the Developmental Welfare State in East Asia. *Development and Change*, 36(3): 477–497.

Kwon, S.-M. (2020), Why Welfare State Building Is of Secondary Importance to Leftists in Japan and South Korea. In J.-J. Yang (Eds), *The Small Welfare State: Rethinking Welfare in the US, Japan, and South Korea*. Cheltenham, UK and Northampton, MA, USA: Edward Elgar Publishing.

Kwon, S.-M. and Hong, I. (2019), Is South Korea as Leftist as It Gets? Labour Market Policy Reforms under the Moon Presidency. *The Political Quarterly*, 90(2): 81–88.

Lee, S., Jensen, C., Arndt, C. and Wenzelburger, G. (2020), Risky Business? Welfare State Reforms and Government Support in Britain and Denmark. *British Journal of Political Science*, 50(1): 165–184.

Lee, S.-H. (2017), The Socialization of Childcare and a Missed Opportunity through Path Dependence: The Case of South Korea. *Social Politics: International Studies in Gender, State and Society*, 24(2): 132–153.

Lee, S.-Y. (2016), Institutional Legacy of State Corporatism in De-Industrial Labour Markets: A Comparative Study of Japan, South Korea and Taiwan. *Socio-Economic Review*, 14(1): 73–95.

Lee, S.-Y., Suh, N. K. and Song, J.-K. (2009), Determinants of Public Satisfaction with the National Health Insurance in South Korea. *International Journal of Health Planning and Management*, 24(2): 131–146.

Lee, Y. J. and Ku, Y. W. (2007), East Asian Welfare Regimes: Testing the Hypothesis of the Developmental Welfare State. *Social Policy and Administration*, 41(2): 197–212.

Lynch, J. and Myrskylä, M. (2009), Always the Third Rail? Pension Income and Policy Preferences in European Democracies. *Comparative Political Studies*, 42(8): 1068–1097.

Meltzer, A. H. and Richard, S. F. (1981), A Rational Theory of the Size of Government. *Journal of Political Economy*, 89(5): 914–927.

Miura, M. (2012), *Welfare through Work: Conservative Ideas, Partisan Dynamics, and Social Protection in Japan*. Ithaca, NY: Cornell University Press.

Nagayoshi, K. and Sato, Y. (2014), Who Supports Redistributive Policies in Contemporary Japan? An Integrative Approach to Self-Interest and Trust Models. *International Sociology*, 29(4): 302–323.

Naumann, E. (2017), Do Increasing Reform Pressures Change Welfare State Attitudes? An Experimental Study on Population Ageing, Pension Reform Preferences, Political Knowledge and Ideology. *Ageing and Society*, 37(2): 266–294.

Neimanns, E., Busemeyer, M. R. and Garritzmann, J. L. (2018), How Popular Are Social Investment Policies Really? Evidence from a Survey Experiment in Eight Western European Countries. *European Sociological Review*, 34(3): 238–253.

Ng, I. Y. H. (2015), Welfare Attitudes of Singaporeans: Ambiguity in Shifting Socio-Political Dynamics. *Social Policy and Administration*, 49(7): 946–965.

Park, K., Park, J., Kwon, Y. D., Kang, Y. and Noh, J.-W. (2016), Public Satisfaction with the Healthcare System Performance in South Korea: Universal Healthcare System. *Health Policy*, 120(6): 621–629.

Peng, I. (2004), Postindustrial Pressures, Political Regime Shifts, and Social Policy Reform in Japan and South Korea. *Journal of East Asian Studies*, 4(3): 389–426.

Peng, I. (2015), The 'New' Social Investment Policies in Japan and South Korea, 142–160, in: Hasmath, R. (Ed.), *Inclusive Growth, Development and Welfare Policy: A Critical Assessment*. London: Routledge.

Peng, I. and Wong, J. (2008), Institutions and Institutional Purpose: Continuity and Change in East Asian Social Policy. *Politics and Society*, 36(1): 61–88.

Pfau-Effinger, B. (2004), *Development of Culture, Welfare States and Women's Employment in Europe*. London: Routledge.

Pierson, P. (1994), *Dismantling the Welfare State? Reagan, Thatcher, and the Politics of Retrenchment*. Cambridge: Cambridge University Press.

Pierson, P. (1996), The New Politics of the Welfare State. *World Politics*, 48(2): 143–179.

Powell, G. B. (2004), The Quality of Democracy: The Chain of Responsiveness. *Journal of Democracy*, 15(4): 91–105.

Ringen, S., Kwon, H. J., Yi, I., Kim, T. and Lee, J. (2011), *The Korean State and Social Policy: How South Korea Lifted Itself from Poverty and Dictatorship to Affluence and Democracy*. Oxford: Oxford University Press.

Rothstein, B. (1998), *Just Institutions Matter: The Moral and Political Logic of the Universal Welfare State*. Cambridge: Cambridge University Press.

Rothstein, B., Samanni, M. and Teorell, J. (2012), Explaining the Welfare State: Power Resources vs. the Quality of Government. *European Political Science Review*, 4(1): 1–28.

Rudra, N. (2008), *Globalization and the Race to the Bottom in Developing Countries: Who Really Gets Hurt?* Cambridge: Cambridge University Press.

Song, J.-E. (2014), *Inequality in the Workplace: Labor Market Reform in Japan and Korea*. Ithaca, NY: Cornell University Press.

Soroka, S. N. and Wlezien, C. (2010), *Degrees of Democracy: Politics, Public Opinion and Policy*. Cambridge: Cambridge University Press.

Sumino, T. (2014), Escaping the Curse of Economic Self-Interest: An Individual-Level Analysis of Public Support for the Welfare State in Japan. *Journal of Social Policy*, 43(1): 109–133.

Swenson, P. A. (2002), *Capitalist against Markets: The Making of Labor Markets and Welfare States in the United States and Sweden*. Oxford: Oxford University Press.

Taylor-Gooby, P. and Leruth, B. (2018), New Challenges for the Welfare State and New Ways to Study Them, 1–28, in: Taylor-Gooby, P. and Leruth, B. (Eds), *Attitudes, Aspirations and Welfare: Social Policy Directions in Uncertain Times*. Basingstoke: Palgrave.

Tsai, P.-Y. (2014), Stability with Change: Work–Family Balance Policies in Taiwan, 45–53, in: Hill, M. (Ed.), *Studying Public Policy: An International Approach*. Bristol: Policy Press.

van Kersbergen, K. and Vis, B. (2014), *Comparative Welfare State Politics: Development, Opportunities, and Reform*. Cambridge: Cambridge University Press.

Vis, B. and van Kersbergen, K. (2007), Why and How Do Political Actors Pursue Risky Reforms? *Journal of Theoretical Politics*, 19(2): 153–172.

Wade, R. (2004), *Governing the Market: Economic Theory and the Role of Government in East Asian Industrialization*. Princeton, NJ: Princeton University Press.

Wang, J. H. (1993), *Capital, Labour and the State: Political and Social Transition in Taiwan*. Taipei: Tonson (in Chinese).

Wang, K. Y.-T., Wong, C.-K. and Tang, K.-L. (2013), Citizens' Attitudes towards Economic Insecurity and Government after the 2007 Financial Tsunami: A Hong Kong and Taiwan Comparison. *International Journal of Social Welfare*, 22(2): 152–163.

Weaver, R. K. (1986), The Politics of Blame Avoidance. *Journal of Public Policy*, 6(4): 371–398.

Weaver, R. K. (2010), Paths and Forks or Chutes and Ladders? Negative Feedbacks and Policy Regime Change. *Journal of Public Policy*, 30(2): 137–162.

Wong, J. (2004), *Healthy Democracies: Welfare Politics in Taiwan and South Korea*. Ithaca, NY: Cornell University Press.

Wu, A. M. and Chou, K.-L. (2017), Public Attitudes towards Income Redistribution: Evidence from Hong Kong. *Social Policy and Administration*, 51(5): 738–754.

Xu, J. (2016), Trust in Government and Preference for Redistribution: An Empirical Study of the Data of China. *Comparative Economic and Social Systems*, 1: 152–163 (in Chinese).

Yang, J.-J. (2017), *The Political Economy of the Small Welfare State in South Korea*. Cambridge: Cambridge University Press.

Yang, K., Peng, H. and Chen, J. (2019), Chinese Seniors' Attitudes towards Government Responsibility for Social Welfare: Self-Interest, Collectivism Orientation and Regional Disparities. *International Journal of Social Welfare*, 28(2): 208–216.

Yeh, C.-Y. (2014), Public–Private Pension Mix in East Asia: An Integrated Political-Economic Explanation. Thesis, University of Southampton.

Yeh, C.-Y. (2018), *East Asian Welfare Regime in Transition*. Hong Kong: City University of Hong Kong Press.

Yeh, C.-Y. and Chen, Y.-F. (2013), Democracy, Capitalism and Pension Development in Taiwan. *Journal of Humanities and Social Science*, 25(1): 45–86.

Yeh, C.-Y. and Ku, Y.-W. (2021), Welfare Attitude and Economic Developmentalism in New Democratic Developmental Welfare State: An Examination of the Taiwanese Case. *Journal of Asian Public Policy*, 14(1): 13–29.

Yeh, C.-Y., Lin, Z.-Y. and Lue, J.-D. (forthcoming), The Micro-Foundation of the National Health Insurance in Taiwan: An Empirical Examination. *Journal of Social Sciences and Philosophy* (in Chinese).

Yeh, C.-Y., Cheng, H. and Shi, S.-J. (2020), Public–Private Pension Mixes in East Asia: Institutional Diversity and Policy Implications for Old-Age Security. *Ageing and Society*, 40(3): 604–625.

Yi, I., Sohn, H.-s. and Kim, T. (2015), Linking State Intervention and Health Equity Differently: The Universalization of Health Care in South Korea and Taiwan. *Korea Observer*, 46: 517–549.

5 The introduction of the "mainland frame" in public policy: a case study on framing and political rhetoric in Hong Kong's climate policy

Tommy Chung Yin Kwan

Introduction

After the handover in 1997, socio-economic integration between Hong Kong and mainland China was deepened gradually under the framework of "one country, two systems". The government and politics of Hong Kong remained comparatively autonomous for a long time, thanks to the promises stipulated in the Basic Law, stating that "the Hong Kong Special Administrative Region shall be a local administrative region of the People's Republic of China, which shall enjoy a high degree of autonomy and come directly under the Central People's Government" (HKSAR, 2022c), the constitution of Hong Kong since 1997. Nevertheless, political integration between the Special Administrative Region (SAR) and mainland China escalated drastically in the aftermath of the 2019 Anti-Extradition Bill Movement, and was arguably the largest social movement in scale since the 1967 riots in Hong Kong. The National Security Law (NSL) was enacted in 2020 as a result of the social movement and it effectively exerted deterrence towards the civil society of Hong Kong. Hong Kong's "high degree" of autonomy was put in doubt after the legislation. In addition to the NSL, there have also been profound changes of the Hong Kong government in terms of its political discourse and political rhetoric despite the bureaucratic structure remaining largely the same after the watershed in 2019. The style and form of governance have changed as a new frame in political communication, which repeatedly emphasizes the relationship and proximity with mainland China and Hong Kong's aspiration to integrate into the National Development, has been adopted by the Hong Kong government since 2019. This "mainland frame" set up by the Hong Kong government can be found across different policies and government documents, ranging from the overarching chief executive's annual Policy Address,[1] anti-epidemic policies in fighting COVID-19, to the city's long-term climate action plan in achieving carbon neutral in the future. A detailed account is needed to evaluate this change of discourse in the SAR government's social and public policy.

This chapter studies the increasing Chinese influence on Hong Kong's social and public policy with a special focus on a relatively less political consensus – i.e. climate policy. The influence of China on Hong Kong's climate policy has been prominent since the accelerated integration in 2019. The influence is two-fold: first, in terms of international participation, Hong Kong failed to send an official delegate to the United Nations Climate Change Conference (COP26) held in Glasgow in 2021. This was also the third meeting of the involved parties to the 2015 Paris Agreement, as it closely followed China's low-key approach in the conference (Rathi & Kan, 2021). In the past, the Secretary of Environment attended the international conferences on behalf of Hong Kong in Paris (2015) and Bonn (2017), respectively. Hong Kong's autonomy in participating in international activities has been limited. Second, the "mainland frame" has been applied in the government's discourse on climate policies; while Hong Kong's climate policy was sometimes criticized as "hiding behind China's coattail" in the past, the autonomy of Hong Kong in climate politics has been further reduced in recent years. In terms of the change in discourse, the chapter studies the application of the "mainland frame" in policy papers by closely comparing two government documents in climate policy: *Hong Kong's Climate Action Plan 2030+* (2017) and *Hong Kong's Climate Action Plan 2050* (2021b), which were published by the Environment Bureau of the SAR government to develop a plan in combating climate change. Although the two long-term climate action plans shared the same policy nature and were both overseen by the same personnel, the 2021 published climate action plan featured an obvious "mainland frame" which had been largely absent in the previous plan. The introduction of the "mainland frame" represents a change in political discourse by the Hong Kong government.

The Chinese influence on Hong Kong's climate policy after 2019 is clearly reflected from the above two perspectives. The chapter is structured as follows. First, it outlines the relationship between Hong Kong and mainland China since the handover of sovereignty and shows the integration process. It also covers the change of the SAR government's participation in the international

---

[1]   For example, in the opening section of the 2021 Policy Address, the chief executive, Carrie Lam (2021), mentioned that Hong Kong citizens should be "striving hard to bring Hong Kong's unique strengths into full play to better integrate into the overall national development".

stage under the influence of mainland China. Second, it lays down the theoretical framework by articulating the essence of government discourse and how the government can introduce "framing" in its discourse. The third part is empirical studies of the two climate policy papers *Hong Kong's Climate Action Plan 2030+* and *Hong Kong's Climate Action Plan 2050*. The chapter highlights the emergence of the "mainland frame" after 2019 by comparing the two climate plans. Finally, it concludes with a section on how the Chinese influence has changed Hong Kong's climate governance.

Integration as a work in progress since 1997

Even though the handover of Hong Kong in 1997 was labelled as "remain unchanged for 50 years", the review of "one country, two systems" and their integration is by no means straightforward. According to Alvin So (2011), a "crisis-transformation perspective" is adopted to evaluate the integration process as there have been multiple "major turning points" of the political system since 1997. The transfer of sovereignty in 1997 materialized the Sino-British Joint Declaration that was signed in 1984. The rise of the Red Bauhinia flag signified the completion of the "national unification" process, however, "integration" between Hong Kong and mainland China was a very long way from complete (So, 2011). Under "one country, two systems", an institutional framework which was designed to define the relationship across the Shenzhen border, the integration process has undergone ups and downs in the past two decades. Ho and Tran (2019) outline that the relationship has gone from "apprehension" before the handover to "integration" after 2003, and then to "clashes" in the Umbrella Movement in 2014. Unfortunately, this "clash" was deepened and intensified in the 2019 Anti-Extradition Bill Movement (Wing-Chung & Emilie, 2019). To monitor the relationship between Hong Kong and mainland China, scholars continuously shed light on both the design of the "one country, two systems" policy and the integration process (Wong & Xiao, 2018). It is without doubt that the "one country, two systems" approach is one of the most innovative designs in politics as it accommodates the oddest pair of systems within a country, i.e. the capitalist economic system of Hong Kong and the socialist system in China. It was designed to ensure and perpetuate both economic prosperity and political stability in Hong Kong after the handover. In a nutshell, "one country, two systems" can be summarized as follows (some of these were also printed in the Basic Law): a high degree of autonomy (Article 2); the previous capitalist system and way of life shall remain unchanged for 50 years (Article 5); the socialist system and policies will not be practised in Hong Kong (Preamble); Hong Kong people will rule Hong Kong; and the continuation of "horse racing and dancing" (HKSAR, 2022c).

While the feasibility and efficiency of the framework were often called into question, integration was not stopped (Lui, 2015). Nevertheless, it is important to highlight that Beijing did for a long time keep its promise and "adopted a hands-off policy" of preserving Hong Kong's autonomy by staying away from the city's own governance (So, 2011). The restrained Chinese government successfully alleviated Hong Kong people's fears and pessimism towards communism (So, 2011, p. 108, 2018). In fact, the integration process was so minimal before 2003 that the pendulum of Hong Kong's political system "began to shift from 'one country' to 'two systems'" (So, 2011). In 2003, together with the outbreak of the Severe Acute Respiratory Syndrome, an underperforming economy and the SAR government's endeavour in pushing the legislation of the freedom-threatening Article 23 under Beijing's initiation, more than half a million people came out to protest against the Hong Kong government (So, 2011; Wing-Chung & Emilie, 2019).[2] In response to the first massive political discontent since the handover, Beijing took the initiative to give Hong Kong an economic boost by first introducing the "Individual Traveller's Scheme", followed by the signing of the Closer Economic Participation Arrangement (Ma, 2015). Hong Kong established an influential role in China's financial development and also served as China's window to global capital (Meyer, 2018; Sung, 2018). It is noteworthy to point out that the economic integration between Hong Kong and mainland China can be dated back as early as China's opening in the late 1970s, but it was refreshed and consolidated by the newly signed cooperation (Wu, 2019). The accelerated economic integration was positively received by the majority of Hong Kong's population from the period of 2003 to 2008, and it marked the heyday of the relationship between Hong Kong and mainland China; there were more Hong Kong people self-identifying as "Chinese" than "Hongkonger" (Wing-Chung & Emilie, 2019). Nevertheless, the overstressing of economic integration soon became a double-edged sword as the city was overloaded by an influx of immigrants and tourists, and ultimately "anti-China" sentiments emerged (Ma, 2015). In this instance, the planning of the Hong Kong–Macao–Zhuhai bridge and the high-speed rail was on the one hand valued by the ambitious Hong Kong government but on

---

[2]   In Article 23 of the Basic Law, it states that the Hong Kong SAR government shall "enact laws on its own to prohibit any act of treason, secession, sedition, subversion against the Central People's Government". The initiation of legislation in 2003 worried Hong Kong people that the likes of freedom of speech and the freedom of press would vanish. A lot of people went on the streets on 1 July 2003 to express their objection and anger.

the other hand it sparked a series of clashes which could be seen as a conflict of identities (Wing-Chung & Emilie, 2019). In explaining the emergence of "anti-China" sentiments, Ma (2015) points out that fostering integration within the framework of "one country, two systems" would be fundamentally paradoxical as the political system was designed to "insert mechanisms of separation between mainland China and Hong Kong".

Political integration and local governance

While it was clear that social integration lagged behind economic integration between Hong Kong and mainland China, political integration was also sparse until the enactment of the NSL. Local governance remained autonomous and political institutions were intact, for instance, the democratic District Council elections were regularly held; meanwhile, half of the Legislative Council was democratically elected until the radical reform in 2021 which scrapped the number of directly elected seats from 35 to 20.[3] At the same time, the autonomy of Hong Kong was guaranteed by the "executive-led" system as the chief executive of the administration was generally perceived as "free to make decisions on Hong Kong internal affairs" (Wing-Chung & Emilie, 2019). The city retained the status of a "global city" and enjoyed a large degree of autonomy in its local governance (Loh, 2006; Meyer, 2018). As promised in the Basic Law, Beijing is mainly responsible for two main areas of Hong Kong, i.e. foreign affairs and defence (Article 13 and 14). Outside of these two areas, Hong Kong "shall enjoy a high degree of autonomy" (Article 12).[4] In truth, Beijing's role in Hong Kong politics is notable in its appointment of personnel in the SAR government as it handpicks the leadership under the façade of the small circle election which is known as the "Election Committee".

While numerous political setbacks, for instance the Umbrella Movement (also known as "Occupying Central"), which fought for universal suffrage in

---

[3]   Before the 2021 reform, the Legislative Council had 70 seats in total, and 35 out of 70 seats were directly elected in five geographical constituencies; in the 2021 reform, the Legislative Council increased the total number of seats to 90, and only 20 seats were directly elected in a total of 10 geographical constituencies.

[4]   According to Article 13, "[t]he Central People's Government authorizes the Hong Kong Special Administrative Region to conduct relevant external affairs on its own in accordance with this Law". This room to conduct external affairs will be shown in the latter example of Hong Kong's participation in international climate conferences (HKSAR, 2016).

2014, showed the lack of democratic development in Hong Kong, Hong Kong remained politically stable and autonomous without explicit interference from Beijing (Yuen, 2015). The annual 4 June candlelight vigil in Victoria Park was one of the remarks footnoting the "unchanged lifestyle" of Hong Kong people. Yet, the outbreak of the Anti-Extradition Bill Movement in 2019 not only rewrote Hong Kong's history as it was labelled "the largest and most long-lasting protest movement" (Lee et al., 2021), it also triggered the enactment of the NSL which had "immediate impacts in the political, social, educational, and judicial spheres"; together with the impact of the pandemic, the strength of civil society shrank significantly (Lo, 2021).

On top of that, political communication of the Hong Kong government has also changed, as an in-depth media report shows that there has been a signifi-cant increase in a number of phrases and words used by the SAR government, for instance, "so-called" (*suowei*) and "hidden agenda" (*bieyou yongxin*), which have also been frequently used by the Chinese central government since 2020.[5] These phrases, carrying a strong character, are easily reminiscent of Chinese officials. In fact, these phrases were not being used by the Hong Kong govern-ment before. The SAR government also started featuring the "mainland frame" as political rhetoric, which often highlights (1) the proximity between Hong Kong and mainland China and (2) the aspiration of Hong Kong in integrating in national development. The deployment of the "mainland frame" which has an emphasis on mainland China in the more recent climate action plan will be addressed in the subsequent section.

In understanding the "one country, two systems" approach, the climate governance of Hong Kong provides a good illustration of how the political system has functioned since 1997. As a SAR of China, Hong Kong's climate governance plays a relatively different and independent role than any other city in China. For instance, through the signatory status of China, Hong Kong voluntarily took part as an observer in the 1997 Kyoto Protocol, the 2007 Sydney Declaration and also the 2015 Paris Climate Conference (Holley & Lecavalier, 2017). Yet, the tangible outcomes of climate policy have arguably been more significant in Chinese cities, such as Shenzhen. Under Beijing's authority, Hong Kong enjoys a high degree of autonomy in taking part on the international stage to combat climate change. As stated on the govern-ment's climate actions webpage, "Hong Kong has been working closely with

---

5   For example, in the report, the frequency of the use of "hidden agenda" by the Hong Kong government was eight times from 2012 to 2018, it increased to 12 times in 2019, 14 times in 2020 and 35 times in 2021 (Li, 2022).

the international community to cope with the impact of climate change and mitigate greenhouse gas emissions" (HKSAR, 2022b). Due to a lack of fuel resources, Hong Kong relies heavily on mainland China's supplies of nuclear energy and natural gas, and the energy trade is guaranteed by the signing of a Memorandum of Understanding (Francesch-Huidobro, 2012; Holley & Lecavalier, 2017). Meanwhile, civil society actors also advocate for more collaboration with mainland China in terms of securing green hydrogen to reduce pollution (Low, 2021).

Hong Kong's participation in international climate conferences

Hong Kong's participation in international climate conferences perfectly shows the increasing Chinese influence in the city's climate governance. In the past, the secretary for the environment participated in the Conference of the Parties to the United Nations Framework Convention on Climate Change on behalf of Hong Kong as a member of the Chinese delegation. Wong went to COP21 in Paris in 2015 and COP23 in Bonn in 2017 to present the *Climate Change Report 2015* and *Hong Kong's Climate Action Plan 2030+*, hosting a Hong Kong session at the China Pavilion in the COP (HKSAR, 2015). However, at COP26, held in Glasgow at the end of 2021, China adopted a comparatively low-key approach in the conference as it was not entirely in line with other countries' ambitions, mainly the developed United States and Western Europe, in terms of the responsibility in combating climate change. For example, unlike previous COPs, China did not set up a pavilion at the conference to network with delegates and observers around the world, neither did President Xi Jinping participate in the conference (UNCC, 2021). As mentioned in a media report, "China's team had just one low-profile briefing with state media and a few foreign organizations selected by its British embassy" (Rathi & Kan, 2021). As a result of China's idle approach to COP26, Hong Kong did not send an official delegate for a duty visit to the conference in Glasgow. Following previous experience, Wong could follow the usual practice and present the newly published *Hong Kong's Climate Action Plan 2050* at the conference. Nonetheless, this was not the case at COP26. This shows Hong Kong's climate governance is heavily influenced by mainland China.

In terms of Hong Kong's autonomy in promoting climate change initiatives, Hong Kong has often been criticized as "hiding behind China's coattail" (Holley & Lecavalier, 2017) and adopting a "passive follower position" in terms of climate change initiatives. However, Hong Kong is a "developed city" which should not follow China's "developing country" standard (Mah & Hills, 2016). The SAR government still has a large degree of autonomy in exercising its climate governance within the city through an extensive and collaborative network which is composed of both state and non-state actors. Business sectors as well as civil society actors work together in response to climate change (Cheung & Fuller, 2022; Francesch-Huidobro, 2012). One example is that the Hong Kong government worked closely with two energy service providers, both private utilities, to ensure their "reliability and environmental performance in providing electricity" (Cheung & Fuller, 2022). The government also promoted the "Feed in Tariff scheme" for different stakeholders, ranging from households to non-government organizations and businesses, to provide financial aid to install rooftop solar panel systems (Cheung & Fuller, 2022). Meanwhile, numerous climate action plans and reports have been published by the Hong Kong government to fight climate change and set a target of achieving carbon neutrality before 2050 (HKSAR, 2022a). However, there has been a significant change in political rhetoric in the discourse of the city's recent climate policies. A "mainland frame" has been introduced in the most recently published *Hong Kong's Climate Action Plan 2050*. Before analysing the emergence and significance of the "mainland frame", an introduction of political rhetoric and emphasis framing is needed.

Political rhetoric and emphasis framing

Regardless of who the political actor is, a politician, a political party or the government, political communication is the key to shaping public opinion and achieving policy outcome (Krebs & Jackson, 2007). According to Reisigl (2008), political communication is defined as "making sense of symbolic exchanges about the shared exercise of power" and "the presentation and interpretation of information, messages or signals with potential consequences for the exercise of shared power". In other words, effective political communication is essential to the effective exercise of power. In order to communicate effectively and efficiently, rhetoric matters as it is described as (1) the "art of speaking and writing well in public spheres through the use of various communicative genres" and (2) "the theory about eloquence" (Reisigl, 2008). Every political actor needs to speak and write, for instance, political speech, party platform and policy paper could determine the popularity, if not the fate, of political actor.

Alan Finlayson (2013) denotes that every political thinking and political message has two faces: first, the internal face, i.e. the political ideology; second, the external face, i.e. the political rhetoric. A political message could be disseminated with different effects, whether elegant or gauche, subtle or blunt, and it could be determined by its rhetoric. In other words, political rhetoric is the "argumentation form" that "is inseparable from ideological content", thus, without the external face, the political message would be incomplete. Therefore, politicians employ rhetoric to manifest their political message and to express their policy positions. It is not surprising that political actors in a democratic regime would have a higher demand to excel in political rhetoric than a political elite in an authoritarian regime as their political career is very much hinged on public opinion. A "rhetorical edge" could enable the political actor to win more support from the general public, for instance, in an election campaign (Jerit, 2008; Reisigl, 2008). Nonetheless, political rhetoric is also important to political actors in an authoritarian regime as it is a unique skill to establish legitimacy, which every political actor is fond of (Krebs & Jackson, 2007). From a linguistic perspective, political rhetoric has an appeal to both ethos and pathos, which ultimately contributes to the "glow of authority and respect" of a political actor (Finlayson, 2013).

Although "rhetoric" sometimes carries a pejorative meaning as it could mean emptiness in disguise, rhetoric is not equivalent to merely flowery language and, more importantly, it is not necessarily deviating from the "truth". There are multiple methods of political rhetoric and "framing" is a common form of rhetoric strategy. Jerit (2008) highlights the importance of "frame" by saying that "subtle differences in how political elites frame a policy proposal can have a dramatic effect on public opinion". The question of "what is framing", however, needs first to be addressed. A political discourse, such as a political speech and a policy paper, often carries multiple messages and issues, some more important, and others less so. "Framing" is a skill to guide citizens' attention in understanding the more central issue and missing the peripheral issue (Kinder, 1998). For instance, every public policy has its intended and unintended outcome. Policy makers tend to put the focus on the intended outcome during policy evaluation in order to show their competence and, ultimately, to achieve their political goal(s). Framing is the "variations in emphasis" with an intention to shape people's thought (Druckman, 2001). Robert Entman (1993) has a formal definition of framing, saying that "[t]o frame is to select some aspects of a perceived reality and make them more salient in a communicating text, in such a way as to promote a particular problem definition, casual interpretation, moral evaluation, and/or treatment recommendation". Political actors have the final say in defining "salience" (Entman, 1993).

As a form of political rhetoric, there are two major types of framing and they significantly differ with each other even though both share the same label of "framing", i.e. (1) equivalency framing and (2) emphasis framing (or issue framing) (Druckman, 2004). Equivalency framing means "the use of different, but logically equivalent, words or phrases" to cause different perceptions by the public, the typical example is 5 per cent unemployment rate and 95 per cent employment rate meaning the same, but yielding different public opinions. The governing party, or a pro-government media, will tend to write "95% employment rate" in the title to try to build an image of a high employment rate, while the opposition party will be more likely to focus on the 5 per cent unemployment rate to accuse the incumbent government (Druckman, 2001). The reality is always like a glass half filled with water, whether it is half full or half empty, the choice of frame could decide which story to tell. Also, emphasis framing means that the policy maker put the focus on different but relevant considerations. Selection of information is therefore needed before the presentation, otherwise the public might not capture the desired meaning(s) of the policy maker (Lee & Chang, 2010). Emphasis framing can usually be found in election campaigns as candidates tend to claim (or sometimes hide) the ownership of specific issue, sometimes for the sake of strengthening a certain image, sometimes to dilute a certain stance. For example, in Taiwan, when the Democratic Progressive Party (DPP) wanted to appeal to middle-class voters in the 2012 election amid a peaceful cross-Strait relationship, the party's pro-independent and "anti-China" stance was lessened. However, in the 2020 election, the DPP wanted to stress its "anti-China" stance in the aftermath of the 2019 Anti-Extradition Bill Movement in Hong Kong. Emphasis framing enables the party to decide which political message to deliver to the general public.

In this chapter, the SAR government choosing to emphasize the proximity of Hong Kong and mainland China in the area of climate policy is an example of "emphasis framing". While equivalency framing is playing around logic to cause, if not confuse, different public opinion, emphasis framing is about focusing on different elements inside the big picture. Many researchers have gauged the effect of framing by studying the change of public opinion in a democratic regime as change can always be reflected in regular elections (Lee & Chang, 2010). This chapter solely focuses on the employment of framing by examining before and after the introduction of a "mainland frame" in Hong Kong's climate policy. It studies the "mainland frame" *per se* as this emphasis framing has not been seen in the past. I defined the "mainland frame" as an emphasis on two elements: (1) the relationship and proximity between Hong Kong and mainland China; and (2) the aspiration of Hong Kong to integrate into the National Development. It is a study of political discourse by analysing the "pattern and commonalities of knowledge and structures" in the two climate action plans (Wodak, 2008). The emergence of "mainland frame" could reflect the updated "core concerns" of the political actor, in this case, the Hong Kong government (Jerit, 2008).

The emergence of the "mainland frame" in climate action plans

In response to the Paris Agreement entered into force in 2016, the Hong Kong government started to set out a long-term climate plan to set out a carbon emissions reduction target. Also, it set a range of initiatives and engaged both state and non-state actors to combat climate change. In January 2017, the Environment Bureau of the SAR government first published *Hong Kong's Climate Action Plan 2030+* and in October 2021, the government published *Hong Kong's Climate Action Plan 2050* with updated targets. Although these two action plans were not the first publications of the SAR government on climate policy, they were the first publications that adopted such a macro perspective in answering the climate problem. In the past, plans like the Energy Saving Plan, the Food Waste and Yard Waste Plan and the Clear Air Plan[6] had been published to tackle different perspectives of climate and environment problems. In both the *2030+* and *2050* climate action plans, a wholistic plan was provided of how the city could cope with the crisis of climate change in the future. It should be noted that even though the *2050 Climate Action Plan* features a "mainland frame", it remains mainly a plan for Hong Kong's local governance as climate change policy is less political in comparison to the likes of education and the media industry.

The climate action plans are a very good pair of cases to study in depth as they were produced by the Steering Committee on Climate Change, and this Steering Committee was chaired by Carrie Lam, the then chief secretary for administration and the current chief executive;[7] at the same time, the main figure in formulating climate policy, Wong Kam-sing, has remained as the secretary for the environment. The same personnel has helped to minimize the difference of writing style in the policy papers which could be a possible factor in contributing to the change of political discourse.

---

[6]   Details and the full report of the above-mentioned plans can be found on the government's "Carbon Neutral @Hong Kong" webpage: www.climateready.gov.hk/?lang=1

[7]   The Steering Committee changed its name to the Steering Committee on Climate Change and Carbon Neutrality in 2021 (HKSAR, 2021a).

Presenting the proximity between Hong Kong and mainland China

The "mainland frame" emerged on two levels in *Hong Kong's Climate Action 2050*. First, it emerged as a form to emphasize the relationship between Hong Kong and mainland China, as well as the leadership of Beijing. In the opening message from the chief executive, Carrie Lam highlighted that, "Our country is committed to achieving peak carbon dioxide emissions before 2030 and carbon neutrality before 2060. As an international city of China, Hong Kong has been an active participant in global efforts to combat climate change" (HKSAR, 2021b). The emphasis of "as an international city of China" is unseen in the much shorter opening message of the *Climate Action Plan 2030+*, which was given by the then chief executive, Leung Chun-ying. In fact, the whole opening message neither mentions "China" nor the relationship between Hong Kong and China. It only focuses on describing the action plan and also its role in Hong Kong's climate policy. In the opening message, he stated that,

> They [the initiatives in the action plan] call for not only the work of Government but also the participation and contribution of business and the community at large …
> Hong Kong's Climate Action Plan 2030+ seeks to make Hong Kong a better and smarter place to live and work. It would also create new economic and social opportunities for Hong Kong. (HKSAR, 2017)

In both action plans' Foreword given by the secretary for the environment, Wong Kam-sing did not mention China in his message. In positioning Hong Kong in the world, he highlighted in the *Climate Action Plan 2050* that "Hong Kong is among the earliest cities in Asia taking actions to combat climate change" (HKSAR, 2021b). Moreover, in the *Climate Action Plan 2050*, two paragraphs are dedicated to reveal China's climate targets (sections 1.5–1.6), for instance, revealing the "State Council has set up a leading group on carbon peak and carbon neutrality to draw up a timetable and roadmap" which has a total of 10 areas of concern; the "Country's Targets" is placed before "Hong Kong's Targets" (section 1.7). Moreover, a quote from President Xi Jinping's statement at the General Debate of the 75th Session of the United Nations General Assembly was put in the heading of the page. In contrast, in the *Climate Action Plan 2030+*, it only has a small section of supplementary information elaborating on "China's Nationally Determined Contributions" in response to the Paris Agreement (HKSAR, 2017). This section came after revealing the details of the Paris Agreement and how they could apply to Hong Kong. In contrast to the *Climate Action Plan 2030+*, the "mainland frame" is newly presented in the *Climate Action Plan 2050* to emphasize the proximity between the SAR and mainland China.

The aspiration of Hong Kong's integration into the National Development

The second level of influence of the "mainland frame" is about Hong Kong's inspiration in integrating into the National Development and it was the main course of the emphasis framing. It provides more substantial details in denoting how Hong Kong could fit into the country's plan. On the one hand it emphasizes the role of Hong Kong in mainland China's development; on the other hand it highlights where Hong Kong is situated in the National Development plan. Again, in the concluding remarks of the opening message from Carrie Lam in the *Climate Action Plan 2050*, she writes:

> In addition, Hong Kong aspires to integrate into the national development. Leveraging our position as a highly-connected international city, we will be a perfect gateway for foreign business to access the Mainland market and for Mainland enterprises to go global, especially to countries along the Belt and Road … For this, we will continue to participate in and work with the international community to combat climate change. We will also partner with our neighbouring cities in the Guangdong–Hong Kong–Macao Greater Bay Area to develop this world-class city cluster into an exemplary liveable and sustainable region. (HKSAR, 2021b)

In 2019, the Outline Development Plan for the Guangdong–Hong Kong–Macau Greater Bay Area was released. Therefore, similar content was not found in the *Climate Action Plan 2030+*, which was published two years before the "Greater Bay Area Development Outline". While most of the sections in the *Climate Action Plan 2050* concerned local climate policy in Hong Kong, the "mainland frame" emerged again in the section on Opportunities to elaborate and repeat multiple policies of the central government, which include the aforementioned Greater Bay Area Outline and the 14th Five-Year Plan. In section 6.3, it reveals how Hong Kong could become a "regional centre for green finance" by issuing green bonds in renminbi (Tsang, 2021):

> The Outline Development Plan for the Guangdong–Hong Kong–Macao Greater Bay Area released in 2019 supported Hong Kong to develop itself into a green finance centre in the GBA and set up internationally recognised green bond certification institutions. The Outline of the 14th Five-Year Plan for National Economic and Social Development of the People's Republic of China and the Long-Range Objectives Through the Year 2035 (the 14th Five-Year Plan) approved this year also reaffirmed its support for Hong Kong to enhance its status as an international financial centre. (HKSAR, 2021b)

Recalling the role of Hong Kong in the national plan, Hong Kong was first included in "the outline of the 12th Five-Year Plan for national economic and social development of the People's Republic of China" as an independent chapter in 2011. An independent chapter on "Hong Kong and Macau" has been included in the national Five-Year Plan ever since (HKSAR, 2011). Another difference can be spotted here again as the 13th national Five-Year Plan (which was published in 2015) was not mentioned in the *Climate Action Plan 2030+*; only a short session on the development of "carbon emission trading" in mainland China is included (HKSAR, 2017). However, in section 6.6 of the *Climate Action Plan 2050*, the 14th Five-Year Plan was mentioned again and this time it was not closely relevant to climate policy.

> The 14th Five-Year Plan promulgated this year has put forward for the first time the support for Hong Kong to develop into a regional intellectual property (IP) trading centre and an international I&T hub, thereby recognising Hong Kong's potential for I&T development; and has named green and environmental protection technology as one of the strategic emerging industries.
>
> Hong Kong's international business environment, comprehensive IP protection regime, and well-developed service sectors such as financial, maritime, trading and legal services, have created extremely favourable conditions for developing green technologies …
>
> Hong Kong and the adjoining GBA cities may complement one another with their own strengths to achieve synergy, with a view to develop an I&T upstream, midstream and downstream industrial chain, thus contributing to our country's advancement towards carbon neutrality. (HKSAR, 2021b)

The above quote shows the enthusiasm of the Hong Kong government in emphasizing the "mainland frame"; nonetheless, it also reflects the lack of sophistication in applying the "mainland frame" effectively and relevantly. As mentioned, the "mainland frame" was not coherent with the initiations and policies of the *Climate Action Plan 2050*. In order to repeatedly stress the role of Hong Kong in the National Development plan, irrelevant content, such as "IP trading centre" and "international I&T hub", were seen in the climate action plan, which was in theory only related to climate change policy.

Conclusion

When evaluating the practice of "one country, two systems" in the past two decades, from 1997 to 2020 before the enactment of the NSL, this period reflected that economic integration was the major repertoire in the relationship between Hong Kong and mainland China, while political integration was comparatively less prominent in the agenda. This enabled Hong Kong to enjoy a "high degree of autonomy" in terms of its policy-making process, such as the case study in this chapter, the climate policy. After the emergence of "anti-China sentiments" and the Umbrella Movement from the early 2010s, the socio-economic relationship between Hong Kong and mainland China changed gradually. The Hong Kong government could still make climate policy in a relatively "autonomous" fashion, which was well reflected in the publication of *Hong Kong's Climate Action Plan 2030+*, published in 2017. Yet, the enactment of the NSL in 2020 significantly changed the politics of Hong Kong on many different fronts, and integration between Hong Kong and mainland China was speeded up. This chapter focuses on how the political rhetoric on climate policy has changed since then. Although the bureaucratic structure of the Hong Kong SAR government remains unchanged, the style of governance is apparently altered by the introduction of a "mainland frame" in the government's political communication. By comparing the 2021-published *Hong Kong's Climate Action Plan 2050* with the previous plan, while there is not a paradigm shift in the content of Hong Kong's climate policy, the new action plan features an abrupt introduction of a "mainland frame" throughout. First, the proximity of Hong Kong and mainland China is emphasized. Second, the aspiration integrating Hong Kong into the central government's plan is underscored.

While Hong Kong still enjoys a relative high degree of autonomy and does, for instance, have the room and capacity to publish its own climate action plan, the degree of autonomy is undoubtedly lower than at any point since 1997. For a long time after the handover, "one country, two systems" was in practice without the frequent presence of the "mainland frame" in the SAR government's political discourse. It coincided with the time of having the most number of Hong Kong people proudly self-identify as "Chinese". Today, the "mainland frame" is almost omnipresent in Hong Kong, even in climate change policy. However, when the "mainland frame" is included in all of Hong Kong's public policies and Hong Kong's governance is completely embedded in the central government's plan, how much autonomy is left? How much of it is a de jure autonomy, or merely a de facto autonomy? It is about the future of Hong Kong and the system of "one country, two systems" and it is the question that Beijing and Hong Kong policy makers need to think about and address.

References

Cheung, T. T. T., & Fuller, S. (2022). Rethinking the potential of collaboration for urban climate governance: The case of Hong Kong. *Area*, 54(3), 408–417.

Druckman, J. N. (2001). The implications of framing effects for citizen competence. *Political Behavior*, 23(3), 225–256.

Druckman, J. N. (2004). Political preference formation: Competition, deliberation, and the(ir) relevance of framing effects. *American Political Science Review*, 98(4), 671–686.

Entman, R. M. (1993). Framing: Towards clarification of a fractured paradigm. In D. McQuail (Ed.), *McQuail's reader in mass communication theory*, pp. 390–397. New York: Sage.

Finlayson, A. (2013). Ideology and political rhetoric. In M. Freeden & M. Stears (Eds), *The Oxford handbook of political ideologies*, 197–213. Oxford: Oxford University Press.

Francesch-Huidobro, M. (2012). Institutional deficit and lack of legitimacy: The challenges of climate change governance in Hong Kong. *Environmental Politics, 21*(5), 791–810.

HKSAR. (2011). *The HKSAR's work in complementing the national 12th Five-Year Plan*. www.cmab.gov.hk/en/issues/12th_5yrsplan.htm

HKSAR. (2015, December 5). *SEN starts duty visit to Paris*. www.info.gov.hk/gia/general/201512/05/P201512050397.htm

HKSAR. (2016, August 22). *The Basic Law*. www.basiclaw.gov.hk/en/index/index.html

HKSAR. (2017). *Hong Kong's Climate Action Plan 2030+*. www.enb.gov.hk/sites/default/files/pdf/ClimateActionPlanEng.pdf

HKSAR. (2021a, October 29). *ENB holds "carbon neutrality" partnership launching ceremony*. www.info.gov.hk/gia/general/202110/29/P2021102900607.htm

HKSAR. (2021b). *Hong Kong's Climate Action Plan 2050*. www.climateready.gov.hk/files/pdf/CAP2050_booklet_en.pdf

HKSAR. (2022a). *Climate actions*.

HKSAR. (2022b). *Cooperation with international community*.

HKSAR. (2022c, August 22). *The Basic Law*. www.basiclaw.gov.hk/en/index/index.html

Ho, W.-C., & Tran, E. (2019). Hong Kong–China relations over three decades of change: From apprehension to integration to clashes. *China: An International Journal, 17*(1), 173–193.

Holley, C., & Lecavalier, E. (2017). Energy governance, energy security and environmental sustainability: A case study from Hong Kong. *Energy Policy, 108*, 379–389.

Jerit, J. (2008). Issue framing and engagement: Rhetorical strategy in public policy debates. *Political Behavior, 30*(1), 1–24.

Kinder, D. R. (1998). Opinion and action in the realm of politics. In D. Gilbert, S. Fiske & G. Lindzey (Eds), *The handbook of social psychology*, pp. 778–867. New York: McGraw-Hill.

Krebs, R. R., & Jackson, P. T. (2007). Twisting tongues and twisting arms: The power of political rhetoric. *European Journal of International Relations, 13*(1), 35–66.

Lam, C. (2021). *The chief executive's 2021 Policy Address*. Hong Kong Special Administrative Region of the People's Republic of China.

Lee, F. L., Cheng, E. W., Liang, H., Tang, G. K., & Yuen, S. (2021). Dynamics of tactical radicalisation and public receptiveness in Hong Kong's Anti-Extradition Bill Movement. *Journal of Contemporary Asia*, 1–23.

Lee, Y.-K., & Chang, C.-T. (2010). Framing public policy: The impacts of political sophistication and nature of public policy. *Social Science Journal, 47*(1), 69–89.

Li, H.-w. (2022, March 14). Chinese style of bureaucratic tone being found in Hong Kong government: Analysis shows the Beijing influence in Hong Kong. *BBC*. www.bbc.com/zhongwen/trad/chinese-news-60672295

Lo, S. (2021). Hong Kong in 2020: National security law and truncated autonomy. *Asian Survey, 61*(1), 34–42.

Loh, C. (2006). Hong Kong's relations with China: the future of "one country, two systems". *Social Research: An International Quarterly, 73*(1), 293–316.

Low, Z. (2021, October 8). Hong Kong to boost share of renewable energy sources, explore using hydrogen for power generation in bid to meet 2050 carbon neutrality target. *South China Morning Post*. www.scmp.com/news/hong-kong/health -environment/article/3151725/hong-kong-boost-share-renewable-energy-sources

Lui, T.-l. (2015). A missing page in the grand plan of "one country, two systems": Regional integration and its challenges to post-1997 Hong Kong. *Inter-Asia Cultural Studies*, *16*(3), 396–409.

Ma, N. (2015). The rise of "anti-China" sentiments in Hong Kong and the 2012 Legislative Council elections. *The China Review*, 39–66.

Mah, D. N.-y., & Hills, P. (2016). An international review of local governance for climate change: Implications for Hong Kong. *Local Environment*, *21*(1), 39–64.

Meyer, D. R. (2018). Hong Kong: China's global city. In T.-l. Lui, S. Chiu & R. Yep (Eds), *Routledge handbook of contemporary Hong Kong*, pp. 414–429. New York: Routledge.

Rathi, A., & Kan, K. (2021, November 6). China's deafening silence speaks loudest at global climate talks. *Bloomberg News*. www.bloomberg.com/news/articles/2021-11 -06/china-s-absence-at-cop26-climate-talks-slow-progress

Reisigl, M. (2008). Analyzing political rhetoric. In R. Wodak & M. Krsyzanowski (Eds), *Qualitative discourse analysis in the social sciences*, pp. 96–120. London: Bloomsbury.

So, A. Y. (2011). "One country, two systems" and Hong Kong–China national integration: A crisis-transformation perspective. *Journal of Contemporary Asia*, *41*(1), 99–116.

So, A. Y. (2018). Hong Kong's integration with mainland China in historical perspective. In T.-l. Lui, S. Chiu & R. Yep (Eds), *Routledge handbook of contemporary Hong Kong*, pp. 494–510. New York: Routledge.

Sung, Y.-w. (2018). Becoming part of one national economy: Maintaining two systems in the midst of the rise of China 1. In T.-l. Lui, S. Chiu & R. Yep (Eds), *Routledge handbook of contemporary Hong Kong*, pp. 66–85. New York: Routledge.

Tsang, J. (2021, November 21). Hong Kong looks to green bonds sale in renminbi as a way of consolidating city's role as global offshore hub for China's currency. *South China Morning Post*. www.scmp.com/news/hong-kong/hong-kong-economy/ article/3156842/hong-kong-government-looks-green-bonds-sale-yuan

UNCC. (2021). *Pavilions at COP 26*. https://unfccc.int/cop26/pavilions

Wing-Chung, H., & Emilie, T. (2019). Hong Kong–China relations over three decades of change: From apprehension to integration to clashes. *China: An International Journal*, *17*(1), 173–193.

Wodak, R. (2008). *Qualitative discourse analysis in the social sciences*. London: Bloomsbury.

Wong, W., & Xiao, H. (2018). Twenty years of Hong Kong and Macao under Chinese rule: Being absorbed under "one country, two systems". *Public Money and Management*, *38*(6), 411–418.

Wu, J.-M. (2019). *Rent-seeking developmental state in China: Taishang, Guangdong model and global capitalism*. New Taipei: National Taiwan University Press.

Yuen, S. (2015). Hong Kong after the Umbrella Movement: An uncertain future for "One Country Two Systems". *China Perspectives*, *1*, 49–53.

6 Child poverty policies in Japan: familial welfare state in transition?

Aya Abe

Introduction

This chapter will examine whether the Japanese welfare model has transformed during the period from 2008 to 2020, especially with regard to policies against child poverty. During this period, there were significant developments of policies and programmes targeting children of poor families. These developments suggest that Japan may be moving away from its traditional welfare model of relying on families (Ochiai, 2009; Osawa, 2007) and prioritising economic development over the provision of social protection (Choi, 2012; Holliday, 2000; Peng, 2000; Yang and Kühner, 2020). To assess if this hypothesis is true, this chapter will examine child poverty policies of Japan before and after 2008, by reviewing statistics, laws, and official statements by the government and politicians.

Child poverty, and poverty in general, is a serious social issue in Japan despite the popular perception that Japan is an equal society (Abe, 2010; Osawa, 2007). In fact, according to the latest government statistics, Japan's relative poverty rate, defined as the percentage of the population whose equivalised household income is less than 50 per cent of the national median, was 15.4 per cent in 2018, which places Japan among the top third of countries of the Organisation for Economic Co-operation and Development (OECD) with a high poverty rate (OECD Income Distribution Database, extracted on 20 November 2021; MHLW, 2019a). The poverty rate of children under 18 is 13.5 per cent (see Figure 6.1).

It is a well-established fact that even in developed nations, poverty is a social issue that poses serious threats to the current and future well-being of children (Duncan and Brooks-Gunn, 1997). In Japan, as many as 5–6 per cent of families with children under 20 years old, and 14–17 per cent of one-parent

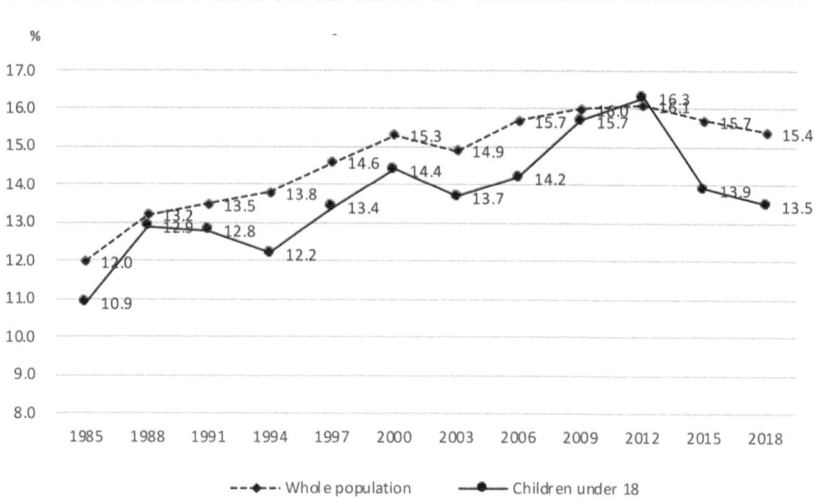

Source: MHLW (2019a).

Figure 6.1   Relative poverty rate of Japan, 1985–2018

families, experience not being able to pay basic utility bills such as electricity, gas, and water (National Institute of Population and Social Security Research, 2018). A survey of 14-year-old children and their parents conducted by Okinawa Prefecture in 2018 showed that 4.4 per cent of the families had experienced stoppage of utility services in the past six months due to financial difficulties (Okinawa Prefecture, 2019). Internationally, Japan ranks among the worst-performing countries among developed nations in terms of child poverty. According to UNICEF, Japan is ranked 21st among 31 developed countries in terms of material well-being in 2013 (UNICEF et al., 2013) and 23rd out of 37 countries in terms of not meeting the 'no poverty' goal of Sustainable Development Goals for children in 2017 (UNICEF, 2017).

The economic standing of families is now related to almost every aspect of children's outcomes. Evidence using data on Japanese children shows that the family income is related to children's weight faltering (Kachi et al., 2018), health (Nakamura, 2014), academic performance (Ochanomizu University, 2014), and physical strength (Ishihara et al., 2015), to name a few. These find-ings are nothing new in many other developed countries, but in Japan they are fairly new findings. Furthermore, the advance in quantitative data analysis has revealed that poverty is transmitted across generations (Ermisch et al., 2012). Also in Japan, a correlation between parents' and children's socio-economic status has been found (Sato and Yoshida, 2007; Kanomata, 2017) and that growing up in poverty increases the probability of material deprivation in adulthood (Abe, 2011; Oshio et al., 2010).

Until 2008, however, child poverty was not given much attention in the social policy discourse in Japan. This is not because child poverty was not a social issue that merited policy response. Rather, it is because the notion that Japan is an equal society, which gained popularity in the 1970s, remained strong in the public discourse long after Japan's inequality and poverty started to rise in the 1980s (Abe, 2010). The Japanese government stopped taking statistics on poverty in the mid-1960s and poverty statistics only became known among academic scholars. Public Assistance to poor families was retrenched to a minimum. In 2007, the social expenditure for Public Assistance as percentages of gross domestic product (GDP), which is Japan's main programme for low-income households, was 0.26 per cent compared to 0.55 per cent in the United States, 0.35 per cent in France, and 0.59 per cent in Sweden (National Institute of Population and Social Security Research, 2008).

Things started to change in 2008 when the global financial crisis hit Japan. Helped by the success of poverty advocates, there was a sharp increase in public awareness that poverty, especially child poverty, was a serious social issue in Japan. This led to the enactment of the Law to Promote Policies against Child Poverty (hereinafter the Law) in 2013. Subsequently, a series of new measures and programmes were introduced in the 2010s in the name of child poverty alleviation.

Such a development, at first glance, seems to indicate that Japan is now eager to tackle two issues on which it had previously not placed much importance: poverty alleviation and support for low-income families with children. Is Japan finally transitioning away from the traditional Japanese welfare model, in which the role of families as welfare providers is strong and social support for people in poverty is minimal?

This chapter is an attempt to answer this question by carefully examining the development of policies against child poverty in Japan before and after 2008. The plan of the chapter is as follows. It will first discuss the Japanese welfare model by reviewing the existing literature and then explain the economic assistance schemes for poor families with children up to 2008. This will help readers understand the extent of the policy shift after 2008. Next, it will analyse the political development from 2008 which led to the enactment of the Law and then it will discuss its characteristics and evaluate if these developments have indeed been a shift away from the traditional Japanese welfare model. It is expected that conceptualising these developments in Japan will not only provide an up-to-date understanding of the welfare model but also shed light on possible developments in other familial welfare states in East Asia.

The Japanese welfare model in the context of child poverty

It is not easy to describe Japan's welfare model as one of the welfare regime typologies. In the past, Japan was defined as a 'hybrid' of the conservative and liberal regimes (Esping-Andersen, 1997) and a 'puzzle' (Powell et al., 2020). This is partly the case because the welfare system is a collection of different policies encompassing income support, healthcare services, education, housing, and labour market protections. For example, Japan's healthcare system is fairly accessible and affordable, while higher education is one of the least accessible systems in East Asia (Yang and Kühner, 2020). Thus, instead of trying to summarise the Japanese welfare system in a single typology, this chapter will concentrate on how the welfare system has defined and addressed the issue of child poverty.

Two characteristics of Japan's welfare system, which are particularly relevant in understanding policy on child poverty are: (1) residual social policy (Peng, 2000; Yang and Kühner, 2020) and (2) reliance on families in providing support and care (Ochiai, 2015; Shizume et al., 2021). The former goes hand in hand with the claim that Japan is an example of a 'productivist' welfare model in which economic development is given the first priority and welfare policy is used as a tool to maintain the workforce, thus enhancing economic development (Choi, 2012; Gough, 2004; Holliday, 2000; Peng, 2000). Its main mechanism of providing security is social insurance (Shizume et al., 2021), yet this protection is only available to those who are in full-time, life-long employment (*Seiki*, or formal employment in Japanese terms) and their families. Those without such employment status are left with little social protection (Abe, 2003). In another words, the 'productive' workforce is protected under social insurance, but for those who are deemed not 'productive', social protection is minimal. Even after 2000, when other East Asian countries such as Korea and Taiwan are expanding its welfare systems and shifting away from this model, Yang and Kühner (2020) argue that Japan has strengthened its 'productive' characteristics by retrenching education and housing services and enhancing work–life balance policies.

The latter characteristics are often labelled as 'familialistic' and highlighted in the literature on Japan (Powell et al., 2020). The 'familialistic' welfare model was first conceptualised in the late 1970s and fully developed in the 1980s when the Japanese government actively put forward the notion of 'the Japanese-style welfare state' as distinct from Western welfare models (Hyodo, 1990; Shinkawa, 2009). The Japanese-style welfare state was announced in the 1979 New Economic Social Seven-Year Plan by Prime Minister Ohira (1978–1980) and was implemented according to the policy developed by the Second Emergency Administrative Research Committee (1981–1983), which was a *de facto* top policy-making institution at the time. The three main features of the 'Japanese-style welfare state' were: acknowledging the limitations of the public sector in providing the welfare needs of citizens; there is an expectation of people's self-help, and help from families, community, and corporations (employers) to provide welfare; and there is an expectation that everyone contributes to maintaining this welfare society (Hyodo, 1990). Although there has been some advancement in defamilialisation in the 1990s and 2000s in the areas of long-term care and childcare (Shinkawa, 2009), in the area of providing support against risks of poverty, these three characteristics are still very much present.

The phrase '*Jijo, Kyojo, Koujo*' (self-help, mutual help, and public help), which was repeatedly used in official documents (Satomi, 2013[1]), summarises the characteristics of the Japanese-style welfare model. It specifies the order in which one should rely in case of need. The first layer of security should come from oneself (including one's family). Next, one's community needs to be sought, and only when these means are exhausted can one ask for help from the state (the public). This three-tier conceptualisation of social security places the utmost responsibility of providing security and care upon families.

The most apparent manifestation of this tiered responsibility is the Public Assistance programme (*Seikatsu hogo*), which has not changed significantly since its enactment in 1951. It is important to note that the Public Assistance programme is based on the right of citizens, as specified in Article 25 of the Japanese Constitution, which states, 'All citizens shall have the right to maintain the minimum standards of wholesome and cultured living'. Thus, all citizens, if they cannot maintain this minimum standard, have a right to claim Public Assistance regardless of the programme's budgetary status. However, the Law states that assistance from family takes precedence before assistance

---

[1]   The first instance of this phrase was in the Diet in 1982, and it then appeared often in official statements by politicians and government institutions, most notably in the *2000 White Paper on Health and Welfare* by the Ministry of Health and Welfare, and again in the *2012 White Paper of Health, Labour and Welfare* by the Ministry of Health, Labour and Welfare (Satomi, 2013).

from the government. In order to apply for Public Assistance benefit, one first has to provide evidence that all members of his/her family, including parents, adult children, and siblings, cannot provide income support. The welfare office, upon receiving an application for Public Assistance, will contact extended family members even if they do not co-reside with the claimant and have been estranged for many years. Even though this practice has been somewhat weakened in recent years (such as foregoing contact to former husbands in cases of domestic violence), such a 'family test' is still required by law. This 'family test' is often pointed out as one of the reasons why many individuals hesitate to apply for the assistance, resulting in low coverage (Iwata, 2021). Public Assistance covered about 1.3 per cent of the population for nearly four decades between the 1970s and 2008 (MHLW, 2020a). The take-up rate of Public Assistance rose from 15 to 32 per cent in 2007 (MHLW, 2010), even by the Ministry of Health, Labour and Welfare's (MHLW) estimate.

To make things worse, Japan's social protection for households in poverty is an all-or-nothing design. Once accepted as a recipient, Public Assistance provides not only income support but also healthcare and long-term care services at no cost, housing assistance, education assistance, and even funeral expenses if one is unfortunate to die while on Public Assistance. The generosity of the programme is much higher than the OECD average. For example, for a jobless couple with two children, the minimum guaranteed income, which in Japan's case resort to Public Assistance, is 47 per cent of the median disposable income, while that of the OECD average is 32 per cent (OECD, retrieved 7 October 2021). Besides this all-inclusive Public Assistance programme, however, there is no other cash-based support programme, such as tax credits, housing subsidies, utility subsidies, and healthcare subsidies, which are often available in other developed countries. Thus, for the small portion of those in poverty who pass all the eligibility criteria of Public Assistance the social protection is strong, yet for the majority of low-income households who do not receive Public Assistance, there is virtually no public support.

Policies for families with children before 2008

In the above context, the government justified the residual social protection by not recognising the prevalence of poverty in Japan. Until 2009, even when members of the opposition party questioned the government's response to rising poverty by quoting poverty rates published by international organisations, the government flatly denied the validity of the statistics and refused to acknowledge that poverty was an issue in Japan. The following dialogues from the Diet between the opposition party and the Minister of State and the Prime Minister in 2005 and 2007 are two examples:

> **Parliament Member Tomoko Abe (pointing to the UNICEF data):** According to this article, Japan's child poverty rate is 14.3%, one of the states with high rate, among the 24 OECD states with data available ... the definition of child poverty is those living in households below 50% of average household.
> **Minister of State Otsuji:** In honesty, I saw this number for the first time, thus I do not know the details of this statistics. (Health and Labour Committee, Diet Session 162, 9 March 2005)
> **Parliament Member Kazuo Shii (pointing to OECD statistics):** Here, I have the OECD Report on the economic survey of Japan published last July and it points out that the child poverty rate of Japan is increasing ... Japan's poverty rate has reached 14.3% and it is above the OECD average.
> **Prime Minister Shinzo Abe:** ... the statistics that the parliament member has cited just now, 2006 Report on Japan by the OECD, needs scrutiny because the rate and the data is dubious. (Budget Committee, Diet Session 166, 13 February 2007)

Until 2008, therefore, there was no recognition within the government that any new policies or programmes were needed to address poverty. In the absence of the recognition of poverty, policies for families with children were developed without paying any attention to the economic needs of raising children. Childcare centres and work–life balance policies, such as maternity and paternity leave, were expanded and enhanced, but economic assistance to low-income families and measures to reduce educational costs were virtually untouched. The policy discourse regarding families with children was almost exclusively on how to raise the fertility rate, as Japan's total fertility rate had decreased steadily since the 1960s and became 1.26 by 2005 (MHLW, 2019b). Thus, it was in the context of encouraging families to have more children that the need to lower the costs of children was discussed.

However, the notion that society should bear a part of the cost of children, as opposed to parents, was not accepted by the public and public spending on family-related policies (Ochiai, 2015) and on education (Nakazawa, 2014) were kept minimal. In 2001, family-related social spending was as low as 1 per cent of GDP compared to 2.6 per cent for the United Kingdom, 3.7 per cent in France, and 2.9 per cent in Sweden. The Child Allowance (*Jido teate*), which is the only cash benefit for two-parent families, started as income support for families with three or more children aged less than three in the 1970s, remaining very small for decades. It was only after 2000, when its purpose was acknowledged as a policy tool to increase the fertility rate, that the programme started to grow to include the first and second children; also, the eligible age was increased gradually from three to 15 (Abe, 2014). However, during this transformation, the effectiveness of the programme as an income support for families vanished because the benefit amount was kept fixed at JPY5,000 (GBP1 = JPY150 in January 2022) from 1972 to 2010 for the first child. With such a small benefit, it had almost no effect in alleviating poverty. In fact, the cash benefit for families with dependent children was so low that throughout the 1980s to 2000s, the net public transfer for poor and near poor families with children was negative, causing the child poverty rate to be higher after government tax and transfers compared to before tax and transfers (Abe, 2008; Whiteford and Adema 2007). Osawa (2008) called this phenomenon the 'Upside-down function of social security (*Shakai hosho no gyaku kinou*)'.

Another cash-based programme for families is the Child Rearing Allowance (*Jido fuyo teate*), which is a cash benefit for low-income single-parent families. It was estimated that about 70 per cent (0.86 out of 1.23 million) of single-mother families received the Child Rearing Allowance in 2018 (MHLW, 2020b). However, the allowance amount is not sufficient to sustain living independently (JPY43,000 = GBP280 per month: February 2022) at maximum, and even though the labour market participation rate of single mothers is more than 80 per cent (MHLW, 2017), the relative poverty rate for single-parent families is strikingly high at 48.1 per cent (MHLW, 2019a).

Japanese scholars highlighted several reasons why the government was so reluctant in providing economic assistance to families with children. Hiroi (2009: 35) argues that the focus of the family policy is not increasing the fertility rate nor reducing the burden of poor families, but raising women's labour participation rate, thus supporting the 'productivist' welfare model. Kita (2002, 2004), in her detailed analysis of the history of Child Allowance, points out that Child Allowance lacked advocators who would promote its cause. The two actors who could have been advocates of the support for families, labour unions and feminist activists, were in fact against public support of families. In her assessment, the labour unions did not push this agenda because in their quest for a living wage, the child benefit borne by the government provided an excuse for employers to keep wages low (Kita, 2004). Feminist scholars and activists were also against it because the allowance was regarded as a way to keep women at home. Without any strong advocators for the expansion, cash-based assistance for families with children remained small. Whatever the reason behind it, the potential that the child benefit had as a way to mitigate child poverty was not developed, and the responsibility to feed, clothe, and house children was left solely as the responsibility of the family.

Familial responsibility was also strong in the area of educational expenses. Mandatory, free-of-cost education in Japan covers nine years (from age six to 15), and the cost of high school and higher education is borne by families.

The percentage of costs borne by public sources for tertiary education as a percentage of GDP was 29th among 31 OECD countries in 2005 (OECD, 2008). Scholarships and student grants were also non-existent except for low-interest loans.

The discovery of poverty in 2008 and change of government

The discovery of 'poverty'

Social policy in Japan took a new turn in 2008. In September 2008, starting from the bankruptcy of Lehman Brothers in the United States, the worldwide financial crisis erupted, which also severely impacted the economy in Japan. The unemployment rate for men, which was around 4.0 until 2008, reached 6.0 in July 2009. The rate was still low in comparison to other countries, but for Japan it was extremely high and was the highest rate since 1945 even to this day. Besides the severity of the impact, what was new in this economic crisis was that, for the first time, poverty became 'visible' in the eyes of the public. For example, during the New Year's holiday season from the end of 2008 to the beginning of 2009, one of the non-profit groups working with homeless people put up a temporary tent village in Hibiya Park in central Tokyo, which was right in front of the MHLW. This gained significant media attention, and scenes of hundreds of 'able-bodied' middle-aged men lining up to receive food and shelter were repeatedly broadcast during the holiday season. Politicians were quick to be at the scene giving sympathetic messages to homeless people. In the end, the MHLW opened its own auditorium to accommodate homeless people until they could be placed in more permanent shelters.

What was interesting was that this was not the first time that such a tent village was put up to shelter homeless people. Every year during the New Year's holiday season, the longest holiday in Japan, many day labourers in construction and manufacturing sectors are laid off because construction sites and factories are closed during the holidays. Since many of these workers are housed in employer-provided dormitories, they lose housing at the same time as losing their job. Thus, tent villages or other forms of temporary shelters are put up by non-profit organisations in major cities including Tokyo, Yokohama, and Osaka. However, at the turn of year 2009, one of the organisations chose Hibiya Park. Together with already nervous public sentiment about an upcoming recession, this media performance placed real fear in the minds of the public that anybody, if struck by bad fortune, had the possibility of becoming homeless. For the first time since the 1960s, poverty became part of the political agenda and the upcoming election resulted in a landslide loss for the Liberal Democratic Party (LDP), which had been in power continuously since the end of the Second World War.

Policies of the Democratic Party government: 2009–2012

The newly elected Democratic Party (DP) government was eager to implement policies to reduce poverty, and its prime policy choice was a universal and generous child benefit. The DP manifesto stated the introduction of a universal 'Kid Allowance' (*Kodomo teate*) with a benefit level much higher than its predecessor, the Child Allowance (*Jido teate*). The reformed Child Allowance ('Kid Benefit') was introduced in 2012, and it started with JPY13,000 (GBP85) per month per child for every child below 16 years old. However, the LDP criticised it harshly as it violated the concept of self-help (Liberal Democratic Party, 2009) and began a large-scale negative campaign, arguing that it would devastate the budgetary balance and that it would be used by 'immoral parents' for their own sake, not for their children's sake (Abe, 2014).

Unfortunately, the DP, which had been a solid supporter of generous social policy and income transfer to low-income households and had constituents favouring liberal social policy, failed to convince the public that the universal child benefit was also effective as a child poverty reduction scheme. Thus, even its main supporters such as labour unions and poverty activists were not too supportive of the party's main policy, *kodomo teate*. Waivered by the loss of public support, politicians even within the DP started to justify the allowance as 'an economic boost' or 'an encouragement to have more children', and *kodomo teate* lost its credibility as an economic assistance to poor families. Furthermore, the 2011 Great East Japan Earthquake shifted the focus of the public and politicians from poverty alleviation to disaster relief. Policies against poverty took a backseat and lost their momentum (Yuzawa, 2015).

In 2012, the DP government lost the general election and the conservative LDP regained power. After coming back to government, the LDP quickly abolished *kodomo teate* and reintroduced the previous *jido teate*. The income threshold was once again put in place, but it was set rather high so that nearly 90 per cent of households were under the threshold. For those above the threshold, a smaller benefit was introduced. Thus, basically, the reintroduced *jido teate* was almost universal coverage, yet it kept the appearance of benefitting both low-income and middle-class households. However, the benefit amount was not doubled as the DP had promised, and rather cut back so that its effectiveness as a poverty reduction scheme was severely compromised.

The Child Poverty Law and its characteristics

The passing of the bill in 2013

The movement to promote policies against child poverty did not pick up again until 2013, but when it came, it was very swift. Ironically, the movement did not start from the DP nor civic activities, but from inside the LDP. In February 2013, the Minister of Education at the time, Hakubun Shimomura (2012–2015), a Liberal Democrat, approached the DP parliament members to pass a non-partisan bill on child poverty, modelled after the 2010 Child Poverty Act in the United Kingdom (Yuzawa, 2015). In just a few months, by May 2013, both the ruling party and opposition party submitted bills for the Law, and a compromised version of the bill passed the Diet in June 2013, with the Law being enacted in January 2014.

The Law to Promote Measures against Child Poverty is a so-called 'principle law', in which the principles that the Japanese government should follow regarding measures against child poverty are specified. Article 1 of the Law states its objective as follows: 'in order to ensure that the future of a child is not influenced by his/her upbringing, the law is intended to promote measures against child poverty by stating its basic principles and clarifying state responsibility in providing an environment for healthy upbringing for poor children and by promoting equal opportunity in education' (Article 1, Objective, author's translation). It then states that 'the measures against child poverty must be promoted through educational assistance, living assistance, employment assistance, and economic assistance whose purpose is to ensure that a child's future is not influenced by his/her upbringing' (Article 2, Basic Principle, author's translation).

Even though the Law broadly specifies four policy areas that need to be addressed, it does not go any further in creating or expanding specific pro-grammes or policy measures. As a 'principle law', its function is to set the tone of the government's position on child poverty and give legal justifications for corresponding ministries to implement measures and programmes. It is up to each ministry to propose measures and programmes as they see fit, and it is up to the Ministry of Finance to allocate budgets to implement them. Thus, even though principle laws create a momentum to implement certain policies, it does not guarantee budgetary allocation to implement these policies. Yet, the Law was a significant milestone in terms of poverty alleviation policies in Japan because there had been no official laws or statements previously which specifically stated that child poverty was a social issue that the government must address.

New policy actor

The Law marks a turning point in policies against poverty in Japan in two aspects. First, for the first time, it places a mandate to address poverty on ministries other than the MHLW. Until then, there was clear demarcation of policy areas and all matters regarding low-income households, including that of education, housing, and nutrition, were under the jurisdiction of the MHLW. The MHLW is responsible for the Public Assistance programme, Child Rearing Allowance, Child Allowance, and all child welfare services including institutionalised care. The MHLW also runs programmes, such as educational assistance for children in families receiving Public Assistance and the Child Rearing Allowance. Thus, these programmes only serve children who belong to families on welfare and the number of beneficiaries was fairly small.

At the same time, the main educational institutions and programmes, such as public and private schools, universities, and other further education institutions, are under the jurisdiction of the Ministry of Education, which was reluctant to address issues arising from poverty. Its stance was that poverty was something the MHLW needed to address, and the Ministry of Education did not and should not get involved in the financial problems of families. Similarly, the Ministry of Land, Infrastructure, Transport, and Tourism, which oversees housing policy, was reluctant to address the housing needs of households in poverty (Hirayama, 2003). The Ministry of Agriculture, Forestry and Fisheries is responsible for food policy but has no policy on food insecurity due to economic constraints. Thus, in Japan, only those on Public Assistance receive housing assistance, income assistance to buy food, and education assistance to meet the educational needs of children (from the MHLW), but there is no other programme to ease the burden of poverty. In short, social policies were divided into those for 'mainstream' households and those for households in poverty. The MHLW took sole responsibility to implement policies to alleviate poverty.

However, the Law specified 'education' at the top of the four policy areas, and this was the first indication that the Ministry of Education, not the MHLW, would be the main actor in implementing actual policies and programmes under the Law. This was made clear in the subsequent Guiding Outline for Child Poverty Policies (hereinafter the Outline), announced in August 2014. The Outline states that 'schools shall be the "platforms" for child poverty policy' (The Outline, p. 4). This was a significant change of policy given the previous position of the Ministry of Education in policies against poverty.

From in-cash to in-kind benefits

The emphasis on education policy as the main tool for child poverty came partly because the minister of education, Shimomura, who grew up in a single-mother family himself (Yuzawa, 2015), was the main actor in enacting the Law, but also focusing on education, instead of economic assistance, fitted well with the LDP's thinking. The LDP was adamant in opposing any expansion of the cash benefit for families in poverty. In fact, at the same time that the Child Poverty Law was enacted and implemented, the LDP government cut the benefit level of Public Assistance for families with children and changed a part of the educational assistance portion of Public Assistance from cash to in-kind benefits (Abe, 2019b). The reason for the LDP's dislike of cash benefits was their distrust of poor parents. It was often mentioned in the Diet debate that there was no guarantee the cash benefit would be used for the sake of children. For example, the disdain against cash benefits was expressed by a parliament member and was confirmed by a government official in the following debate in the Diet:

> **Parliament member Shintani (LDP):** However, I fear that any policy based on in-cash benefit, in the end will not be used for the sake of children's future, and it will bring distortion.
> **Vice-Minister of MHLW Tokashiki:** We believe that it is important to implement measures so that children's future is not influenced by their upbringing. For this, we expanded educational assistance to children receiving the Public Assistance from grade 9 to grade 10 ... These assistance, and not economic assistance, catered to each family's needs, will be provided. (183rd Diet, Committee on Health, Labour and Welfare, No. 15, 29 May 2013)

This stereotyping of low-income parents as immoral who would use the child benefit for their own pleasure, typically gambling and alcohol, was common and accepted as a valid reason against the cash benefit (Yuzawa, 2015).

Thus, even though economic assistance was one of the four policy areas that the Law specified, its priority was placed last among the four. In the Outline, the section on economic assistance was minimal. It merely mentioned already existing programmes and research. The following six measures were mentioned as 'economic assistance' in the Outline:

1. Re-examination of benefit adjustment while receiving Child Rearing Assistance and pensions: The government recently modified the rule for adjustment of the Child Rearing Assistance while receiving pensions and will implement this modification smoothly.

2. Research on one-parent family policies: The government will examine if research on the effects of policies for employment assistance for single-parent families is necessary.
3. Expansion of the special loan to single-father families: The government recently expanded the eligibility for the loan to single-mother families to include single-father families and will implement this modification smoothly.
4. Payment of education assistance to families on Public Assistance: In the payment of education assistance in the Public Assistance programme, it is possible to pay fees directly to schools, and the government will use this method more vigorously so that the assistance is used for the purpose intended.
5. Assistance to high school students in families on Public Assistance: The government will pay the entrance fee and entrance exam fees of high schools for children belonging to families on Public Assistance. The government will not deduct the income earned by students from Public Assistance if the income is to be used for college education.
6. Assistance to receive child support: After divorce, it is desirable that divorced parents pay child support to fulfil his/her duty as a parent and to promote the well-being of children, thus the single-parent support centres and such will provide consultation support in this matter. (The Outline 2014, pp. 20–21, translated and numbers added by the author)

Items 1, 2, 3, and 5 were modifications that were already in place by the time the Law was enacted; item 2 is research, item 6 is consultation without any measures to actually receive child support, and item 4 is another manifestation of distrust of parents to use the benefit for children.

Without expansion of cash assistance for poor families with children, the net social transfer continued to be negative for two-parent nuclear families. Figure 6.2 shows that in 2015, for two-parent nuclear families, the poverty rate 'after tax and transfers' (calculated using household disposable income after subtracting income and other direct taxes and adding public cash transfers including child benefit) was higher than the poverty rate before tax and transfers, indicating that the net transfer for these families was negative.

Steering away from the cash benefit also meant steering away from the relative poverty rate as the indicator to monitor poverty. Following the examples of the European Union and the United Kingdom, both ruling and opposition parties agreed that there should be a set of indicators which show the state of child poverty. However, there was a fierce debate on what indicators to include and whether to set policy targets. The LDP was against using the relative poverty

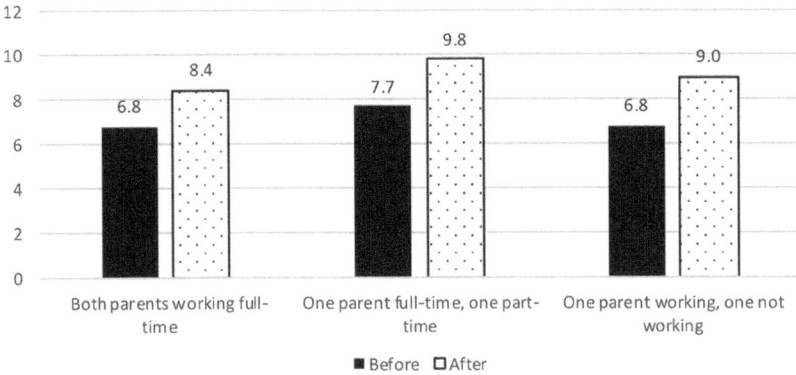

Source: Abe (2019a).

Figure 6.2   Poverty rates before and after tax and transfers (two-parent, two-generation families), 2015

rate since only cash benefits or reductions of tax and social security premiums would reduce the poverty rate (Yuzawa, 2013). The opposition DP was keen to set the target for a reduction in the poverty rate, but the ruling LDP was not only against setting the target but also against using the relative poverty rate as the indicator to monitor child poverty.

> **Minister of State Tamura (LDP):** PM Yamanoi keeps mentioning the poverty rate, and I think it is one of the indicators. However, the poverty rate does not tell the whole story of poverty, for example, even if income of parents is above the poverty line, if parents have some issues and children might be suffering. On the other hand, even if the income flow is not much, one might receive a lot of assistance from grandparents and living standard might be quite high …
> **PM Yamanoi (DP):** … Of course, it [the poverty rate] is not the only indicator, however, if the poverty rate a few years after the enactment of the Law continues to get worse, it would be very disappointing … It is a historical event that child poverty is debated so much in the Diet and the poverty rate keeps increasing and we need to demonstrate that the government and parliament members will do everything possible to reverse the trend.
> **PM Furuya (Komei):** The ruling coalition of the Komei party and LDP has submitted the bill for the Law to Promote Measures against the Child Poverty. However, I have a question regarding setting the target. The poverty rate is calculated only using the disposable income and in-kind benefits such as childcare services and education assistance will not improve the poverty rate and thus will not lead to expansion of in-kind benefits. Also, the asset is not reflected, and thus [the poverty rate] is not an adequate indicator. (183rd Diet, Committee on Health, Labour and Welfare, No. 15, 29 May 2013)

In the end, 14 indicators were chosen as child poverty indicators in the Outline. The indicators range from the employment rate for single parents, high school entrance rate of children in families receiving Public Assistance, and the number of school social workers. The child poverty rate using disposable income data and poverty rate for single-parent families is included among the 14; however, its significance was mostly diluted as one of many indicators.

Development in policy to reduce educational cost

Initially after the enactment of the Law, the programmes implemented under the Law were modest, such as the increase of school social workers and mandating municipalities to make an action plan for child poverty reduction. However, several major expansions were gradually put in place in education. In 2014, a bill to make fees for early childhood education and daycare centres for three–five-year-old children free was put forward, and it became effective in 2019. Whether this policy reduced the economic burden of poor families is not certain. There is a two-tier system for pre-school children in Japan: daycare centres for children of working parents and kindergartens for other children. The daycare centres are part of child welfare services and the cost is determined according to the income of parents, whereas kindergartens are mainly private institutions and costs are higher. Since most single parents are those on low-income work, they are likely to be using daycare centres, and the fees were already zero or low even before the reform. Thus, this policy was more beneficial to middle- and high-income families and also to the kindergarten sector, which had been experiencing a decrease in enrolment due to the declining birth rate and a shift to daycare centres.

Another policy reform since the enactment of the Law is the reduction of costs for higher education. In 2014, high school tuition was made free for all children going to a state school and tuition assistance for private school students for the same amount as state high school tuition. Mandatory education in Japan is up to grade 9 (junior high school), and high schools (grades 10 to 12) require tuition regardless of their public or private status.[2] Moreover, bursaries for high school students were introduced to cover educational expenses other than tuition. Since 98.8 per cent of all children enter high school (Ministry of Education, 2020), the cost of high school education was a burden on low-income families.

---

[2]   According to the Ministry of Education, 25.8 per cent of high schools are private, and tuition for private schools is higher than tuition for public schools (www .mext.go.jp/a_menu/koutou/shinkou/main5_a3.htm, last accessed 30 September 2021).

Furthermore, starting in 2020, university tuition became free for students from low-income families. Until then, Japan was one of the OECD countries with the highest private share in meeting the cost of tertiary education (Figure 6.3). The 2020 reform waived or reduced both the entrance fee and tuition depending on income level. The waiver applies to both public and private universities but the benefit amount does not cover the entire tuition for private universities. To cover costs other than tuition, a grant-based scholarship for university students was also introduced. Until then, Japan had student loan schemes with subsidised interest rates but not grant-based scholarships.

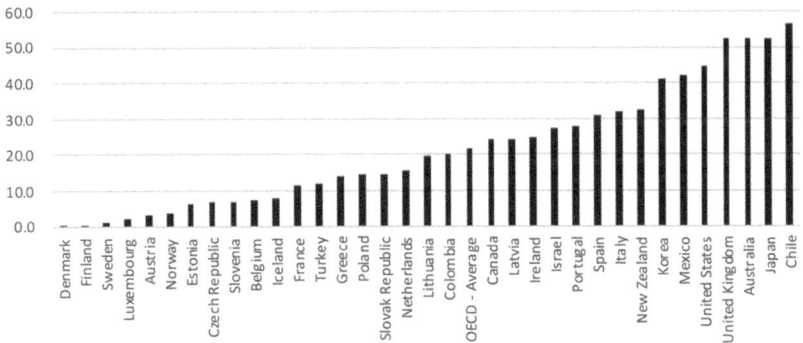

Source: OECD (retrieved 6 October 2021).

Figure 6.3   Percentage of share of education cost borne by households (tertiary education)

Mobilising the private sector

Another new development in child poverty policy after the Law is that the government started to actively mobilise and engage the private sector in funding and implementing programmes for children in poverty. In 2015, Prime Minister Abe inaugurated the National Movement for the Future of Children (*Kodomo no mirai ouen kokumin undo*) with various economic leaders. The main mechanism of the Movement was the Fund for the Future of Children (*Kodomo no mirai ouen kikin*), in which donations were collected from companies and individuals and the Fund, managed by the Cabinet Office, channelled the fund to non-profit organisations engaged in activities for children. By September 2019, more than JPY1 billion was collected and JPY0.8 billion was disbursed to various non-profit organisations (Cabinet Office, 2019). The

Movement also matches enterprises that would like to donate money and goods to organisations doing certain activities.

For the government, the Movement has an obvious advantage in that its funding is from the private sector and does not put pressure on the budget, and that the programmes are carried out by non-profit organisations and not public institutions. However, it steers the responsibility of addressing child poverty away from the government, and at the same time allows the government to influence how the private charity is spent. Also, the implementation and continuation of programmes is not mandated on the government and is completely dependent on the whim of the private sector.

Conclusion: familial welfare state in transition?

Did the introduction of the Child Poverty Law change the fundamental nature of the Japanese welfare model? From the description presented above, it is hard to conclude that it did. First, even though the Japanese government acknowledged the existence of (child) poverty, its rationale for the need to address this social issue is limited to that of the future productivity of children. Thus, the policy choices for child poverty are overwhelmingly on education. Income assistance that could raise the current living standard of children was deliberately shunned. Even the objective of the Law was stated as 'in order to ensure that *future of a child* is not influenced by his/her upbringing', which carefully does not mention the state of poor children's *current* living standard or the violation of their human rights. The fact that financial assistance for higher education, even though it is progress, only targets children who are regarded as having high potential of becoming productive members of society is further evidence that the government's main interest is in the future productivity of the Japanese labour force, and it can be argued that this is the typical mindset of the 'productivist' welfare model.

Second, the political discourse of the Law disintegrated policies for poor children from policies for poor families with children. While policies that directly benefit children (without going through parents) are favoured, policies that benefit households as a whole were shunned. The rationale behind this disintegration is prejudice against poor households, especially poor parents, who are not capable of giving their children decent living standards and education. During the discourse of policies against child poverty, the issues surrounding adult poverty, such as duality of the Japanese labour market into protected formal workers and unprotected informal workers (Shizume et al., 2021), income-support policies for the working poor, and easing the requirements of the family and work test in the Public Assistance programme were not mentioned. Thus, the Japanese governments managed to justify the development of policies against child poverty within the framework of the familial welfare model by branding poor families as a failure and providing assistance only to children.

It is interesting that this focus on children is not based on children's rights either, since there has been no expansion of programmes that assure rights of all children. Nor did it spur any expansion of assistance for families with children in general, except for the waiver of fees for kindergartens and daycare centres for three–five-year-old children. Since this waiver was heavily advocated by the kindergarten industry, it is not clear if the motivation of the government was in reducing the cost of raising children or in subsidising this failing industry. The only cash benefit that reaches a significant share of families with children, Child Allowance, remained fixed at the 2012 level. Thus, policies against child poverty in Japan remain a residual and small programme, which reach only children who are from 'failed families' who do not fulfil their responsibility to care for their children.

In the 2019 Revision of the Law, some of the above-mentioned points were addressed. The objective of the Law was revised as 'in order to ensure that *current* [conditions] *and the future of the child* is not influenced by his/her upbringing' (Article 1, translated by the author) after protests by scholars and activists. At the same time, three new indicators that reflect current living standards and hardship are added to the list of child poverty indicators: the percentage of families with children who have arrears in paying utility (electricity, gas, water) bills; the percentage of families with children who experience not being able to afford food or clothes; and the percentage of individuals belonging to families with children who have no one to count on, emotionally and financially.[3] In the original list, there was no indicator in the field of living standards, so the addition of the three can be considered as a significant improvement. However, six more indicators were added in the area of education and three in the area of economic and employment assistance, and the number of indicators in the new list became 22, so the significance of the three indicators was watered down. Further, even after the 2019 reform, there was no significant expansion of the programmes to raise the current living standard

---

[3]   These indicators were chosen from research on material deprivation, which was inspired by the vast body of previous research in the United Kingdom, notably by Peter Townsend and David Gordon.

and assure the rights of children. Now we are faced with the new challenges of the COVID-19 pandemic. It is beyond the scope of this chapter to discuss the responses to the pandemic and their ramifications to child poverty policies in Japan; however, it is sufficient to note that the pandemic brought about a new turning point in the social policy of Japan.

References

Abe, A. (2003) 'Low income people in social security systems in Japan', *Japanese Journal of Social Security Policy*, 2(2), 59–70.

Abe, A. (2008) *Kodomo no Hinkon: Nihon no Fukohei wo kangaeru* (Child Poverty: Rethinking Japan's inequality), Tokyo: Iwanami (in Japanese).

Abe, A. (2010) 'The myth of egalitarian society: Poverty and social exclusion in Japan', in P. Saunders and R. Sainsbury (eds) *Social Security, Poverty and Social Exclusion in Rich and Poorer Countries*, Mortsel: Intersentia Publishing, 175–199.

Abe, A. (2011) 'Kodomoki no hinko ga seijin go no seikatsu konnan (deprivation) ni ataeru eikyo no bunseki' (Analysis of the effect of childhood poverty on adult deprivation), *Shakai Hosho Kenkyu (Social Security Research)*, 46(4), 354–367 (in Japanese).

Abe, A. (2014) 'Is there a future for universal programs in Japan: A case of child benefit', in T. Yamamori and Y. Vanderborght (eds) *Basic Income in Japan: Prospects for a Radical Idea in a Transforming Welfare State*, New York: Palgrave Macmillan, 49–67.

Abe, A. (2019a) *Kodomo no Hinkonritsu no Doko: From 2012 to 2015*, www.hinkonstat .net/ (last accessed 6 October 2021) (in Japanese).

Abe, A. (2019b) 'Seikatu Hogo Seido ni okeru Kodomo no Shien no Genjo to Arikata' (Assistance for families with children under the Public Assistance programme), *Jinbun Gakuho*, 15–32 (in Japanese).

Cabinet Office (2019) *Kodomo no Hinkon Taisaku* (Child Poverty Policies), 18 December, www8 .cao .go .jp/ kodomonohinkon/ ouen -forum/ r01/ pdf/ tokyo/ naikakufu.pdf (last accessed 30 September 2021) (in Japanese).

Choi, Y.J. (2012) 'End of the era of productivist welfare capitalism? Diverging welfare regimes in East Asia', *Asian Journal of Social Science*, 40(3), 275–294.

Duncan, G.G. and Brooks-Gunn, J. (eds) (1997) *Consequences of Growing Up Poor*, New York: Russell Sage Foundation.

Ermisch, J., Jantti, M. and Smeeding, T. (eds) (2012) *From Parents to Children: The Intergenerational Transmission of Advantage*, New York: Russell Sage Foundation.

Esping-Andersen, G. (1997) 'Hybrid or unique? The Japanese welfare state between Europe and America', *Journal of European Social Policy*, 7(3), 179–189.

Gough, I. (2004) 'East Asia: The limits of productivist regimes', in I. Gough, G. Wood, A. Barrientos, P. Bevan, P. Davis and G. Room (eds) *Insecurity and Welfare Regimes in Asia, Africa and Latin America*, Cambridge: Cambridge University Press, 169–201.

Hirayama, Y. (2003) 'Housing policy and social inequality in Japan', in M. Izuhara (ed.) *Comparing Social Policies: Exploring New Perspectives in Britain and Japan*, Bristol: Policy Press, 151–172.

Hiroi, T. (2009) 'Shoshika wo meguru Kazoku Seisaku: Kazoku ha naze hihan sareru-noka' (Family policies for low fertility: Why are families criticized), *Nihon Kyoiku Seisaku Gakkai Nenpo*, 30–38 (in Japanese).

Holliday, I. (2000) 'Productivist welfare capitalism: Social policy in East Asia', *Political Studies*, 48(4), 706–723.

Hyodo, T. (1990) 'Tenkanki ni okeru Shakai Seisaku Shisou: "Nihongata Fukushi Shakai Ron" wo megutte' (Social policy ideology in turning point: Discourse around 'Japanese style welfare society'), *Shakai Seisaku Sosho*, 14, 135–157 (in Japanese).

Ishihara, Y., Tomita, Y., Hirade, K. and Mizuno, M. (2015) 'Nihon no kodomo ni okeru Hinkon to Tairyoku Undo Noryoku no kankei' (The relationship between poverty and physical strength and ability of children), *Hokkaido University Department of Education*, 122, 93–105 (in Japanese).

Iwata, M. (2021) *Seikatsu Hogo Kaitai Ron* (Demolishing Public Assistance System), Tokyo: Iwanami Shoten (in Japanese).

Kachi, Y., Fujiwara, T., Yamaoka, Y. and Kato, T. (2018) 'Parental socioeconomic status and weight faltering in infants in Japan', *Frontiers in Paediatrics*, 6, Article 127.

Kanomata, N. (2017) 'Hinpu no Sedaikan Saiseisan to Chii Tassei Katei' (Inter-generational transmission of wealth and poverty and social class achievement process), *Shakaigaku Hyoron*, 68(2), 283–299 (in Japanese).

Kita, A. (2002) 'Nihon no Jido Teate Seido no Tenkai to Henshitsu (2)' (Development and changing nature of Japan's Child Allowance Part 2), *Ohara Shakai Mondai Kenkyusho Zasshi*, 526/527, 39–55 (in Japanese).

Kita, A. (2004) 'Nihon no Jido Teate Seido no Tenkai to Henshitsu (3)' (Development and changing nature of Japan's Child Allowance Part 3), *Ohara Shakai Mondai Kenkyusho Zasshi*, 547, 32–47 (in Japanese).

Kobayashi, M. (2018) 'Koto Kyouiku no Mushoka wo meguru Seisaku' (Policies surrounding free tuition of higher education), *Recruit College Management*, 213, 47–51 (in Japanese).

Liberal Democratic Party (2009) 'Gimon darake no Kodomo Teate' (Kid Allowance full of questions), www.jimin.jp/policy/policy_topics/recapture/pdf/013r.pdf (last accessed 26 November 2022).

Ministry of Education (2020) *Koto Gakko Kyoiku no Genjo nit suite* (Current State of High School Education), www.mext.go.jp/a_menu/shotou/kaikaku/20201027-mxt_kouhou02-1.pdf (last accessed 12 December 2021) (in Japanese).

MHLW (Ministry of Health, Labour and Welfare) (2010) *Seikatu Hogo Kijun Miman no Teishotoku Setaisu no Suikei ni Tsuite* (About the Estimate of Low-Income Households below the Public Assistance Threshold), www.mhlw.go.jp/shingi/2010/04/dl/s0409-2d.pdf (last accessed 7 October 2021) (in Japanese).

MHLW (Ministry of Health, Labour and Welfare) (2017) *Zenkoku Hitorioya Setai to Chosa Kekka Hokoku* 2016 (The Report of the National Survey of Single Parent Families 2016), www.mhlw.go.jp/stf/seisakunitsuite/bunya/0000188147.html (last accessed 6 October 2021) (in Japanese).

MHLW (Ministry of Health, Labour and Welfare) (2019a) *2019 nen Kokumin Seikatsu Kiso Chosa Kekka no Gaiyo* (The Summary Report of 2019 Comprehensive Survey of Living Conditions), www.mhlw.go.jp/toukei/saikin/hw/k-tyosa/k-tyosa19/index.html (last accessed 30 November 2021) (in Japanese).

MHLW (Ministry of Health, Labour and Welfare) (2019b) *Reiwa 1 nen Jinko Dotai Tokei Geppo* (The Summary of 2019 Population Dynamis Monthly), www.mhlw.go.jp/toukei/saikin/hw/jinkou/geppo/nengai19/index.html (last accessed 3 December 2021) (in Japanese).

MHLW (Ministry of Health, Labour and Welfare) (2020a) *Reiwa 2 Nendo Kosei Rodo Hakusho* (White Paper of Health, Labour and Welfare), www.mhlw.go.jp/stf/wp/hakusyo/kousei/19/index.html (last accessed 3 December 2021) (in Japanese).

MHLW (Ministry of Health, Labour and Welfare) (2020b) *Tokei Yoran Reiwa 2 Nendo* (Main Statistics FY2021), www.mhlw.go.jp/toukei/youran/ (last accessed 16 July 2021) (in Japanese).

Nakamura, S. (2014) 'Parental income and child health in Japan', *Journal of the Japanese and International Economies*, 32, 42–55.

Nakazawa, S. (2014) 'Naze Nihon no Kokyo Kyoikuhi ha Sukunainoka' (Why is the public expenditure on education is so low in Japan?), *Keiso Shobo* (in Japanese).

National Institute of Population and Social Security Research (2008) *Shakai Hosho Kyufuhi 2008* (Social Security Expenditure 2008), Tokyo: NIPSSR (in Japanese).

National Institute of Population and Social Security Research (2018) *Dai 2 kai Seikatsu to sasaeai ni kansuru Chosa Kekka no Gaiyo* (The Report of the National Survey on Social Security and People's Life), www.ipss.go.jp/ss-seikatsu/j/2017/seikatsu2017summary.pdf (last accessed 30 November 2021) (in Japanese).

Ochanomizu University (2014) *Heisei 25 Nendo Zenkoku Gakuryoku Gakushu Jokyo Chosa no Kekka wo katsuyo shita Gakuryoku ni eikyo wo ataeru youin bunseki ni kansuru chosa kenkyuu* (2013 Report on the Research of the factors affecting academic performance using National Academic and Learning Survey), Ochanomizu University (in Japanese).

Ochiai, E. (2009) 'Care diamonds and welfare regimes in East and South-East Asian societies: Bridging family and welfare sociology', *International Journal of Japanese Sociology*, 18, 60–78.

Ochiai, E. (2015) 'Nihon-gata Fukushi Regimu ha naze Kazoku Shugi no mamananoka' (Why is the Japanese welfare still familialistic?), *Kazoku Shakaigaku Kenkyu*, 27(1), 61–68 (in Japanese).

OECD (2008) 'Graph B3.1 – share of private expenditure on educational institutions (2005)', in *Education at a Glance*, Paris: OECD Publishing.

Okinawa Prefecture (2019) *Heisei 30 nendo Okinawaken ShoChugakusei Chosa Kekka Hokoku* (Report of the Survey of Elementary and Junior High Students in 2018), Okinawa-ken (in Japanese).

Osawa, M. (2007) 'Comparative livelihood security systems from a gender perspective, with a focus on Japan', in S. Walby, H. Gottfried, K. Gottschall and M. Osawa (eds) *Gendering the Knowledge Economy*, London: Palgrave Macmillan, 81–108.

Osawa, M. (2008) 'Reply: Gendai Nihon no Seikatu Hosho System' (Reply: Livelihood security system of modern Japan), *Shakai Fukushi Gaku* (Social Welfare Studies), 48(4), 214–216 (in Japanese).

Oshio, T., Sano, S. and Kobayashi, M. (2010) 'Child poverty as a determinant of life outcomes: Evidence from nationwide surveys in Japan', *Social Indicators Research*, 99, 81–99.

Peng, I. (2000) 'A fresh look at the Japanese welfare state', *Social Policy and Administration*, 34(1), 88–114.

Powell, M., Kim, K. and Kim, S. (2020) 'The puzzle of Japan's welfare capitalism: A review of the welfare regimes approach', *Journal of International and Comparative Social Policy*, 36(1), 92–110.

Sato, Y. and Yoshida, T. (2007) 'Hinkon no Sedaikan Rensa no Jissho Kenkyu' (Empirical research on the inter-generational transmission of poverty), *Nihon Rodo Kenkyu Zasshi* (Japanese Labour Research Journal), 563, 75–83 (in Japanese).

Satomi, K. (2013) 'Kosei roudou sho no "Jijo Kyojo Koujo" no tokui na shin kaishaku' (Peculiar interpretation of self-help, mutual-help, public-help by the Ministry of Health, Labour and Welfare), *Shakai Seisaku* (Social Policy), 5(2), 1–4 (in Japanese).

Shinkawa, T. (2009) 'Fukushi Regimu Bunseki no Kanousei: Sengo Nihon Fukushi Kokka wo jirei to shite' (Perspectives on welfare regime analysis: A case of welfare state experiences in postwar Japan), *Shakai Seisaku* (Social Policy), 1(2), 49–63 (in Japanese).

Shizume, M., Kato, M. and Matsuda, R. (2021) 'A corporate-centred conservative welfare regime: Three-layered protection in Japan', *Journal of Asian Public Policy*, 14(1), 110–133.

Suetomi, K. (2017) 'Kodomo no Hinkon Taisaku ha naze Zeijaku nanoka?' (Why are the policies for child poverty so fragile?), *Kyoikugaku Zasshi*, 53, 19–31 (in Japanese).

UNICEF (2017) *Building the Future: Children and the Sustainable Development Goals in Rich Countries* (Innocenti Report Card 14). www.unicef-irc.org/publications/890-building-the-future-children-and-the-sustainable-development-goals-in-rich-countries.html (last accessed 30 November 2021).

UNICEF, Abe, A. and Takezawa, J. (2013) *Child Well-being in Rich Countries: Comparing Japan* (Innocenti Report Card 11 Japan), www.unicef-irc.org/publications/714-child-well-being-in-rich-countries-comparing-japan-j apanese-version.html (last accessed 30 November 2021).

Whiteford, P. and Adema, W. (2007) *What Works Best in Reducing Child Poverty: A Benefit or Work Strategy?* OECD Social, Employment and Migration Working Papers, 51, Paris: OECD.

Yang, N. and Kühner, S. (2020) 'Beyond the limits of the productivist regime: Capturing three decades of East Asian welfare development with fuzzy sets', *Social Policy and Society*, 19(4), 613–627.

Yuzawa, N. (2013) 'Kodomo no Hinkon Taisaku ni kansuru Horitsu no seitei keii to kongo no kadai' (The political process and issues of the passing of the law to promote measures against child poverty)', *Hinkon Kenkyu*, 11, 50–60 (in Japanese).

Yuzawa, N. (2015) 'Kodomo no Hinkon wo meguru SeijiDoko' (Political movement around child poverty), *Kazoku Shakaigaku Kenkyu*, 27(1), 69–77 (in Japanese).

Diet reports

183rd Diet, Committee on Health, Labour and Welfare, No. 15, 29 May 2013.
https://kokkai.ndl.go.jp/txt/118304260X01520130529/21
https://kokkai.ndl.go.jp/txt/118304260X01520130529/206

7

The role of housing in successful and sustainable youth transitions in Japan and South Korea

Misa Izuhara and Bongjo Yi

Introduction

Youth transitions to residential independence have been extended in many post-industrial societies over the last two decades. East Asian societies are no exception. The struggle of young adults not making 'successful' transitions to adulthood has exacerbated social issues, especially since the 2008 Global Financial Crisis. In Japan, the trend started earlier after the burst of the economic bubble in the early 1990s. Thus, the 'lost generation' who were the victims of the post-bubble recession have already reached their 40s. On the other hand, young Koreans have faced double pressures from the adverse labour market and high housing price inflation due to the aftermath of the Asian Financial Crisis in 1997 and the subsequent Global Financial Crisis. As a result of the economic and labour market transformation, young adults currently benefit much less from the features of post-war welfare development such as job security, seniority-based salary, and corporate welfare compared to their parents' generation (Iwata and Miyakawa, 2003; Kim et al., 2020). In this vein, young adults have been experiencing an observed delay in achieving full independence.

It is not only their employment status and working conditions that have shifted, but this is also the case in the housing context. Economic crises and precarious labour markets have indeed jeopardised the conventional upward housing trajectories – from parental home to independent household, from private rental to home ownership – which have become no longer the normative pathways for the current younger generation. A prolonged departure from the parental home including never leaving their parental home or returning to it after a period of independent living has indeed become an unprecedented phenomenon for young adults, while many studies articulate the diverse trajectories and dynamic nature of parent–child relations (Kim, 2014; Kublikowski and Rodrigues, 2016; Ronald and Hirayama, 2009; South and Lei, 2015). This is a global issue alongside stagnated access to home ownership among young adults, which has been well documented in various national contexts (Forrest and Yip, 2013; Hirayama and Izuhara, 2018; McKee, 2012).

The aim of this chapter is therefore to bring the housing dimension more fully into the analysis of youth transitions in the post-financial crisis context in East Asia. This is because youth studies tend to be dominated by the analysis of precarious labour market experiences, the 'second demographic transition' of late marriage and low fertility, or stagnated 'education to work' trajectories (Brinton, 2011; Inui, 2009; Nahm and Namgoong, 2012; Yamada, 2004). The term 'housing career' provides a perspective linking housing needs and life stages, even though the concept has been criticised for its implication of 'linear' housing trajectories (Beer and Faulkner, 2011). In the global context, urbanisation has fuelled the constant demands for housing in large cities, driven partly by new household formations of young adults. In more advanced economies, which exhibit a mature stage of urbanisation, however, such new household formations have stagnated due to precarious labour market conditions and housing affordability. Since neoliberal policies have shaped housing markets for the last few decades, housing inequality has widened within and between generations in those societies. In this global context, young adults have become the major victims having been excluded from access to adequate and affordable housing both owned and rental (Aalbers, 2015). The focus of the chapter is, however, not on young adults in the 'fast track' of their life-course (Bynner et al., 2002) moving up the housing ladder to home ownership. Instead, it focuses on those individuals remaining in the parental home, defined in the housing pathway typologies as 'pre-pathway' by Ford and colleagues (2002). Leaving the parental home often represents something significant in youth transitions. As Mulder (2009) argues, for example, leaving the family home is an important marker since it requires young adults to take on substantial adult responsibilities such as managing their own finances, making consumption decisions, and managing domestic chores independent of their parents. However, such perspective could not explain the heavy reliance of young adults on parental resources, illustrated as the phenomenon of 'dependent independence', during life transitions towards adulthood (Druta and Ronald, 2017; Izuhara, 2015).

Japan and the Republic of Korea (hereafter Korea) are chosen for comparative analysis in this chapter because they are both mature home-ownership societies with similar tenure patterns. Youth transitions have equally stagnated, although the timing of economic growth and crisis which impacted on housing markets and social policy developments have been staggered (see, for example, Takegawa, 2013). Yet, different housing systems, housing stock, and different ranges and levels of housing policy and regulations exist in the two societies, which will stimulate comparative analysis. Common to both societies are minimal state intervention in terms of direct provision of social or public housing and similarly heavy reliance on family resources (Forrest and Yip, 2013; Hirayama and Izuhara, 2018). As we examine in the subsequent sections, many unmarried young adults, often on low incomes, live with their parents. Where possible, we include an analysis on Tokyo and Seoul, which are both capital and global cities in East Asia, since the delay in housing transitions and associated housing problems tends to be more acute in large cities with booming housing markets. In this context, the chapter is aimed at examining how young adults can achieve successful and sustainable residential transitions; and what are the roles of families, the state, and market assisting or hindering the processes. It will also analyse the conflictive yet inter-related concepts of autonomy and dependence of young adults in the housing context. In doing so, the chapter will make a significant contribution to the understanding of the role of housing in youth transitions and draw policy implications in the post-growth social context.

The methodology used for the analysis in this chapter includes a review of relevant policies, existing academic literature, and national/sample surveys including periodic housing surveys of the two countries as well as the authors' own primary research. In particular, qualitative fieldwork, which was conducted in 2018 among 32 young adults in their 30s in Seoul, helped to inform the analysis (Yi, 2022). After this introduction, the chapter first defines key terms such as 'young adults' and conceptualises changing youth transitions in the housing context. It then examines comparable datasets of Japan and Korea in order to ascertain the current living arrangements and tenure patterns of young adults. The main body of the chapter will argue distinctive and shared factors influencing their stagnated residential transitions under three themes: housing stock and housing practices as barriers for youth transitions; cultures and institutions influencing or hindering youth transitions; and autonomy and family dependence. Finally, conclusions will be drawn by discussing the key role of housing in successful and sustainable youth transitions as well as policy implications in the East Asian context.

Conceptualising 'youth transitions' in the housing context

It has been more than two decades since Arnett (2000, 2006) first conceptualised 'emerging adulthood' as a new stage of the life-course between adolescence and adulthood. Defining the age band of 'youth' or 'young adults' is a matter of academic and policy debate as the age category is often fluid rather than fixed across cultures and societies as well as over time. For statistical consistency, for example, the United Nations defines youth or young people narrowly as those aged between 18 and 25. In Japan, 20 years old was the legal coming of age (to celebrate with cultural significance and to be allowed to drink and smoke) although the legal age was lowered to 18 in 2022 following the lowering of the voting age in 2016. In Korea, the age threshold of young adults is equally complex. For example, the new 2020 Youth Basic Act defines 'youth' as persons aged 19 to 34, while other acts such as the Special Act on the Promotion of Youth Employment define it more narrowly as those aged between 15 and 29. In a sense, although not consistent across different acts and programmes, legislative definitions of young adults give clear age thresholds. Ambiguity usually lies where we consider the social construction of young adults such as social norms and age-related expectations. For example, a Japanese saying, 'owning one's home is the rite of passage to full adulthood' used to indicate home ownership as a material precondition to becoming an adult. Such post-war cultural norms also implied the departure from the parental home as an achievement of youth transition as well as financial independence in the form of home ownership.

In the current economic climate, however, young adults have more leeway in not following standardised paths into adulthood (see Furlong, 2012). Moreover, the demographic status of traditional role requirements no longer captures the diversity and uncertainty of the lives of young adults (Arnett, 2007). In contemporary societies, 'emerging adulthood' has become a lengthy and unsettling period when young adults explore identity, lifestyles, career opportunities, and individual conceptions of autonomy rather than simple traditional markers of maturity such as getting stable jobs, marriage, and parenthood (Arnett, 2000). In Japan, the post-war life-course was first 'institutionalised' with the development of the male-breadwinner family model, the corporate-centred employment system, as well as the social security system. Then, the life-course model was 'standardised' when men and women started following distinctive but separate life-courses (Shimazaki, 2008). In Korea, the period of youth transition, such as from graduation to family formation, tends to be shorter than that of the previous generation due to a prolonged period of education, although the rates of marriage have significantly declined (Moon, 2010). Moon's studies particularly highlighted the prevalence of this trend among young women. Achieving the precondition of securing adequate housing for marriage and subsequent family formation has become much more difficult for men (and their family) who are often expected to be financially responsible in the traditional male-breadwinner societies such as Korea.

Furthermore, for the familial societies of Japan and Korea, the legitimacy of marriage still holds strongly, but the hurdle for marriage has risen considerably due to the required financial responsibilities in an increasingly precarious labour market. The marked decline and delay in marriage are some of the consequences. In fact, the average age of first marriage has risen to approximately 30 in both societies (29.6 years for women and 31.2 years for men in Japan by 2019, and 30.8 and 33.2 respectively in Korea by 2020) (Korea Statistics, 2021; Ministry of Health, Labour and Welfare, 2020). The average age of women having their first baby is similarly extended to 30.7 in 2015 compared to 26.7 in 1985 in Japan, which was 32.2 in 2019 in Korea. In relation to such 'second demographic transition' of late marriage and low fertility, 'wakamono' ('young adults' in Japanese) are increasingly defined in policy terms much more broadly to include those aged between 16 (the end of compulsory education) and 39 or even 44 in some programmes. Although expanded individual choices are partly the driver for the change in many aspects of youth transitions, the process is fundamentally shaped by more structural factors such as labour market instability borne out of deregulation in the globalising world as well as exclusion mechanisms of social policy such as benefit cuts driven by austerity politics (Bynner, 2005).

Housing plays a significant role in youth transitions. Residential transitions may involve changes in living arrangements (e.g. from parental home to private sharing, co-habiting or independent living; back to co-residency with parent/s after a period of independent living) and also housing consumption including tenure change (e.g. from private rental to home ownership). In the life-course, housing transitions are recognised as parallel but inter-related pathways with work and life-stage progression (Beer and Faulkner, 2011; Clapham, 2004). In other words, housing is not consumed separately, but closely linked to other aspects of life-course transitions including entering and leaving the labour market, family formation and dissolution, and changes in health or financial status. Housing transitions are indeed often driven by employment status, level of income, and changing household need. Marriage and employment (and higher education, albeit temporary) are the conventional reasons for young adults to leave the parental home in East Asian societies. In particular, marriage and new household formation are strongly connected in both Japan and Korea, compared to reasons such as the search for identity and lifestyles found in Western societies like the United Kingdom (Heath, 2008; Hirayama and Izuhara, 2008). Housing literature also highlights that home ownership still plays an important role in pursuing marriage and parenthood, while private rental is an inevitable housing choice for those of a lower socio-economic status when they leave their parental home (Fuster et al., 2019; Izuhara, 2015).

While 'achieving' youth transitions in the above key areas is challenging enough in the current socio-economic climate, 'sustaining' such transitions also requires different levels of commitment, employment status, and
resources of individuals (and their family). Sustainable youth transitions do
not simply mean achievements of such conventional life-course markers, as
some of the transitions are temporary and highly at risk of reverting to the
previous position in the life-course. 'Yo-yo transitions' (young adults moving
back and forth between independent household and the parental home) are
a good example of the lack of sustainability in youth transitions (see France et
al., 2021). Sustainable transitions need to be underpinned by progress in other
domains such as income, employment, and relationships. For example, own
income from a secure employment can be a precondition for residential independence, which would also support or lead to partnership and/or family formation. Moreover, the concept also signifies autonomy and control of young
adults making life-course decisions. In other words, such decision-making
autonomy for their lives – when to move out of the parental home, what
accommodation to live in, whether or when to get married or have children
– is an important marker for independence. Such autonomy and control over
their lives, however, are increasingly challenged due to the precarious labour
market and associated incomes, which is one of the explanations for the
growing phenomenon of prolonged co-residence with their parents (Arundel
and Ronald, 2016; Lennartz et al., 2016). For young adults who cannot afford
to manage independent lives, their parental home accommodates them longer
while waiting to find and fund stable and affordable housing (Hochstenbach
and Boterman, 2015).

Extended youth housing transitions in the comparative context

This section examines key housing trends of young adults comparatively. In
order to highlight the distinctiveness and changing patterns of housing situations of the age groups, we identified two reference points: the latest Housing
and Land Survey in Japan (2018) and the equivalent in Korea (2015); and the
pre-financial crisis Japanese data in 1988 and the 1995 Korean survey as the
comparator (Ministry of Internal Affairs and Communications, 1988, 2018;
Statistics Korea, 2007, 2017). The 2018 and 2015 survey results are the latest
datasets capturing the current situations for the two societies. For Japan, we
examined both the 1978 and 1988 datasets. Although the 1978 housing survey
shows more compelling evidence for the expansion of household numbers and
the shift to home ownership during the economic growth and urbanisation

period in the 1970s, we chose the 1988 datasets to remain comparable to the equivalent period in Korea. As Korean society reached a stable stage of urban and economic development in the early 1990s, the 1995 survey results exhibit a more complete case to capture the demographic and tenure changes. It is significant to note that there was some 20-year gap between the two societies in terms of urban and economic development.

The number of households (the age of household heads as a reference group) is used as a unit of measurement rather than the proportion of tenure distribution within each age group. This is because it is critical to observe the prevalence of households headed by young adults, reflecting the trends of household formation and stagnation. The latest figures in both societies clearly show that the number of households headed by young adults in their 30s has significantly declined over the period of two to three decades. We included the age cohort of 40–49 in our analysis especially because in the post-financial crisis context the initial entry of this cohort to the labour market was impacted by the financial crisis in the 1990s.

Japan

As is evident in Figure 7.1, there was a significant drop in the number of households headed by those aged between 30 and 44. During the 1970s, those in their 30s experienced a period of great household expansions and upward tenure mobility. The number of households headed by the 30–34 age group started dropping in 1988 and by 2018 the household number among 35–39 became significantly fewer (3 million households) compared to approximately 4.8 million in 1988. This can be partly explained by the shrinking cohort but is also an indication of stagnated residential transitions to independent households. No significant change in the number of younger households headed by under 25s over the last three decades was observed, which implies that residential youth transitions usually occur from the late 20s onwards.

Tenure patterns tell another compelling story of youth transitions. A significant decline in home ownership among all the age groups was evident (see Figure 7.1). Private renting is a dominant tenure among young adults in their 20s. Considering this cohort includes university students and new graduates, the patterns are similar between 1988 and 2018 data; and also between Japan and Korea. More alarming shifts can be observed among those in their 30s and 40s over the decades. The figures show that the shift to owner occupation which used to occur in their 30s (38 per cent among 30–34) in 1988 has stagnated as indicated by the 2018 figure (26.2 per cent). The number of owner occupiers in the 45–49 age cohort dropped from 3.37 million to 2.76 million despite the number of households remaining similar, around 4.6 million over the two periods.

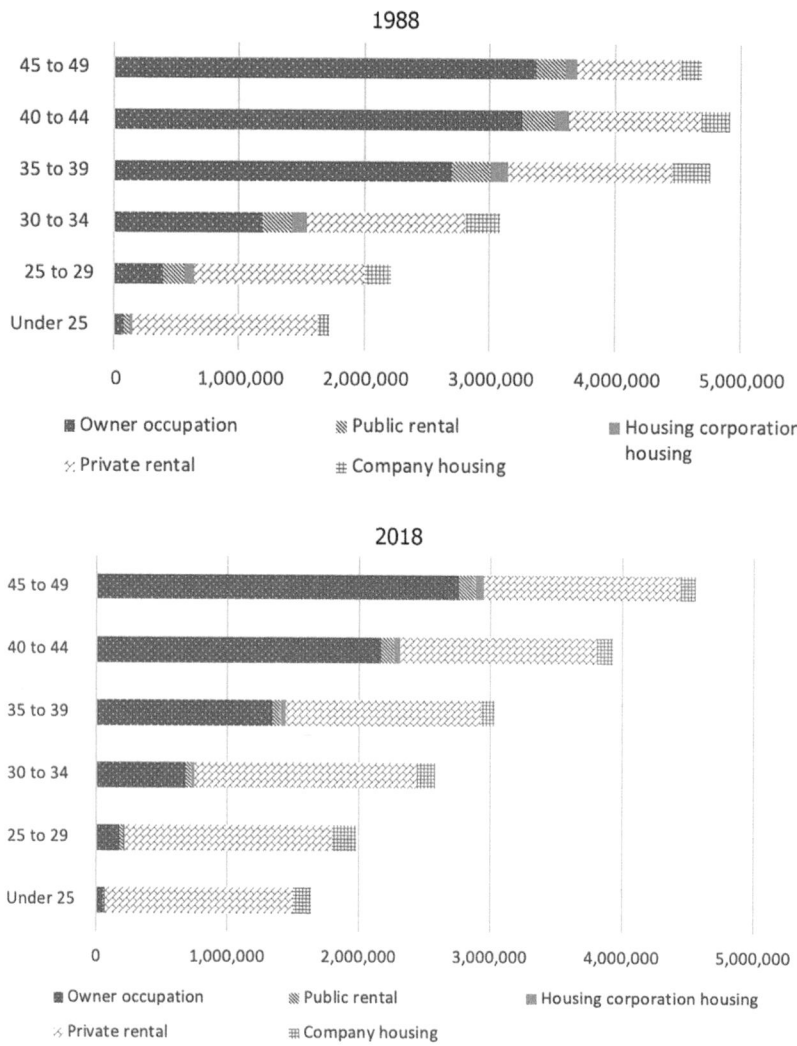

Source: Ministry of Internal Affairs and Communications (2018).

Figure 7.1   Tenure patterns by age of household reference person in Japan in 1988 and 2018

Figure 7.1 also includes all household types (single, couple, and family) as long as the age of household head falls in the age groups. Comparing the two reference years, a higher number (and larger proportions) of households were housed in public housing in the 1980s. This is because the 1970s was the period when the construction of public housing occurred to house 'new families' (nuclear families with children). Such housing provision has become insignificant in the 2018 figure as the resident profile of public housing has shifted. Moreover, company housing used to have a distinctive role in the economic growth period as part of occupational welfare and also offered young adults a stepping stone to access home ownership. In the increasingly precarious labour market, company housing is a much less significant form of tenure in 2018 compared to the 1980s.

Moreover, the 2014 National Survey on Household Change showed a significant and widening gender difference in patterns of home leaving (Suzuki, 2017). Among younger women (aged 20–34) who were unmarried in the previous survey (2009), an increasing proportion (77.1 per cent) remained unmarried and continued to live at the parental home, while 15.7 per cent got married and only 5.5 per cent formed an independent household without marriage. Such patterns were more diverse among single men; and the rate of those who formed an independent household without marriage has increased from the previous two surveys: 9.8 per cent (2004) and 9.6 per cent (2009) to 12.7 per cent (2014).

Korea

In Korea, the post-war baby boom period occurred between 1955 and 1963 after the end of the Korean War (1950–1953). This translates to a high volume of baby-boomer households who entered their 30s in 1995 (see Figure 7.2). The number of households has increased significantly over the decades following similar but delayed trends in Japan. Also, the transition included the shift from three-generation co-residency to nuclear family households in the 1980s and the subsequent rise of the single-person household in the early 2000s. At the same time, a significant reduction in new household formation among young adults (25–39) is evident between 1995 and 2015 due largely to their stagnated entry into the labour market and delay in marriage. For example, the number of households aged under 49 rose only 230,000, while the number of entire Korean households rose from 12.9 to 19.1 million over the two decades (Statistics Korea, 2007, 2017). Such a trend is particularly evident among those in their 30s, which confirms youth transitions have been extended since the two financial crises. Like Japan, the reduction in household numbers indicates that many young adults have remained in their parental home, which is a common form of living arrangement. However, the stagnated growth of household formation may be somewhat associated with the inaccuracy in data collection. For example, the statistical data may not fully capture some independent single youth adults living away from their parental home due to the tendency that initial independent living (e.g. students or informal renting) is considered temporary and thus not formally registered.

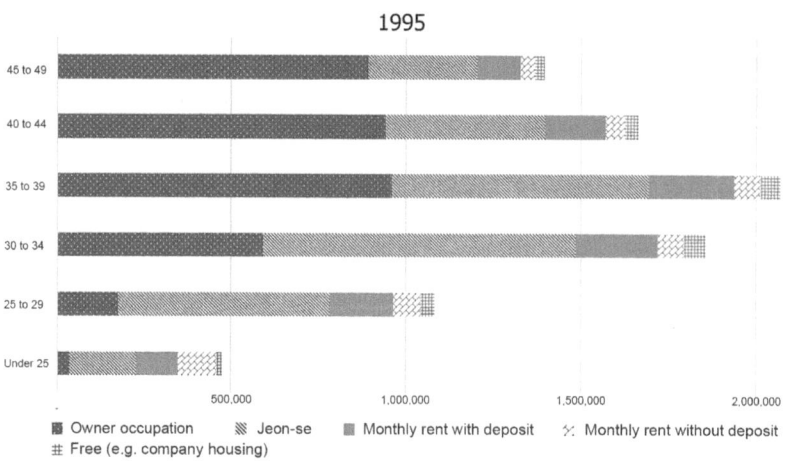

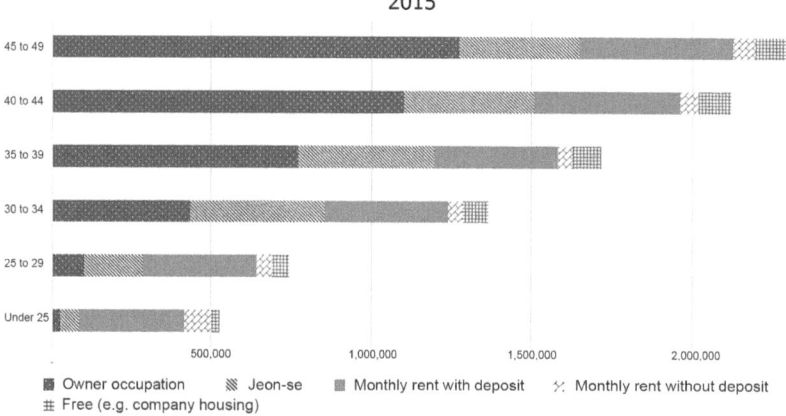

Source: Statistics Korea (2007, 2017).

Figure 7.2   Tenure patterns by age of household reference person in Korea in 1995 and 2015

In terms of tenure, the rate of home ownership by age did not exhibit a dramatic change over the two decades, even though there was a slight decline in home ownership among the cohorts, including the 40s. The number of owner occupiers under 40 has dropped despite the steady increase in the housing stock and household ratio between the total number of houses and that of households from 86 in 1995 to 103 in 2020 (Ministry of Land, Infrastructure and Transport, 2015, 2020). This means that the constant and high volume of new housing construction did not benefit young adults in their access to home ownership. Also, the private rented sector in Korea shows a significant change in tenure type over the decades: in 1995, '*Jeon-se*' was the most dominant tenure for young adults under 35, while monthly rents were dominant for those in their 20s. '*Jeon-se*' is a unique Korean system, which refers to a term of lease where the tenant pays a deposit in advance, typically from 30 to 70 per cent of the property value, without the requirement for periodic rent payment. The number of monthly rent types exceeded *Jeon-se* among young adults including those in their 40s. As *Jeon-se* is conventionally used as a stepping stone to home ownership for those who cannot yet afford to purchase their own home (Ha and Ro, 2016), the increase in the number of monthly rents indicates the struggle of young adults in the precarious housing market.

Housing stock and housing practice as barriers for youth transitions

Housing supply and housing stock influence housing practice in society, including how people consume housing. Housing supply is often driven by demand but equally constrains people's housing choices. In this vein, this section will examine how current housing stock and housing policy of the two societies fail to support or facilitate the residential transitions of young adults. The idea of a 'housing ladder' indicates linear upward mobility in housing quality and tenure as people progress in their life-course. The ladder entails a series of steps as young adults leaving their parental home for the first time do not move straight into a high-quality, owner-occupied accommodation. As youth transitions involve a period of fluidity and temporality such as spending time in higher education, their first entry to the labour market often mirrors the nature of their residential transitions.

For young adults who are making residential transitions, what sorts of housing typically accommodate them? What characteristics are shared or differ between Japan and Korea? Private rental is the most common tenure among Japanese and Korean young adults moving out of the parental home. As indicated in

Figures 7.1 and 7.2, for example, 65 per cent of the households headed by the 30–34 age group lived in private rental accommodation in 2018 in Japan and such proportion is slightly higher in Korea (68.1 per cent). Typical rental units for single-person households are studio flats for single occupancy, which is popular although such construction has been regulated in urban areas such as in the central Tokyo wards. In the Japanese housing market, private renting is considered an 'atomised and formalised' tenure (Ronald and Izuhara, 2016), which requires signing a formal contract, a large initial fee (e.g. deposit, key money, and agency fee), and providing one's own white goods and furniture as unfurnished accommodation is the norm in both the public and private rented sectors. Thus, residential independence in the form of renting requires significant financial commitment and thus is a higher hurdle for young adults on low incomes, which is not equivalent to renting a room in a shared accommodation in other housing markets. This is part of the reason for young adults not leaving the parental home more readily, although rental accommodation without requiring a guarantor or initial fees are on the increase.

In Korea, since the dominance of new housing construction is to accommodate nuclear families, housing provision for single-person households has often been overlooked and under-regulated. In response to the rise of single-person households since the early 2000s, deregulation in the housing market and tax incentives have fuelled the construction of small housing units to accommodate those households (Shin and Lee, 2019). This type of housing unit provides young tenants with relatively affordable and accessible housing, although safety and security issues often surround the units (Jung and Lee, 2018).

In particular, many young Koreans on low incomes in Seoul live in houses of multiple occupation (HMOs), called *Gosi-won*, a compound word ('*Gosi*' means national examinations such as civil servant recruitment exams and '*won*' means accommodation used for students). Despite the initial purpose of a short-term let for students taking exams, low-income individuals have started to live in such accommodation for longer periods due to its affordable rents compared to the formal rents charged in the private rental sector. Meanwhile, housing policy continues to neglect the phenomenon of long-term dwellers in HMOs, resulting in the rapid increase of the number of *Gosi-won* across large cities, especially in Seoul. *Gosi-won* resembles a beehive due to their cluster of extremely small single rooms (normally 3.3–10m^2) without windows or private bathrooms. In such extreme living environments, dwellers face multiple housing deprivations such as overcrowding, lack of basic facilities, safety, and security (Yi, 2022). The period of time living in such deprived housing is prolonged for many young adults due to the precarious labour market, particularly if they cannot draw upon parental financial support, even though young dwellers do not always foresee the difficulty of leaving such accommodation (Yi, 2022).

The dichotomy between parental homes and one-room rental housing units as housing options for young adults, highlighted above in the case of Japan, suggests a lack of transitional accommodation to support young adults leaving the parental home. In countries like England (Roberts, 2013), using social networks and contacts was identified as a pull factor to draw young adults out of their parental home and the culture of a flat share with a 'family of choice' such as friends is considered an important stepping stone facilitating youth residential transition. Instead, housing careers of young adults lack a transitional phase between the parental home and an established independent household in East Asia. Roberts (2013) argues that flat shares for young adults are the 'collective dimension' of housing transitions and provides them with a stepping stone to full residential independence in the English context. In Japan, such a transitional phase existed previously in the economic growth period in the form of company housing and dormitories, although this was a more institutionalised approach. Opportunities to enter such a transitional phase were not necessarily driven by social capital, including the availability and strength of social networks and friendships, although the strength of social capital tends to lead them to more prestigious employment (which may grant access to housing).

Flat shares are a growing business and a number of estate agencies are now operating, dealing particularly with the construction of shared flats in the private rental sector in Japan. According to the Japan Share House Association, 22,000 units were available in 2015 which was a 10 per cent increase from the previous year. Even a large corporation such as Daiwa House has been constructing or converting unused office complexes into shared flats in urban areas since 2015 (*Nihon Keizai Shinbun*, 10 September 2016, p. 13). The first one was in Nagoya with the capacity of 130 rental units in 2015, while the house maker was planning to launch ten complexes each year. These are purpose-built complexes in accessible locations with high specs and communal facilities such as futsal courts and a BBQ area to facilitate social interactions among residents. The inclusive rents (no separate charge for utility bills) are more expensive compared to a studio flat in the local market thus these new developments are geared towards a lifestyle choice rather than just economising on rents by sharing. They certainly differ from the more informal, transitional nature of flat shares in countries like England.

Indeed, the large majority of single young adults on low incomes in the 'pre-pathway' (remaining at their parental home) is partly as a consequence of a combination of the lack of affordable housing in the public and private sectors and the lack of cash-based housing benefits to support residential transitions for young adults. While such housing affordability continues to escalate, there are millions of residential properties currently unoccupied in Japan. Since the rising number of vacant properties hit the headlines in 2014, when the 2013 Housing and Land Survey identified 13.5 per cent of the total dwellings as vacant properties nationally (Ministry of Internal Affairs and Communications, 2014), 'revitalising unused or under-used housing stock' has become a popular discourse in Japan. Considering the rising level of vacant properties, it seems reasonable to question why those properties are not effectively used to accommodate people in housing need, including young adults. The mismatch of housing supply can be explained as the nature of vacant properties is often 'difficult to sell or difficult to rent out' due to their location, accessibility, ownership title, or state of repair. Residential location is an important criterion for housing choice of any household in any age, but for young adults looking for employment, in particular, good access to the work-place is crucial to minimise commuting time and cost (Yi, 2022).

Cultures and institutions supporting or hindering youth residential transitions

Following the earlier discussion on the importance of balanced transitions across different spheres of work, housing, and relationships, this section examines factors influencing or hindering sustainable residential transitions to independent living including the stagnated parallel transitions in the labour market as well as the lack of state support. Achieving residential independence from their parental home is linked to successful and sustainable labour market participation, but also it is strongly linked to financial support from parents. In other words, although residential independence is an important marker of youth transitions, it is not strongly supported by the welfare state in either society. In fact, non-state intervention in youth residential transitions has always been the case in Japan and Korea. Housing is not firmly located in the heart of social policy, or welfare provision, in particular. Housing policy tends to be pro-family in both countries. Thus, state provision is channelled into priority need groups with low 'workability' (less able to earn income from the labour market) such as older people, single parents with dependent children, and people with disabilities. While the supply of company housing has shrunk in the post-growth period, the role of families has been re-emphasised in the provision of housing for young adults.

Stagnated residential transitions of young adults are evident in relation to some of their precarious employment statuses. There are a growing number of employment support agencies which offer various services and schemes in Japan. The agencies are a key contact point for many young adults including those not in education, employment, or training seeking more secure employment. They often act as a one-stop shop providing a range of services including skills training, CV clinics, and other relevant advice on personal finance and housing. In Korea, on the other hand, such services are still underdeveloped and access to employment is largely left to individual responsibility. Nevertheless, knowledge and understanding of contemporary youth transitions at the local level highlighted that stagnated residential independence did not always derive from financial factors such as being on no or low income, but could also involve cultural, attitudinal, and structural constraints. For example, compared to Western societies, there is a lack of social norms or expectations that young adults leave home by a certain age in East Asia. As traditionally marriage and new household formation have a strong link, the concept of 'children should be independent from the family of origin by a certain age' does not necessarily exist as residential independence is tightly linked to parallel events such as marriage, moving to a different locality for higher education, albeit temporary, and employment-related moves including gaining accessibility for commuting.

It is often understood that countries with familial welfare systems tend to achieve residential independence when they get married, as opposed to other welfare systems which facilitate youth residential transitions before marriage (Lesthaeghe, 2010). As Saraceno and Keck (2010) argue, however, the link between familialism and generosity of welfare states cannot necessarily be explained in such a simplistic way. On the one hand, it is certainly true that the lack of housing support by the state, cash or in kind, does not incentivise youth residential independence. On the other hand, however, family dependence is a norm and thus there is a level of social acceptance of unmarried adult children remaining at home. As argued by Kublikowski and Rodrigues (2016) with the term 'kangaroo generation', co-habitation between parents and adult children during the mature stage of the family life cycle is not necessarily associated with a dysfunctional character.

In Japan, the supply of public housing is extremely low at 3.6 per cent in 2018 (Ministry of Internal Affairs and Communications, 2018) as the persistence of the post-war market dominance signified the highly marginalised social housing sector. In the economic growth period in the 1960s and 1970s, many young families were accommodated in subsidised rental units provided by housing corporations and private companies offering employees housing as a stepping stone for young adults to move up the housing ladder, although this can be considered as part of economic growth strategies rather than mere housing welfare (Hirayama and Izuhara, 2018). Due to the limited provision of social housing, conditionality is indeed attached to the ways in which the units are allocated to households in need. In the familial welfare state, policy had tended to restrict single people from accessing public housing until 1980 when the eligibility criteria were relaxed to accept some single older households into public housing. Similarly, in Korea, new public housing programmes provide some young adults with no or low incomes limited access to housing. Such direct provision of housing is also minimal in Korea as both governments tend to focus on market investment and stimulation through tax incentives and (de) regulation as housing policy.

In societies where the direct public housing provision is limited, rent subsidies can be another means to support households in housing need using the private rented sector. Reviewing other social contexts, the availability of cash-based housing allowances for young adults facilitates distinctive patterns of youth transition. In France, for example, housing benefits are widely available to young adults over 18 years old. Since their own income (not that of their parents) is means tested, housing allowances are routinely used to support university students (Chevalier and Palier, 2014). In 2006, for example, 42 per cent of all households under the age of 30 received housing benefit, which represented 30 per cent of the total recipients across the age groups (Kesteman, 2010, cited in Chevalier and Palier, 2014). In contrast, family wealth is explicitly counted as means of young adults in both societies. Cash-based housing allowances are only available within the public assistance scheme in Japan. A recent initiative is Emergency Housing Allowances in 2009 helping the victims of the 2008 Global Financial Crisis. Apart from the public assistance, there had been no purpose-orientated cash benefit to cover rents in place previously at the national level. Albeit at a small scale and an emergency nature, this was a significant step forward in Japanese housing policy.

Autonomy and family dependence

The term autonomy often embraces an act of making a choice or a decision and the sense of self-motivation behind such actions. Thus, the concept of 'housing autonomy' is associated with multiple layers of freedom and control including the ability to choose and determine one's current living situation and residential mobility (Schapiro et al., 2021). In addition, housing autonomy is strongly linked to an aspect of youth transition to independent living out of the parental home. In the current housing market, however, young adults are experiencing significant constraints in making their housing choices and are exposed to poor housing conditions, indicating their compromised autonomy (see Ronald et al., 2018).

Young adults relying heavily on family resources to secure their housing has become a phenomenon in the Global North (Christophers, 2018; McKee, 2012; Ronald and Hirayama, 2009). In order to consume adequate housing according to their life stages in home-ownership societies like Japan and Korea, young adults need to raise sufficient funds, in some cases beyond their own incomes earned in the labour market. Home ownership is still considered to be desirable housing tenure for those progressing through the life-course to marriage and family formation, although housing types have shifted from the post-war ideal of single-family homes to condominiums, at least in Japan (Hirayama and Izuhara, 2018). Purchasing a condominium unit is considered to be a precondition in order to form an independent family household. Despite the more favourable housing finance including ultra-low interest rates and the availability and accessibility of mortgage products for the last two decades, as Figures 7.1 and 7.2 indicate, their access to home ownership has stalled. Parental material support has become crucial in this context.

In both societies, family ties between parents and offspring are bound by the social norms of love, duty, obligations, and reciprocity (see also Chapter 9 by Yamashita and Soma in this volume). The relationships between generations are mutual and the direction of support is not one way but reciprocal. Considering the cycle of post-war economic boom and bust, the current parent generation with more financial resources tend to be the net providers who can accommodate their adult children in both societies. In this context, becoming a full adult not only means the departure from the parental home but also indicates the transfer of responsibility from their retiring or retired parents to working children for family support. The traditional role change between parents and their adult children has been an important social expectation to meet filial duty. During the period of economic growth and stability, such role change between generations has taken place despite a lack of state assistance (Choi, 2012). For example, the stable and secure labour market underpinned the financial means of the younger generation to support their family members (Ronald and Hirayama, 2009). The current economic climate and associated new social risks, however, mean that some adult children are unable to take on such responsibility, and instead their reliance on their parents may have become heavier and longer. The lack of social policy targeted at young adults means that there is an expectation for families to absorb new social risks surrounding young adults in those societies. However, as family resources can be limited, there is a risk that extensive material support by ageing parents would eat into their own resources in retirement (Kim and Lee, 2020).

Although parental financial support or co-residency often plays a positive role in assisting youth transitions to independent living and access to home ownership (Druta and Ronald, 2017), the delicate balance of power between parents and adult children may result in the compromised autonomy of adult children. When young adults try to leave their parental home, some parents may intervene and influence their housing choices, especially if they were financing their residential move. Lee and Lee (2019) argue that parents who support rents of their children are the powerful decision makers when it comes to housing choice such as location, quality, and the timing of leaving home. In particular, young adults such as undergraduate students are more likely to be controlled by the decisions of parents in Korea because the parents tend to think that their offspring are not ready for independent living (Lee and Lee, 2019). Young independent households could gradually gain autonomy over their housing choices by entering the labour market and securing their own income. Otherwise, parental intervention may continue to impact the lifestyles of young adults in co-residency. In this regard, we found that such parental intervention is a push factor for adult children to leave their parental home, although financial dependency has been prolonged due to housing unaffordability (see also Yi, 2022). The degree of intervention by parents may be more profound for single women (Izuhara, 2015; Lee and Lee, 2019). In both societies, unmarried women tend to have difficulties in leaving the parental home without their own means partly because of the conservative and gendered social norms in relation to morality as much as the safety and security of independent living.

Despite parental expectations of achieving residential independence through marriage, achieving full adulthood is not always linked to family formation. Although marriage is still one of the critical and defined life events in youth transitions away from the family of origin, the assumptions of the conventional life-course, e.g. entry to the labour market leading to marriage, have been severely challenged among the current younger generation. Full and secure employment usually guarantees financial autonomy, which supports the progress of other strands of youth transitions. However, it has become increasingly difficult to get a foothold in the labour market, which does not ensure reasonable income, and thus financial support from parents has become a precondition to consume appropriate housing (Kim et al., 2020; Lee et al., 2015). In Korea, for example, Moon et al. (2020)'s research revealed the prolonged financial dependency of young adults on their parents when their parents support their rents. A question remains whether the social and economic independence of young adults can really be achieved in the context of adverse labour and housing markets. Moreover, the accentuated (mutual) dependence may also be a cause of the hindrance of youth transitions. The lack of housing opportunities, derived from minimal government support, is one of the main reasons mentioned by young adults. Living at the parental home is normalised and not necessarily considered to be inappropriate for this age group in those societies. Not only young adults themselves but their parents may also need to shift their attitudes to encourage and facilitate youth residential transitions out of the parental home. In the current economic climate and housing market, stagnated youth transition has become a serious and longer-term social issue, although it may not be considered as a policy priority while parental resources last.

Comparative discussion and conclusions

This chapter argued that not only economic factors such as low incomes but also cultural, institutional, and market factors have influenced the stagnated residential transitions of young adults. In societies where residential independence is more privatised and heavily linked to success in employment and family wealth, the lack of direct public measures, the lack of a collective nature of transition through house share, or under-regulated markets pose considerable challenges to young adults. Many issues are shared between Japan and Korea, while some are distinctive to one society.

Tenure options in Japan have become more dichotomous between owner occupation and private rental as public and social housing as well as company housing have been further marginalised. This is also the case for Korea and the balance between *Joen-se* and monthly rents has been shifted towards monthly rents indicating harder access to home ownership. Moreover, within the two housing markets, we observed the dualism of formal and informal as well as regulated and deregulated approaches to housing provisions, which combined to present young adults with differentiated challenges. The more formal and regulated market places a higher hurdle for young Japanese adults to leave their parental home as the private rental sector requires stable financial resources and commitment. In Korea, on the other hand, the availability of more informal and substandard housing options such as *Gosi-won* has opened up opportunities for youth residential transitions, but the experiences of housing deprivation are more pronounced in this context.

Both countries suggest in their social norms the outcomes of successful youth transitions to full adulthood as marriage, financial independence, and departure from the parental home. In the current economic climate, however, without parental financial assistance, many young adults find it difficult to make such transitions, in particular, the residential transition. In this context, despite the advantages which family resources often bring to youth transitions, parental intervention in the form of financial support could also undermine the autonomy and control of young adults over their lives and decision making, including housing choice. Such family dependence in this process also contradicts with the expectation of them gaining independence through youth transitions. Moreover, family support is not always available to everyone. Thus, a combination of a heavy reliance on family wealth and a lack of policy measures is the source of widening social inequality among young adults. As discussed, some individuals without strong family support could remain in informal and substandard accommodation for a prolonged period. While tackling housing affordability remains a critical policy agenda in East Asian societies, in relation to youth transitions we suggest exploring opportunities for transitional housing by expanding housing options as a new research agenda. More housing options including shared and collective living for those at this stage of the life-course will potentially make the current divided society between home owners and private tenants more inclusive.

Moreover, youth residential transitions need new conceptualisation. In societies where late or no marriage has become a contemporary phenomenon, it is important to reconsider what 'successful' youth transitions entail for those who are not married or unpartnered well into their 30s and 40s. Also, questions such as whether the phenomenon of the 'kangaroo generation' constitutes a failed life path and whether a return to the parental home means that young adults are 'parasites' require critical discussion. This chapter argued that financial support from parents is often a prerequisite for young adults to access the formal housing market. For the baby-boomer generation, it was common that their incomes alone were enough to move up the housing ladder to home ownership, supported by low-interest, long-term government loans as well as companies in the post-war growth period in Japan. As incomes which are earned in the labour market are not necessarily the only incomes, however, how can we conceptualise youth transitions supported by family resources? Such 'independent' living achieved through family 'dependency' paints a more complex picture and thus it is hard to conceptualise the phenomenon. Intergenerational relations based on filial piety are still relatively robust in both societies. However, it is not uncommon that some young adults remaining at the parental home provide substantial care and support to their ageing parents and contribute to their household finance significantly. Cultural values underpinning family relations and practices thus need to be taken into account to evaluate success in youth transitions in the East Asian context. Despite the policy concerns of low marriage and low fertility rates, young adults play a pivotal role in families and society by supplementing the incomes of some retired parents and filling a gap in social security. The position and the role of family wealth in youth transitions need to be considered when theorising their autonomy. Finally, despite the rapid demographic transitions, the age category of young adults, expected social roles, and the timing of transitions are still relatively fixed. However, young adults are a diverse group of people. In this regard, the measures of success in youth transitions often ignore the diversity of lifestyles, relationships, and housing choices. Examining what successful and sustainable youth transitions entail will contribute to the understanding of contemporary youth transitions in relation to autonomy and dependence in familial welfare systems.

References

Aalbers, M.B. (2015) The great moderation, the great excess and the global housing crisis, *International Journal of Housing Policy*, 15(1): 43–60.

Arnett, J.J. (2000) Emerging adulthood: A theory of development from the late teens through the twenties, *American Psychologist*, 55(5): 469–480.

Arnett, J.J. (2006) Emerging adulthood in Europe: A response to Bynner, *Journal of Youth Studies*, 9(1): 111–123.

Arnett, J.J. (2007) Emerging adulthood: What is it, and what is it good for?, *Child Development Perspectives*, 1(2): 68–73.

Arundel, R. and Ronald, R. (2016) Parental co-residence, shared living and emerging adulthood in Europe: Semi-dependent housing across welfare regime and housing system contexts, *Journal of Youth Studies*, 19(7): 885–905.

Beer, A. and Faulkner, D. (2011) Housing over the life course: Housing histories, careers, pathways and transitions, in A. Beer and D. Faulkner, with C. Paris and T. Clower (eds), *Housing Transitions through the Life Course: Aspirations, Needs and Policy*, Bristol: Policy Press, 15–37.

Brinton, M.C. (2011) *Lost in Transition: Youth, Work, and Instability in Postindustrial Japan*, Cambridge: Cambridge University Press.

Bynner, J. (2005) Rethinking the youth phase of the life-course: The case for emerging adulthood?, *Journal of Youth Studies*, 8(4): 367–384.

Bynner, J., Elias, P., McKnight, A. and Huiqi, P. (2002) *Young People's Changing Routes to Independence*, York: Joseph Rowntree Foundation.

Chevalier, T. and Palier, B. (2014) The dualisation of social policies towards young people in France: Between familism and activation, in L. Antonucci, M. Hamilton and S. Roberts (eds), *Young People and Social Policy in Europe*, Basingstoke: Palgrave McMillan, 189–209.

Choi, Y.J. (2012) End of the era of productivist welfare capitalism? Diverging welfare regimes in East Asia, *Asian Journal of Social Science*, 40: 275–294.

Christophers, B. (2018) Intergenerational inequality? Labour, capital, and housing through the ages, Antipode, 50(1): 101–121.

Clapham, D. (2004) Housing pathways: A social constructionist research framework, in K. Jacobs, J. Kemeny and T. Manzi (eds), Social Constructionism in Housing Research, Farnham: Ashgate, 93–116.

Druta, O. and Ronald, R. (2017) Young adults' pathways into homeownership and the negotiation of intra-family support: A home, the ideal gift, Sociology, 51(4): 783–799.

Ford, J., Rugg, J. and Burrows, R. (2002) Conceptualising the contemporary role of housing in the transition to adult life in England, Urban Studies, 39(13): 2455–2467.

Forrest, R. and Yip, N.-M. (eds) (2013) Young People and Housing: Transitions, Trajectories and Generational Fractures, London: Routledge.

France, A., Giancola, O., Maestripieri, L. and Visentin, M. (2021) Introduction to the special section. Mastering youth transitions: Italy as a case for the contemporary complexities, Italian Journal of Sociology of Education, 13(2).

Furlong, A. (2012) Youth Studies: An Introduction, London: Routledge.

Fuster, N., Arundel, R. and Susino, J. (2019) From a culture of homeownership to generation rent: Housing discourses of young adults in Spain, Journal of Youth Studies, 22(5): 585–603.

Ha, S.J. and Ro, S. H. (2016) Analysis of the assets structure of Jeonse households, Housing Studies Review, 24(1): 5–26.

Heath, S. (2008) Housing Choices and Issues for Young People in the UK, York: Joseph Rowntree Foundation.

Hirayama, Y. and Izuhara, M. (2008) Women and housing assets in the context of Japan's home-owning democracy, Journal of Social Policy, 37(4): 641–60.

Hirayama, Y. and Izuhara, M. (2018) Housing in Post-Growth Society: Japan on the Edge of Social Transition, London: Routledge.

Hochstenbach, C. and Boterman, W.R. (2015) Navigating the field of housing: housing pathways of young people in Amsterdam, Journal of Housing and the Built Environment, 30: 257–274.

Inui, A. (2009) NEETS, freeters and flexibility: Reflecting precarious situation in the new labour market, in A. Furlong (ed.), Handbook of Youth and Young Adulthood: New Perspectives and Agendas, Abingdon: Routledge, 176–181.

Iwata, K. and Miyakawa, T. (2003) Ushinawareta 10 nen no Shin'in wa nanika [What are true reasons behind the 'lost decade'], Tokyo: Toyo Keizai Shinpo Sha.

Izuhara, M. (2015) Life-course diversity, housing choices and constraints for women of the 'lost' generation in Japan, Housing Studies, 30(1): 60–77.

Jung, Y.H. and Lee, Y.M. (2018) The impact of the physical status of urban life-type housing and the characteristics of single-person households on the anxiety of crime in housing, KIEAE Journal, 18(6): 51–60.

Kesteman, N. (2010) Le lodgement des jeunes: synthèse des études statistiques récentes, Politiques Sociales et Familiales, 99: 113–120.

Kim, E.J. (2014) 'Emerging adulthood' as the new developmental stage: Understanding the new way of coming of age in Korea, Discourse 201, 17(3): 83–129.

Kim, J.Y. and Lee, H.J. (2020) A study on the parents' experience and consciousness in support of housing costs for independent children, Journal of the Korean Housing Association, 31(3): 99–107.

Kim, S.Y., Ha, E.S. and Kim, Y. (2020) Reconsidering the economic-oriented discourses of precarious work: Through a case study on voluntary nonstandard workers, Korean Social Policy Review, 27(1): 89–127.

Korea Statistics (2021) Vital statistics, https://kosis.kr/statHtml/statHtml.do?orgId=101&tblId=DT_1B83A05&conn_path=I3

Kublikowski, I. and Rodrigues, C.M. (2016) 'Kangaroo generations': New contexts, new experiences, *Estudos de Psicologia*, September.

Lee, J.S. and Lee, Y.M. (2019) Homes on the border between 'routes' and 'roots': Home-making practices and the meaning of homes for the young adult living alone, *Journal of the Korean Urban Geographical Society*, 22(2): 93–109.

Lee, S.S., Park, J.S., Lee, S.Y., Oh, M.A., Choi, H.J. and Song, M.Y. (2015) *The 2015 National Survey on Fertility and Family Health and Welfare*, Sejong: Korea Institute for Health and Social Affairs, www.kihasa.re.kr/publish/report/view?type=all&seq=27737

Lennartz, C., Arundel, R. and Ronald, R. (2016) Younger adults and homeownership in Europe through the Global Financial Crisis, *Population, Space and Place*, 22: 823–835.

Lesthaeghe, R. (2010) The unfolding story of the second demographic transition, *Population and Development Review*, 36(2): 211–251.

McKee, K. (2012) Young people, homeownership and future welfare, *Housing Studies*, 27(6): 853–862.

Ministry of Health, Labour and Welfare, Japan (2020) Vital statistics, www.mhlw.go.jp/toukei/saikin/hw/jinkou/kakutei20/index.html

Ministry of Internal Affairs and Communications (1988) *Housing and Land Survey*, Tokyo: Statistics Bureau.

Ministry of Internal Affairs and Communications (2014) *2013 Housing and Land Survey*, Tokyo: Statistics Bureau.

Ministry of Internal Affairs and Communications (2018) *Housing and Land Survey*, Tokyo: Statistical Bureau.

Ministry of Land, Infrastructure and Transport (2015) Housing supply ratio, https://stat.molit.go.kr/portal/cate/statFileView.do?hRsId=29&hFormId=&hSelectId=&sStyleNum=&sStart=&sEnd=&hPoint=&hAppr=

Ministry of Land, Infrastructure and Transport (2020) Housing supply ratio, https://stat.molit.go.kr/portal/cate/statFileView.do?hRsId=29&hFormId=&hSelectId=&sStyleNum=&sStart=&sEnd=&hPoint=&hAppr=

Moon, C.Y., Park, S.H., Lee, Y.S. and Lee, H.J. (2020) Young single-person households' housing situation and housing expectations according to subjectively assessed income levels of themselves and their parents, *Korean Journal of Human Ecology*, 29(3): 421–435.

Moon, H.J. (2010) A study of the life-course perspective: The exploratory analysis of transitions to adulthood, Korean Journal of Welfare Studies, 41(3): 349–378.

Mulder, C.H. (2009) Leaving the parental home on young adulthood, in A.G. Furlong (ed.), *Handbook of Youth and Young Adulthood*, Abingdon: Routledge, 203–210.

Nahm, C.H. and Namgoong, M.H. (2012) A research on the de-standardisation of life course: Focused on the structural change in the transition to adulthood, Journal of Regional Studies, 20(2): 91–128.

Roberts, S. (2013) Youth studies, housing transitions and the 'missing middle': Time for a rethink?, *Sociological Research Online*, 18(3): 11.

Ronald, R. and Hirayama, Y. (2009) Home alone: The individualisation of young, urban Japanese singles, *Environment and Planning A: Economy and Space*, 41(12): 2836–2854.

Ronald, R. and Izuhara, M. (2016) Emerging adulthood transitions in Japan: The role of marriage and housing careers, *Asian Journal of Social Sciences*, 44(3): 391–415.

Ronald, R., Druta, O. and Godzik, M. (2018) Japan's urban singles: Negotiating alternatives to family households and standard housing pathways, *Urban Geography*, 39(7): 1018–1040.

Saraceno, C. and Keck, W. (2010) Can we identify intergenerational policy regimes in Europe?, *Journal of European Societies*, 12(5): 675–696.

Schapiro, R., Blankenship, K., Rosenberg, A. and Keene, D. (2021) The effects of rental assistance on housing stability, quality, autonomy, and affordability, *Housing Policy Debate*, DOI: 10.1080/10511482.2020.1846067

Shimazaki, N. (2008) *Life Course no Shakai Gaku* [Sociology of the Life Course], Tokyo: Gakubun sha.

Shin, M.C. and Lee, J.S. (2019) Examining the factors affecting residential satisfaction of the residents of the urban residential housing in the Seoul Metropolitan Area, *Appraisal Studies*, 18(3): 167–195.

South, S.J. and Lei, L. (2015) Failures-to-launch and boomerang kids: Contemporary determinants of leaving and returning to the parental home, *Social Forces*, 94(2): 863–890.

Statistics Korea (2007) Population census, Daejeon: Statistics Korea, https://kosis.kr/statHtml/statHtml.do?orgId=101&tblId=DT_1GA8507&conn_path=I3

Statistics Korea (2017) Population census, Daejeon: Statistics Korea, https://kosis.kr/statHtml/statHtml.do?orgId=101&tblId=DT_1PE1511&conn_path=I3

Suzuki, T. (2017) Setai Keisei Kaitai no Doukou [The trends of household formation and dissolution], *Journal of Population Problems*, 73(3): 155–171.

Takegawa, S. (2013) Between Western Europe and East Asia: Development of social policy in Japan, in M. Izuhara (ed.), *Handbook on East Asian Social Policy*, Cheltenham, UK and Northampton, MA, USA: Edward Elgar Publishing, 41–64.

Yamada, M. (2004) *Parasaito Shakai no Yukuei* [The Fortune of Parasite Society], Tokyo: Chikuma Shobo.

Yi, B.J. (2022) *Housing poverty and housing choice: The experiences of young South Koreans*, PhD thesis, University of Bristol.

8 The marketisation of long-term care in East Asia

Wenjing Zhang

Introduction

Marketisation is a worldwide trend across different fields of social welfare, such as education (Lowrie and Hemsley-Brown 2011) and health care (Collyer and White 2011; Ho and Lee 2017). The marketisation of welfare has various forms, including the transfer of welfare provision from the state to independent agencies or individuals (e.g. charity, private care agencies), purchasing services from independent providers (regardless of using public or private funding), and relocating responsibilities to individuals (Powell 2007).

Like other welfare-related sectors, long-term care is increasingly shaped by global ageing and rising care needs (Bone et al. 2018), in conjunction with urbanisation and industrialisation that prolonged the lifespan of the population with better living conditions, education, and accessibility to health care (Bergman et al. 2013). The rapidly ageing population, changing socio-demographic patterns, and economic pressures also provide the rationale for care systems progressively shaped by a growing market in a global context. Regarding the provision of long-term care in East Asia, increasing attention has been paid to the shifting role of the market in the care sector in recent years (Williams and Brennan 2012; Yamane 2019).

The key analytical framework used in this chapter – marketisation of care – focuses on the application of markets, market principles, and market mechanisms in the field of adult social care (i.e. long-term care) (Glendinning 2012; Shutes and Chiatti 2012; Bolton and Wibberley 2014). The marketisation of care is a considerably complicated and multi-faceted process, which involves increasing applications of market principles in the care sector and shifts in the balance of different sectors including the state, market, family, and not-for-profit providers (Daly and Lewis 2000). This inevitably leads to mixed outcomes. On the one hand, positive outcomes of the marketisation of care have been claimed, including saving expenditure (Bolton and Wibberley

2014), empowering purchasers and prompting greater individual choice (Daly and Lewis 2000; Greener 2008; Shutes and Chiatti 2012; Williams and Brennan 2012), and improving competition and efficiency (Drakeford 2007; Greener 2008). On the other hand, the marketisation of care introduces different forms of risks and failures embedded in a market system (Forder et al. 1996; Greener 2015), such as inequality (Brennan et al. 2012), the minimum care quality (Forder and Allan 2014), as well as the lack of consideration of public interests (Drakeford 2007) and care relationships (Lewis and West 2014).

Care policy, provision, and practice are path dependent and vary across countries, which are embedded in the context of shifting balances of the state, market, family, and not-for-profit provision, and influenced by ideational movements and cultural practice. Similarly, the marketisation of care is also path dependent, emphasising different historical pathways of care provision and changing demographic, political, cultural, and socio-economic contexts (Williams and Brennan 2012). However, previous literature and theoretical discussions about the marketisation of care predominantly focus on European countries based on the categorisation of European care systems. For example, Brennan et al. (2012) and Shutes and Chiatti (2012) summarised three care models in Europe: the 'familial' model in Mediterranean countries involving high levels of unpaid care in families and low levels of institutional care; the 'public' model in Nordic countries with a high volume of public services involved; and the 'means-tested' model in the United Kingdom with public care provision being allocated based on the economic background of older people.

Although sharing some cultural principles in traditionally family-centred care provision for older people and an emphasis on 'filial piety', there are significant differences among East Asian societies in their organisation and provision of care (Peng and Yeandle 2017). Distinct socio-cultural and institutional factors shape government care policies as well as the provision, organisation, and marketisation of care (Peng 2018). There is also no single model of the marketisation of care in East Asia. Instead, the processes, characteristics, and outcomes of the marketisation of care are varied and shaped by their different historical pathways of care provision, institutional contexts, and movements.

This chapter provides an overview of the marketisation of long-term care in East Asian societies, as well as exploring convergences and diversities among different models. It begins by introducing the background of the marketisation of long-term care in East Asia, which includes changes in socio-demographic trends and the mixed economy of care. The second section examines key processes and policy schemes of marketisation in different East Asian societies and the impacts of these strategies on care regimes, care markets, and participants, as well as exploring the factors that might explain different outcomes. The third section further contributes to the theoretical discussions on the marketisation of care in East Asia in a global context, exploring the similarities and distinctiveness of the marketisation models. The final section summarises the key messages of this chapter and suggests future research needs in examining different marketisation models and evaluating market-oriented care policies in contemporary East Asia.

Socio-demographic changes and the mixed economy of care in East Asia

The family, as a traditionally influential provider in caring for older people, which is especially evident in East Asian societies, plays a vital role in providing emotional, financial, and direct care support (Ochiai 2009). With traditional family-centred care arrangements for older people in East Asia, the family has had the primary responsibility for providing and financing care (Yamashita et al. 2013; see also Chapter 9 by Yamashita and Soma in this volume). However, rapid demographic changes in East Asia, including the drastic ageing process, large-scale ageing population, and changing family structures, challenge these family-centred care arrangements.

As shown in Figure 8.1, most East Asian societies have experienced an extension of life expectancy with low fertility rates in recent decades. The fertility rate, the average number of children born to women at reproductive age, is much lower across these East Asian societies (e.g. the lowest of 0.92 in South Korea and the highest of 1.7 in China) when compared to replacement-level fertility – at which a population exactly replaces itself from one generation to the next, which is roughly 2.1 for most countries depending on mortality rates (United Nations 2017). This accelerates the process of population ageing. In this context, the number of older people and the proportion of older people have been dramatically rising in East Asian societies. For example, Japan has become a super-aged society and the world's oldest society with 28 per cent of its population aged 65 or over (World Bank 2021), while other East Asian societies also have turned into ageing or aged societies in recent years (e.g. in China 11.47 per cent of the population is 65 years or older, in South Korea it is 15.06 per cent), according to the definition made by the World Health Organization and the United Nations ('ageing society' is defined as more than 7 per cent of the total population consisting of those aged 65+; 'aged society' with more than 14 per cent; and 'super-aged society' with more than 21 per cent).

In addition to demographic changes, care arrangements in East Asia have also experienced dramatic socio-economic changes in a short period. Family care provision is not increasing alongside the growing care needs with decreasing household sizes, increasing female participation in the labour market (except for China: despite remaining one of the highest in East Asia, the female participation in China's labour market is decreasing together with growing gender pay gaps since its market-oriented reforms from 1978 (Dasgupta et al. 2015)). As Ochiai (2009) argued, the traditional responsibilities of adult children are changing from direct care provision to financial support for purchased care in East and Southeast Asian societies. These changes in the family sector have led to plenty of risks to society as well as a push for reform (Soma et al. 2011; Chan et al. 2016).

Regarding key providers of care for older people, the significance of the role of each sector (e.g. the state, the market) in the mixed economy of care is shifting under changing socio-economic conditions and policy directions (Daly and Lewis 2000; Soma et al. 2011). In response to the changing families, other sectors such as the market and the community were required to be developed. Like its substantial role in the mixed economy of care in Europe and other welfare states across the world (Powell 2007; Glendinning 2012; Williams and Brennan 2012; Lewis and West 2014), the market is playing an increasingly significant role in care provision for older people in East Asia (Williams and Brennan 2012; Yamane 2019; Zhang 2022). For example, as an important element in the marketisation of care and as alternatives to family members, paid care workers are performing an active role for older people in different care settings, including care homes and domiciliary care. Specifically, foreign migrant care workers widely participate in care provision in some East Asian societies like Japan, South Korea, Singapore and Hong Kong (Peng 2018), while internal rural–urban migrants play a vital role in urban China's care provision (Zhang 2018).

Meanwhile, the community in the East Asian context includes a variety of forms of local support groups. For example, Ochiai (2009) highlighted the vital roles of different forms of the community in East Asian societies, which include regional networks (e.g. urban neighbourhoods and housing complexes in China); voluntary or informal networks (e.g. mothers' associations in Korea and Japan); and officially or deliberately formed function groups (e.g. *shequ*: functional organisations established as the fundamental social unit of the government in urban China). The community, albeit in different forms, provides care to older people via informal networks or non-governmental and non-profit organisations (Soma et al. 2011), and takes an increasingly important role while more market-oriented care policies and schemes are brought into the care sector (Zhang 2018).

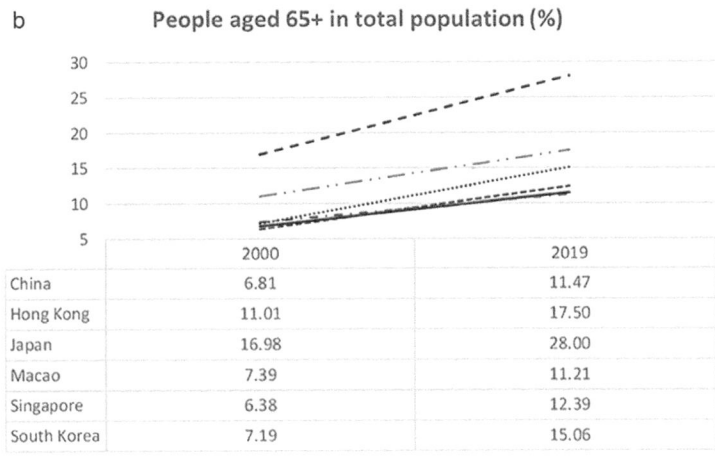

a   Life expectancy

	2000	2019
China	71.40	76.91
Hong Kong	80.88	84.93
Japan	81.08	84.36
Macao	80.41	84.12
Singapore	77.95	83.30
South Korea	75.91	83.23

b   People aged 65+ in total population (%)

	2000	2019
China	6.81	11.47
Hong Kong	11.01	17.50
Japan	16.98	28.00
Macao	7.39	11.21
Singapore	6.38	12.39
South Korea	7.19	15.06

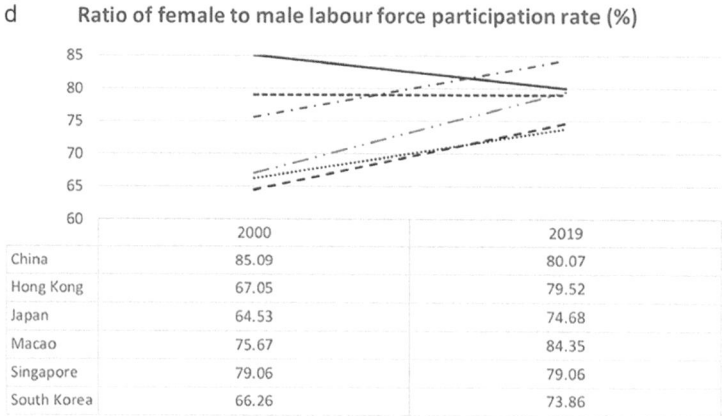

c   Fertility Rate

	2000	2019
China	1.60	1.70
Hong Kong	1.03	1.05
Japan	1.36	1.36
Macao	0.95	1.23
Singapore	1.60	1.14
South Korea	1.48	0.92

d   Ratio of female to male labour force participation rate (%)

	2000	2019
China	85.09	80.07
Hong Kong	67.05	79.52
Japan	64.53	74.68
Macao	75.67	84.35
Singapore	79.06	79.06
South Korea	66.26	73.86

Source: World Bank (2021).

Figures 8.1a–d Life expectancy, population ageing, fertility rate, and female labour participation rate in East Asia

The marketisation processes of care for older people in East Asia

The care market has been developing rapidly in many East Asian societies since the 2000s. In the context of significant socio-demographic changes, unsurprisingly, ageing and care issues have become central to social policy debates. Policy makers have started to pay more attention to developing social care for older people. For example, the Long-Term Care Insurance in Japan was launched in 2000 after the enactment of the Long-Term Care Insurance Act 1997 (Shimizutani and Suzuki 2007; Shimizutani 2014; Yamane 2019), while China has enacted various market-oriented care policies in urban areas since the 2000s (Zhang 2022). The latter includes contracting out care projects to independent care providers and providing cash and non-cash subsidies to older people to purchase care services (Shanghai Municipal Government 2016).

The 'path-dependent' model of marketisation of care is shaped by historical pathways of care provision and changing demographic, political, cultural, and socio-economic contexts (Williams and Brennan 2012). As a result, the processes, characteristics, and outcomes of the marketisation of care are varied in different countries with different emphases and practical schemes. However, even though the model of marketisation of care is distinct in each society, there are several key marketisation processes and strategies identified across different care regimes. For example, Williams and Brennan (2012) demonstrate that the forms of marketisation of care include contracting out from governments to independent providers (including for-profit and not-for-profit organisations), financial support to encourage individuals to enter the care market, long-term care insurance, tax reductions for individuals and families, cash or vouchers for home care, and subsidies or tax reductions to care providers.

Marketisation strategies applied in care policy and practice in East Asian societies share common features with the processes in many other countries as well as having distinct characteristics associated with their political, cultural, and socio-economic contexts. For instance, based on cases in the United Kingdom and Mediterranean countries, Shutes and Chiatti (2012) illustrate three processes of the marketisation of care for older people: contracting out care services to private or non-profit providers; applying cash transfers to prompt older people and their families to employ care workers; and private funding of care. These key processes were also found in the home care market in East Asian societies. For example, more than 70 per cent of care agencies for older people are private providers in South Korea (Jeon and Kwon 2017); research in urban China identified contracting out from the state to independent providers (private or non-profit), financial support from the state to older people and their families to purchase care services or employ care workers, and the direct purchasing by older people and their families in the care market (Zhang 2018).

Contracting out care services and entry of private care providers

Contracting out services from the state to independent (e.g. private, charitable, not-for-profit) providers is identified as a major process of the marketisation of care across welfare states, which is also observed as a key trending change in many East Asian societies. Independent care providers are playing a significant role in fulfilling care demands of the large older populations in East Asian societies. For example, Japan has allowed participation by independent non-profit, for-profit, and public providers to compete for customers in the care provision market, since the introduction of its long-term care insurance in 2000 (Kanaya et al. 2015), while the market was further opened up to private care providers in 2006 (Broadbent 2014). Similarly, the strategy of contracting out services was initially implemented in Shanghai as a pilot in China in 1998, which then became representative in the field of care for older people in many urban areas in China (Xu and Xia 2014). More significantly, the provision of care for older people is predominantly private in South Korea (Kwon 2009), representing 70–80 per cent of providers (Jeon and Kwon 2017).

Various strategies and principles are used in contracting out care services, which in turn shapes the care market as well as state–market relations. For example, Zhang (2018) identified three models representing different relationships between the state and the market and specific contracting-out strategies applied by local governments in urban China, including the state-controlled model, the limited competition model, and the free market model (see Table 8.1). Each model is shaped by different contracting-out strategies (e.g. open bidding or selective providers) and the embedded hierarchies of power between the state and providers in the care market.

Table 8.1   Three models of the care market in Shanghai, China

Models	Competition	State control	Local government priorities	Contracting-out methods
State controlled	Low	High	Local interests (e.g. supporting local agencies)	Pre-determined one agency
Limited competition	Medium	Medium	Comparisons and combined considerations	Several chosen agencies
Free market	High	Low	Efficiency	Open bidding

Regarding the outcomes of contracting out services, although it was claimed to save expenditure of the state (Bolton and Wibberley 2014) and service users (Nyssens et al. 2012), research evidence does not fully support these claims in the field of long-term care. As identified from an international systematic review (Petersen et al. 2018), cost savings have been much greater in technical services than in social services, including care for older people. This raises the question of whose costs have been saved via contracting out services. Based on a study in England, Lewis and West (2014) argue that contracting out care services does save money for the state, but the financial burden of families is not reduced alongside this.

Controlling or reducing public spending is also a key attraction for policy makers to apply marketisation schemes in East Asian societies (Peng and Yeandle 2017). Similar to evidence from European countries, Broadbent (2014) argued that Japan's policies around contracting out state-run home care services and opening the care market to private care agencies, together with changes in funding allocation via its Long-Term Care Insurance scheme, reduced some of the financial burdens of the Japanese government. Kwon (2009) also highlighted the potential challenge of increasing financial burdens on older people when investigating the impacts of for-profit incentives of private providers in South Korea. Nevertheless, there is still limited economic evidence in the East Asian context, which calls for more research to investigate the impacts of contracting out on costs of the state and older people and their families in East Asian countries.

Furthermore, the increasing involvement of private care providers unavoidably leads to debates with regard to the impacts on care recipients, care providers, and care workers, such as inequality among service users in accessing information and other resources (Brennan et al. 2012) and care quality (Forder and Allan 2014). Some negative outcomes are related to the characteristics of the marketisation of care. For instance, contracting out services leads to the extended market taking over public provision, which would lead to less attention to public interest and equality; inequalities are embedded in the marketisation of care due to contracting out public provision to the market and different levels of purchasing power among care users. Similar to the dualism of the care labour market found in England (Ungerson 1999; Shutes and Chiatti 2012), studies in East Asian societies found a disparity in care labour markets and care quality. For example, the growth of the home care market involves both high-end care with an all-round care workforce and 'standard' care provided by low-paid and more casual care workers in the markets since home care services opened to private companies in Japan (Broadbent 2014).

In this context, some researchers highlighted the importance of strengthening the guiding role of the government (Jia et al. 2016) and the urgency to establish standards for care agencies and care quality after contracting out (Ding 2013) in the large-scale marketisation context in East Asian countries.

Financial support for older people and their families

Alongside contracting out care services and promoting the accessibility and supply of private care providers, governments increasingly encourage older people and families to purchase care services via financial support, including both cash and non-cash schemes.

First, 'cash-for-care' policies allocate ring-fenced money to older people and their families to purchase care services in the care market as consumers (Nyssens et al. 2012). By doing so, cash-for-care schemes seek to empower care recipients with more choice and autonomy to make their own care arrangements (Ungerson and Yeandle 2007), boost care markets, promote home care and family care, and increase cost effectiveness and efficiency (Woolham et al. 2017). For example, financial support in China includes various forms of care vouchers and cash-for-care benefits provided by local governments based on the care needs of older people and their income (Hu et al. 2020). Local governments usually pay the care users' money into their personal bank accounts. For example, in 2000, the Shanghai government started to conduct home care support schemes for older people in selected local jurisdictions of 12 *jiedaos* (sub-districts) in six districts. The Shanghai government provided the funding for this scheme, with a start-up fund of CNY30,000 (GBP3,589; GBP1 = CNY8.36 in May 2022) to each *jiedao* for care facilities and purchasing home care services from independent providers. Since the pilots in Shanghai, many cities have begun trials of home care schemes for older people in China.

Second, non-cash financial support includes various strategies in care practice. For example, long-term care insurance schemes established in Japan and South Korea help to pay care service fees for older people who have participated in the schemes (Izuhara 2003; Bode et al. 2011). Japan has launched mandatory long-term care insurance since 2000, which allows the marketisation of the care sector (Ochiai 2009; Tamiya et al. 2011; Broadbent 2014; Fu et al. 2017; Yamane 2019). The long-term care insurance scheme is also being piloted in China, where Jiangsu was the first province in China to establish a long-term care insurance plan in 2006 (Shen et al. 2014), and a national pilot was launched in 15 cities in 2016.

Long-term care insurance schemes in East Asian countries share some key principles that contribute to the marketisation of care, especially home and community-based care. For example, Japan's long-term care insurance focuses on supporting older people in deciding which services to use, encouraging private companies, cooperatives, and non-profit organisations to provide care services to older people, and promoting and improving home care and community-care quality and quantity (Kurimoto and Kumakura 2016). The newly piloted long-term care insurance in China brings in a co-payment idea for care services based on needs assessments: a co-payment of 10 per cent for home care services and 15 per cent for institutional care for those aged 60 and over based on eligibility assessments (Feng et al. 2020).

In addition to long-term care insurance, various non-cash schemes (e.g. tax concessions) are employed to fund personal care (Bode et al. 2011) and to encourage adult children to support older people, which has become commonly applied in some East Asian societies (e.g. Hong Kong, Singapore) (Ng 2011). The tax concessions and housing discounts policy encourage family members to live together with older people as well as enable the employment of care workers at home (Brennan et al. 2012). For example, Hong Kong applies a Dependent Parent and Dependent Grandparent Allowance to co-residents with older people (Hong Kong Government 1999) as well as tax deductions to adult children or grandchildren who pay fees to care homes for older family members (Hong Kong Government 2000), while Singapore has introduced the Proximity Housing Grant on purchasing houses to people who live with or near their older parents since 2015 (Housing and Development Board of Singapore 2021) to encourage and support families to care.

Cash and non-cash schemes and different schemes within each category could either co-exist or work separately in each society. For example, Japan has put more effort into Long-Term Care Insurance rather than a cash-for-care scheme (Campbell and Ikegami 2000; Tamiya et al. 2011), while China attempts to enable older people and their families to purchase care services from the market by providing both cash and non-cash financial support (Zhang 2018).

Referring to the impacts on service recipients, both cash and non-cash financial support schemes influence users' choice and care provision. Cash and non-cash care schemes also contribute to the maintenance and development of home care for older people. The private, familial, economic, and social life of older people turn from traditional unpaid care to paid care services supported by different financial support schemes across welfare states (Ungerson and Yeandle 2007). Similarly, it is especially representative in East Asian societies where 'ageing in place' and home care remain priorities for both older people and their families and the governments. For example, Japan's long-term care insurance promotes the involvement of care workers as home helpers (Ochiai 2009) and emphasises home-based care (Tamiya et al. 2011); Hong Kong's Dependent Parent and Dependent Grandparent Allowance encourages co-residence and family care, while the majority of 'cash-for-care' schemes in China also focus on promoting and expanding home care services for older people.

The application of different schemes and contexts in each country, of course, leads to diverse outcomes that shape their care regime and older people's lives. For example, unlike the nationwide long-term care insurance policy in Japan, local governments take the key responsibility of providing cash-for-care schemes in China, and the benefits level and coverage are highly associated with local economic backgrounds, which contributes to the growth of regional disparities in welfare provision in China. Considering the impacts on providers, the employment of care workers is also influenced by financial support schemes. For example, paid care workers are playing an increasingly important role in care provision for older people across East Asian societies, where financial support schemes like long-term care insurance and cash-for-care support some older people and their families to purchase care services or employ care workers (Zhang 2018; Yamane 2019).

Direct purchasing by older people and families in care markets

Older people and their families act as direct purchasers (also known as self-funding) in the care market, without financial support from the state or with a need to top up using their own money in addition to state-funded care services. Direct purchasing by service users contributes to the increasing use of residential care and the employment of care workers in their own homes. The private financial support to older people is significant in 'familial' countries (those with high levels of unpaid care provided by family members and low levels of institutional care) (Shutes and Chiatti 2012), which is especially evident in East Asian societies based on their traditionally family-centred care regimes.

Direct purchasing allows older people and their families to make decisions in the care market and offers more choices for those economically advantaged groups. However, on the one hand, this increases the financial burden for many older people and their families. Like the case in England, families are bearing increasing burdens during the marketisation process (Lewis and West 2014). This is also evident in some East Asian societies where governments' financial support could only provide a limited amount of public-funded care services. For example, it is not uncommon in some local authorities in China that hours of home care services covered by 'cash-for-care' schemes cannot fulfil older people's care needs, and older people and their families have to top up from their own pockets (Zhang 2018). Considering the increasing ageing population and related care needs in most East Asian societies, publicly funded support is not widely accessible for the majority of older people, leaving older people and their families to source care from the market (Peng and Yeandle 2017).

On the other hand, the increasing accessibility of and choices in the care market allow older people and their families to look for more cost-effective services. This creates new ways for older people and their families to purchase care from less-paid and more casual migrant care workers in many East Asian societies (Broadbent 2014; Peng 2018; Yamane 2019). For example, the participation of foreign migrant workers in the care labour market is evidently found in some East Asian societies, including more regulated institutional care in Japan and South Korea and less regulated domestic care in Hong Kong and Singapore (Peng 2018). Similarly, rural–urban migrants within China play a significant role in providing care in both residential care and home and community care in its urban areas (Ochiai 2009; Zhang 2018).

In this context, some East Asian governments make policies to cater to the trend of employing migrant care labour. For example, Japan has eased its immigration policy control to recruit foreign migrant care workers (mainly from the Philippines, Indonesia, and Vietnam) to cope with the labour short-age in the care market (Broadbent 2014; Miyazaki 2019; Yamane 2019). This includes Japanese policies of the Economic Partnership Agreement in 2008 and its expansion in 2016, which allow qualified foreign care workers to work permanently in Japan as long as they complied with a five-year status renewal (Yamane 2019). There is also a growth of the grey market, in which unskilled migrant workers join the care labour market via direct purchasing from older people and their families (Miyazaki 2019).

Consequently, a better understanding of the care market, accessibility of infor-mation for older people and their families, and regulations in care provision and the care labour market are urgently required in East Asian societies in terms of protecting the rights of service recipients and care workers. Compared to European welfare states, where new regulatory frameworks have been set up to reduce the risk of market failure and guarantee competition and empowerment in the context of the marketisation of care (Pavolini and Ranci 2008), although they still require further development (Lewis and West 2014), the regulatory systems have a long way to develop in many East Asian societies. Therefore, it is important for the state and individuals to gain a better understanding of the care market and the potential risks embedded in it.

Before widely applying marketisation strategies, it is important for policy makers to evaluate the existing evidence, identify distinct pathways for their local contexts, take and review pilot schemes, and set up regulations at an earlier point in response to embedded risks in the care market. It is also important to balance the tension between more regulations of the market and counterproductive burdens being placed on providers, which is actively a debate in some welfare states. Meanwhile, service users could benefit by recognising 'information failures' in the care market when they make decisions, which will not only require older people and their families to seek information, but also asks the state and care providers to proactively offer transparent information and monitor the availability and quality of information available for older people and their families.

Is there an East Asian model of the marketisation of care?

In Eurocentric discussions of welfare states and care regimes, some researchers treat East Asia as a whole and try to fit it into existing Eurocentric classifications. For example, Japan and East Asia were allocated in the category of 'conservative southern European regimes' in Hill (2007)'s categorisation of care regimes or 'familial' model. However, despite sharing some cultural principles in traditionally family-centred care provision for older people and an emphasis on filial piety, care systems and their pathways of the marketisation of care are diverse in East Asia. For example, Soma et al. (2011) argue that the unitary definition of the family-centred welfare regime in East Asia is not accurate, as sources and the organisation of financial resources, care provision, and regulations are all distinct in different periods in each society. Similarly, as discussed in this chapter, there is no single model for the marketisation of care in East Asian societies. For example, Peng (2018) identified two distinct forms of care markets in four East Asian societies: (1) a regulated institutional approach via universal long-term care insurance in Japan and South Korea; and (2) a liberal private market via tax and policy incentives that encourage families to purchase care in Hong Kong and Singapore. This section discusses the similarities and distinctiveness of the marketisation approaches in East Asia.

On the one hand, regarding the marketisation of long-term care provision in East Asia, there is an evident and increasing marketisation trend across many societies in this region, involving some similarities in marketisation schemes and characteristics. For example, investigating the care systems in South Korea, China, Taiwan, Thailand, Singapore, and Japan, Ochiai (2009) identified a co-existence of the large family sector and the large market sector in most East and Southeast Asian societies, which represents a prevalent model of the combined familistic and liberalist welfare regime; except for Japan, which she argued as only having a significant family system with a stagnated marketisation. However, since the application of the Long-Term Care Insurance scheme in 2000 and the easing of restrictions of immigration policies to recruit foreign care workers to work in the care sector in 2008, the marketisation of care is also becoming significant in Japan (Broadbent 2014; Yamane 2019).

Based on traditionally family-centred care regimes, those marketisation strategies and processes in familial welfare states in Europe (e.g. Italy) are also found in East Asia, such as the familial care model of 'migrant in the family', employing migrant care workers to provide care at home in Italy (Shutes and Chiatti 2012), which is increasingly seen in Japan (Broadbent 2014; Yamane 2019) and China (Zhang 2018). Meanwhile, although developing in a different way, the role of the state remains comparatively strong in East Asian societies during the transition from the 'familial care regime' to increasingly involving the market sector. For example, the expansion of social care in South Korea and Japan has been introduced in conjunction with economic and labour market reforms since the 1990s, during which these governments have increased social investment and support for social care (Peng 2012).

In this context, the marketisation processes in many East Asian societies represent a 'quasi-market' (Zhang 2018, 2022; Yamane 2019) – a market with competitive independent agencies replacing the monopolistic state providers while differing from the conventional free market in one or more of three ways: not-for-profit and for-profit organisations co-exist and compete in the market; applying vouchers for purchasing; and agents representing service users in the market (Le Grand 1991; Le Grand and Bartlett 1993). With contracting out previously publicly funded care services (e.g. China) and diverse forms of financial support (e.g. care allowances and tax credits in Singapore and Taiwan), older people and their families are increasingly getting involved in the quasi-care market in East Asia (Peng and Yeandle 2017). For example, the quasi-marketisation characteristics emerge in the field of long-term care in urban China: independent care providers are increasingly involved in care provision; not-for-profit and for-profit organisations compete in the market; there are care services for older people to purchase from the care market; and community officials or care managers represent older people to make decisions in the quasi-market (Zhang 2018).

On the other hand, as a path-dependent concept, the processes and outcomes of the marketisation of care are influenced by different and changing demographic, political, cultural, and socio-economic contexts, the historical pathways of care provision, and trending challenges in care practice and policy (Williams and Brennan 2012). As discussed in the above sections, the processes, characteristics, and outcomes of the marketisation of care are varied in different East Asian societies with different emphases and practical schemes. For example, even if Japan, South Korea, and China all have long-term care insurance schemes, their insurances not only are at different development and coverage levels, but also reflect differences in their tax systems, welfare systems, and political systems. Thus, there also come along mixed outcomes and variations in different contexts when applying different marketisation strategies or even when adopting similar policies.

Conclusion

This chapter provided an overview of key processes and strategies of the marketisation of long-term care applied by different societies in East Asia, as well as exploring convergences and diversities among different models of marketisation of care. It examined key marketisation processes with specific care policy schemes in different East Asian societies and the impacts of marketisation processes on care recipients and providers and shifts in the care regimes. It identified quasi-market characteristics in many East Asian societies where independent and private agencies compete in providing care services with strong control and regulations from the state. While the family remains the key supporter for older people, physically, mentally, and financially, market-oriented care schemes in East Asian societies especially focused on promoting home and community-based care.

This chapter also emphasised the need to take into account the impacts of these marketisation strategies on older people and their families, care providers, care workers, and other stakeholders in the growing care market, which require better government regulations in shaping and monitoring the care markets. Considering the rapid development of the marketisation of care in East Asia, future work is required to explore and evaluate the application of marketisation strategies and market-oriented care policies in East Asian societies. It is important to analyse the East Asian model and distinctive marketisation models in each society based on their distinct pathways compared to other Western countries and contribute to international comparative discussions.

References

Bergman, H., Karunananthan, S., Robledo, L.M.G., Brodsky, J., Chan, P., Cheung, M., and Bovet, P., 2013. Understanding and meeting the needs of the older population: a global challenge. *Canadian Geriatrics Journal*, 16 (2), 61–65.

Bode, I., Gardin, L., and Nyssens, M., 2011. Quasi-marketisation in domiciliary care: varied patterns, similar problems? *International Journal of Sociology and Social Policy*, 31 (3/4), 222–235.

Bolton, S.C. and Wibberley, G., 2014. Domiciliary care: the formal and informal labour process. *Sociology*, 48 (4), 682–697.

Bone, A.E., Gomes, B., Etkind, S.N., Verne, J., Murtagh, F.E.M., Evans, C.J., and Higginson, I.J., 2018. What is the impact of population ageing on the future provision of end-of-life care? Population-based projections of place of death. *Palliative Medicine*, 32 (2), 329–336.

Brennan, D., Cass, B., Himmelweit, S., and Szebehely, M., 2012. The marketisation of care: rationales and consequences in Nordic and liberal care regimes. *Journal of European Social Policy*, 22 (4), 377–391.

Broadbent, K., 2014. 'I'd rather work in a supermarket': privatization of home care work in Japan. *Work, Employment and Society*, 28 (5), 702–717.

Campbell, J.C. and Ikegami, N., 2000. Long-term care insurance comes to Japan: a major departure for Japan, this new program aims to be a comprehensive solution to the problem of caring for frail older people. *Health Affairs*, 19 (3), 26–39.

Chan, R.K.H., Takahashi, M., and Wang, L.L.-R., 2016. *Risk and Public Policy in East Asia*. London: Routledge.

Collyer, F. and White, K., 2011. The privatisation of Medicare and the National Health Service, and the global marketisation of healthcare systems. *Health Sociology Review*, 20 (3), 238–244.

Daly, M. and Lewis, J., 2000. The concept of social care and the analysis of contemporary welfare states. *British Journal of Sociology*, 51 (2), 281–298.

Dasgupta, S., Matsumoto, M., and Xia, C., 2015. *Women in the Labour Market in China*. Geneva: International Labour Organization.

Ding, J.-D., 2013. The home care service: recognizing mistakes, rational principles and perfecting measures. *Journal of Renmin University of China*, 27 (2), 20–26.

Drakeford, M., 2007. Private welfare. In: M. Powell, ed. *Understanding the Mixed Economy of Welfare*. Bristol: Policy Press, 61–82.

Feng, Z., Glinskaya, E., Chen, H., Gong, S., Qiu, Y., Xu, J., and Yip, W., 2020. Long-term care system for older adults in China: policy landscape, challenges, and future prospects. *The Lancet*, 396 (10259), 1362–1372.

Forder, J. and Allan, S., 2014. The impact of competition on quality and prices in the English care homes market. *Journal of Health Economics*, 34 (1), 73–83.

Forder, J., Knapp, M., and Wistow, G., 1996. Competition in the mixed economy of care. *Journal of Social Policy*, 25 (2), 201–221.

Fu, R., Noguchi, H., Kawamura, A., Takahashi, H., and Tamiya, N., 2017. Spillover effect of Japanese long-term care insurance as an employment promotion policy for family caregivers. *Journal of Health Economics*, 56, 103–112.

Glendinning, C., 2012. Home care in England: markets in the context of under-funding. *Health and Social Care in the Community*, 20 (3), 292–299.

Greener, I., 2008. Markets in the public sector: when do they work, and what do we do when they don't? *Policy and Politics*, 36 (1), 93–108.

Greener, J., 2015. Embedded neglect, entrenched abuse: market failure and mistreatment in elderly residential care. *Social Policy Review 27: Analysis and Debate in Social Policy*, 149–313.

Hill, M., 2007. The mixed economy of welfare: a comparative perspective. In: M. Powell, ed. *Understanding the Mixed Economy of Welfare*. Bristol: Policy Press, 177–198.

Ho, K. and Lee, R.S., 2017. Insurer competition in health care markets. *Econometrica*, 85 (2), 379–417.

Hong Kong Government, 1999. LCQ18: Dependent parent or grandparent allowances. www.info.gov.hk/gia/general/199906/16/0616128.htm

Hong Kong Government, 2000. Deduction for elderly residential care expenses. www .gov.hk/en/residents/taxes/salaries/allowances/deductions/elderly.htm

Housing and Development Board of Singapore, 2021. Living with/near parents or child. www .hdb .gov .sg/ residential/ buying -a -flat/ resale/ financing/ cpf -housing -grants/ living-with-near-parents-or-child

Hu, B., Li, B., Wang, J., and Shi, C., 2020. Home and community care for older people in urban China: receipt of services and sources of payment. *Health and Social Care in the Community*, 28 (1), 225–235.

Izuhara, M., 2003. Social inequality under a new social contract: long-term care in Japan. *Social Policy and Administration*, 37 (4), 395–410.

Jeon, B. and Kwon, S., 2017. Health and long-term care systems for older people in the Republic of Korea: policy challenges and lessons. *Health Systems and Reform*, 3 (3), 214–223.

Jia, M., Zhou, Y., and Lin, J., 2016. The privatisation and the unbalanced spatial development of residential care for the elderly: the case of Beijing, China. *Applied Spatial Analysis and Policy*, 11 (1), 59–80.

Kanaya, N., Takahashi, H., and Shen, J., 2015. The market share of nonprofit and for-profit organizations in the quasi-market: Japan's long-term care services market. *Annals of Public and Cooperative Economics*, 86 (2), 245–266.

Kurimoto, A. and Kumakura, Y., 2016. Emergence and evolution of co-operatives for elderly care in Japan. *International Review of Sociology*, 26 (1), 48–68.

Kwon, S., 2009. The introduction of long-term care insurance in South Korea. *Eurohealth*, 15 (1), 28–29.

Le Grand, J., 1991. Quasi-markets and social policy. *The Economic Journal*, 101 (408), 1256–1267.

Le Grand, J. and Bartlett, W., 1993. *Quasi-Markets and Social Policy*. London: Macmillan International Higher Education.

Lewis, J. and West, A., 2014. Re-shaping social care services for older people in England: policy development and the problem of achieving 'good care'. *Journal of Social Policy*, 43 (1), 1–18.

Lowrie, A. and Hemsley-Brown, J., 2011. This thing called marketisation. *Journal of Marketing Management*, 27 (11–12), 1081–1086.

Miyazaki, R., 2019. Migrant care workers and care-migration policies: a comparison between Italy and Japan. *Asia Europe Journal*, 17 (2), 161–177.

Ng, K.-H., 2011. Review essay: prospects for old-age income security in Hong Kong and Singapore. *Journal of Population Ageing*, 4 (4), 271–293.

Nyssens, M., Picchi, S., and Simonazzi, A., 2012. The process of marketisation in home care and its consequence on welfare mix: a comparative analysis. 2nd International Conference on Evidence-Based Policy in Long-Term Care, London.

Ochiai, E., 2009. Care diamonds and welfare regimes in East and South-East Asian societies: bridging family and welfare sociology. *International Journal of Japanese Sociology*, 18 (1), 60–78.

Pavolini, E. and Ranci, C., 2008. Restructuring the welfare state: reforms in long-term care in Western European countries. *Journal of European Social Policy*, 18 (3), 246–259.

Peng, I., 2012. Social and political economy of care in Japan and South Korea. *International Journal of Sociology and Social Policy*, 32 (11/12), 636–649.

Peng, I., 2018. Culture, institution and diverse approaches to care and care work in East Asia. *Current Sociology*, 66 (4), 643–659.

Peng, I. and Yeandle, S., 2017. Eldercare policies in East Asia and Europe: mapping policy changes and variations and their implications. *UN Women*, 19, 1–76.

Petersen, O.H., Hjelmar, U., and Vrangbæk, K., 2018. Is contracting out of public services still the great panacea? A systematic review of studies on economic and quality effects from 2000 to 2014. *Social Policy and Administration*, 52 (1), 130–157.

Powell, M., 2007. The mixed economy of welfare and the social division of welfare. In: *Understanding the Mixed Economy of Welfare*. Bristol: Policy Press, 1–22.

Shanghai Municipal Government, 2016. *Implementation Advice on the Construction of Care Institutions for Older People in the 13th Five-Year Plan Period in Shanghai.* Shanghai.

Shen, S.Y., Li, F., and Tanui, J.K., 2014. Long-term care insurance in China: public or private? *Social Work in Health Care*, 53 (7), 679–692.

Shimizutani, S., 2014. The future of long-term care in Japan. *Asia-Pacific Review*, 21 (1), 88–119.

Shimizutani, S. and Suzuki, W., 2007. Quality and efficiency of home help elderly care in Japan: Evidence from micro-level data. *Journal of the Japanese and International Economies*, 21 (2), 287–301.

Shutes, I. and Chiatti, C., 2012. Migrant labour and the marketisation of care for older people: the employment of migrant care workers by families and service providers. *Journal of European Social Policy*, 22 (4), 392–405.

Soma, N., Yamashita, J., and Chan, R.K.H., 2011. Comparative framework for care regime analysis in East Asia. *Journal of Comparative Social Welfare*, 27 (2), 111–121.

Tamiya, N., Noguchi, H., Nishi, A., Reich, M.R., Ikegami, N., Hashimoto, H., Shibuya, K., Kawachi, I., and Campbell, J.C., 2011. Population ageing and wellbeing: lessons from Japan's long-term care insurance policy. *The Lancet*, 378 (9797), 1183–1192.

Ungerson, C., 1999. Personal assistants and disabled people: an examination of a hybrid form of work and care. *Work, Employment and Society*, 13 (4), 583–600.

Ungerson, C. and Yeandle, S., 2007. *Cash for Care in Developed Welfare States.* New York: Palgrave.

United Nations, 2017. *World Fertility Report 2015 – Highlights.*

Williams, F. and Brennan, D., 2012. Care, markets and migration in a globalising world: introduction to the special issue. *Journal of European Social Policy*, 22 (4), 355–362.

Woolham, J., Daly, G., Sparks, T., Ritters, K., and Steils, N., 2017. Do direct payments improve outcomes for older people who receive social care? Differences in outcome between people aged 75+ who have a managed personal budget or a direct payment. *Ageing and Society*, 37 (5), 961–984.

World Bank, 2021. DataBank. https://databank.worldbank.org/home.aspx

Xu, A. and Xia, Y., 2014. The changes in mainland Chinese families during the social transition: a critical analysis. *Journal of Comparative Family Studies*, 45 (1), 31–53.

Yamane, S., 2019. Formal-care work under the Japanese quasi-market: towards a care-friendly gender regime. In: J. Liu and J. Yamashita, eds. *Routledge Handbook of East Asian Gender Studies*. London: Routledge, 169–184.

Yamashita, J., Soma, N., and Chan, R.K.H., 2013. Re-examining family-centred care arrangements in East Asia. In: M. Izuhara, ed. *Handbook on East Asian Social Policy*. Cheltenham, UK and Northampton, MA, USA: Edward Elgar Publishing, 472–490.

Zhang, W., 2018. *Home Care for Older People in Urban China*. Bristol: University of Bristol.

Zhang, W., 2022. Market-oriented policies on care for older people in urban China: examining the experiment-based policy implementation process. *Journal of Social Policy*, 51 (2), 284–302.

9 Gendered responsibility of multigenerational care: examining 'defamilialisation' policies in family-centred welfare regimes in East Asia

Junko Yamashita and Naoko Soma

Introduction

Demographically, the segment of the population that is called on to respond to both the demands of childcare and elderly care is increasing. A growing proportion of women experience childbirth much later than before, which has led to the mean age of women at first birth reaching 30 years old among Organisation for Economic Co-operation and Development (OECD) countries in 2019, 4.5 years older than that in 1995 (OECD, 2021). It is the highest in South Korea (henceforth Korea) at 31.6 years old (OECD, 2021). This trend of childbirth at a later age is creating a crossover period in their life-course when they provide both childcare and elderly care (Yamashita and Soma, 2015; Soma et al., 2020). That is, for example, when their parents become 75 years old and the probability of needing to be cared for significantly increases, their children are still of primary school age or younger.

This is an emerging yet under-researched social and demographic phenomenon. A large body of literature on intergenerational care, care policy or family sociology exists. However, it tends to focus on one type of intergenerational caring relationship, i.e., adult children and parents or parents and children, with some exceptions that examine sandwich generations which will be reviewed in the next section. This trend is also observed in the development of policy fields, such as family policies for childcare and long-term care policies related to elderly care. The underlying assumption behind this perception of intergenerational caring relationships as being between two generations is that people engage with childcare and elderly care at different periods of their life-course and with varying matters of concern (Song, 2014). Childcare is for people in their 20s, 30s and 40s, and key themes concern work–life balance and parenting (motherhood and fatherhood). On the other hand, elderly care is for people in their 50s and 60s and key themes are informal caring, family obligation, financial and health issues and quality of care. By placing the multigenerational carers at the centre of the analysis, our research connects childcare and elderly care and provides a holistic approach to investigating caring relationships and practices beyond dyadic relations.

This chapter examines the impacts of recent policy reforms on the care responsibilities of women who provide both childcare and elderly care, what we term 'multigenerational care', in East Asian societies. Drawing on considerable and comparative evidence from Hong Kong, Japan, Korea and Taiwan, it reveals that there are significant differences among women's experiences of multigenerational care. Our findings suggest that recent generous care policy reforms have not clearly relieved the sense of responsibility that multigenerational carers feel, especially in Japan and Korea. We critically review the discussion on defamilialisation approaches in comparative welfare regime studies and provide insight into why the expansion of state roles in financing and arranging care provision has not lessened women's responsibility for care.

East Asian societies are excellent cases for examining social policy interventions and the gendered responsibility of care. Under the demographic pressure of ageing populations and low fertility rates, East Asian governments have been implementing policy reforms in the last two to three decades that aim to redress the family responsibility to provide both financial and care support to older people and children. This has resulted in a shift in the care arrangements of each society, moving from a heavily family-centred one to one in which a larger part of care responsibility is shared across the state, the market, the community/voluntary sector and family (see, for example, Yamashita et al., 2013). Yet East Asian societies appear to maintain gendered social institutions and relations that reinforce the family household as the locus of care (Shire and Nemoto, 2020; Song, 2020; Yamane, 2020). Thus, investigating multigenerational care is timely and crucial for understanding the effect of recent care policy reforms on the gendered responsibility of caregiving in East Asia.

In the first part of this chapter, we provide an overview of multigenerational caregiving and relations in Europe and East Asia. Then, the concept of defamilialisation is discussed as a theoretical approach to analysing recent policy reform effects on women's sense of care responsibility in the second section. After a brief explanation of the methodology for the collection and analysis of the primary data that we have generated on multigenerational carers in the third section, we discuss our findings with a focus on why women in Japan and

Korea, where defamilialisation policies have been recently implemented, feel a heavier burden when providing multigenerational care. In the concluding discussion, we argue that the defamilialisation policies have a limited impact on the gendered division of care when implemented without intervening in unjust gender relations.

Multigenerational care

'Sandwich generation' is a term that incorporates multigenerational caring relationships. The sandwich generation refers to a middle generation, typically of women, who are caught 'in the middle' of two generations who require their care. The existing studies on the sandwich generation in European societies argue that multigenerational care is more challenging than dyadic caring as multiple difficulties and conflicts need to be negotiated (Mitchell, 2014; O'Sullivan, 2015; Suh, 2016; Halinski et al., 2018; Zelezna, 2018). Fingerman et al. (2010) and Grundy and Henretta (2006) state that assisting one family member does not decrease the responsibility of supporting other family members, and care responsibilities tend to keep accumulating for those who already provide care. These have an adverse impact on carer wellbeing (Boyczuk and Fletcher, 2016; Gillett and Crisp, 2017). Multiple challenges and difficulties include responding to different types of care (Halinski et al., 2018), roles as mother and daughter clashing (Steiner and Fletcher, 2017), feeling squeezed and pulled as time is constrained (Rubin and White-Means, 2009; Mitchell, 2014), experiencing limited and exhausted resources (Mitchell, 2014; Boyczuk and Fletcher, 2016) and coping with changes in relationships (Daatland et al., 2010; Steiner and Fletcher, 2017). In short, multigenerational carers are squeezed and pulled between the simultaneous and accumulating demands of caring for elderly parents and children. The literature suggests that in European societies, intergenerational support typically flows down the generations (Fingerman et al., 2010; Suh, 2016), but if parents or parents-in-law have a disability or illness, then more support is likely to be provided to them (Fingerman et al., 2010; Zelezna, 2018).

Studies on multigenerational care in East Asian societies also discuss the difficulties and complexities that multigenerational care involves (Song, 2014; Baek et al., 2018; Chan and Wong, 2018; Tan, 2018; Soma et al., 2020; Song, 2020; Yamashita and Soma, 2020), and suggest that women generally view caring for young children as their priority (Song, 2014; Tan, 2018). However, differentiated experiences of multigenerational care in East Asian contexts from those in European ones are also discussed, specifically in relation to a sense of obligation to elderly care, namely filial piety. Tan (2018) argues that in East Asian societies where expectations of filial piety are high, financial and care support are more likely to be involuntary and the product of social pressure. Tan (2018) thus claims that this sense of obligation may explain the lower life and marital satisfaction among married women who provide both elderly and childcare. Song (2014) reveals the ambivalence that multigenerational carers feel when prioritising either elderly care or childcare. The ambivalent feelings become most stressful when they provide elderly care based on the sense of obligation even though they wish to prioritise childcare (Song, 2014). Yamashita and Soma (2020) argue that women who provide multigenerational care experience structured difficulties derived from conflicting norms of filial obligation, gendered division of work and strong expectations for mothers to shoulder the sole responsibility of taking care of children. The literature suggests that the tension with prioritising between childcare and elderly care is higher in East Asian societies where filial piety is practised. It was noted that in Japan, the caring relationships have seen a dramatic shift from daughter-in-law to daughter as the primary carer in the last two decades (Yamashita and Soma, 2020). This shift is also under way in Korea (Song, 2014). Despite these changes in caring relationships, filial piety remains influential as a frame of normative reference when providing elderly care in the region (Song, 2014).

The analysis of these existing studies on multigenerational care and carers in European and East Asian societies reveals a number of difficulties and challenges that women experience providing this care. Yet few studies have attempted to explore how social policy, especially care policy, might influence this experience. This chapter is one of the first attempts to examine the impact of care policy on multigenerational carers' sense of responsibility for providing care.

Welfare regimes and the arrangement of care: the concept of defamiliarisation and gendered division of care

How care is arranged in each society differentiates people's experience of providing and receiving care. Earlier studies documented that social policy is a critical factor that matters for the arrangement of both elderly and childcare, along with other socio-economic and political factors, including social norms and institutions shaping gender and intergenerational relations (e.g., Bettio and Plantenga, 2004; Kalmijn and Saraceno, 2008; Chan et al., 2011; Lohmann and Zagel, 2016; Kurowska, 2018). The arrangement of care is also linked to the (in)equality nature of gender relations (Ungerson, 1987; Fraser, 1994; Gornick and Meyers, 2008; Orloff, 2009).

The welfare regime literature from feminist perspectives provides ample theoretical and empirical knowledge on the links between social policy and gender relations. The defamilialisation concept has been developed as a key concept to examine how countries respond to the issues of financial and care dependencies between family members (Lister, 1990; Orloff, 1993; Leitner, 2003; Saraceno and Keck, 2010; Saxonberg, 2013; Kurowska, 2018; Zagel and Lohmann, 2021). Though the definition varies among scholars (Lohmann and Zagel, 2016), we can loosely define defamilialisation as a degree of support (often statutory support) of individual independence from family relationships in sustaining a standard of living, especially with receiving and providing care and financial support. Discussions on its conceptual development now span more than three decades. The concept of defamilialisation is still considered one of the most useful tools for analysing and comparing welfare states' role in forming family relationships of responsibility and dependence (Lohmann and Zagel, 2016; Saraceno, 2016; Kurowska, 2018). The current debate centres around how to appropriately measure defamilialisation and to what extent defamilialisation policy interrelates with gender relations. In this section, we first discuss the development of the defamilialisation concept and then consider the effects of defamilialisation on gender relations with care.

The defamilialisation concept was originally developed by feminist social policy scholars in the critical examination of Esping-Andersen's (1990) analysis of welfare regimes and its key analytical concept of decommodification (see, for example, Lister, 1990; Lewis, 1992; Orloff, 1993; McLaughlin and Glendinning, 1994). The concept of defamilialisation was proposed to capture both economic independence from family relationships (Lister, 1990) and independence from familial care responsibility (McLaughlin and Glendinning, 1994). Later, Esping-Andersen (1999) incorporated the concept of defamilialisation into his welfare regime theory but limited the concept to the dimension of economic independence from family relationships and employment. In more recent years, various scholars criticised this narrowing focus of the defamilialisaiton approach to the labour market. Although the analytical scopes vary, they use the defamilialisation concept to examine financial and/ or care dependencies among family members in different welfare regimes. For example, whereas Leitner (2003) solely focuses on the influence of social policy on family caring functions, others propose to examine family functions in terms of both care and income provisions (Saraceno, 2016; Kurowska, 2018; Zagel and Lohmann, 2021). Lohmann and Zagel (2016: 52) define defamilialising policies as 'welfare state provision (social policies and regulations) that reduce care and financial responsibilities and dependencies between family members'. Kurowska (2018: 33–34) suggests a more detailed definition, proposing two angles to assess social policy from defamilialisation perspectives: (1) the extent to which the welfare of the dependent individuals in the family such as children or elderly people is supported by the state; and (2) the extent to which the state reduces the burden of traditional kinship/family obligations, including care, and the provision of income, goods or services.

The main debating point on the defamilialisation approach lies in its analytical power on social policy roles in maintaining or transforming the existing gender relations. Even though the defamilialisation concept was originally developed to assess social policy impacts on gender relations in different welfare regimes, scholars increasingly argue that defamilialisation policies do not directly lead to a reduction in gender inequality (Ferragina et al., 2013; Saxonberg, 2013; Kurowska, 2018). Ciccia and Sainsbury (2018) state that the effects of defamilialisation should be carefully assessed against the feminist assumptions regarding the liberating effects of unravelling care work from women's unpaid domestic work. Kurowska (2018: 36) argues that 'gender roles clearly intersect with, but are not necessarily tantamount to defamilialisation'. Mathieu (2016) argues that to 'genderise' the comparative analysis of welfare states, the analytical focus should shift from the effect of social policy on the caring responsibilities of families to the caring responsibilities of mothers, as the distribution of care responsibility between the state, market and families will not affect the caring responsibility of women. Chybalski and Marcinkiewicz (2021) further claim that the defamilialisation concept is gender blind.

To capture gendered impacts of defamilialisation, Leitner (2003) differentiates between two types of defamilialisation with and without intervention in gender relations: 'gendered familialism' and 'degendered familialism'. Focusing on how defamilialisation recognises and intervenes in gendered responsibility of care, Saraceno and Keck (2008: 8) also argue that:

> the familisation–defamilisation dichotomy must, therefore, be articulated at two levels: one that concerns the degree to which norms and policies shape and acknowledge the degree and duration of family interdependencies; the other that concerns the way these norms and policies take for granted incentive or disincentive gender specific behaviours with regard to these same responsibilities.

We argue that the defamilialisation concept can be a valuable framework to analyse social policy interventions in family responsibilities of care. However, following the recent debate on the limits of this approach to analyse policy impacts on gender relations, our analysis pays close attention to what extent the defamilialisation policies that have been recently implemented in East Asian societies intervene in the existing gender relations with regard to care responsibilities. We now discuss the arrangement of care among East Asian welfare regimes and examine the recent care policy reforms.

The expansion of elderly and childcare provision in family-centred welfare regimes in East Asia

A family-centred welfare regime has been considered one of the main characteristics of East Asian welfare regimes since the early stage of the debates on whether there is such a model as an 'East Asian welfare regime' (Goodman et al., 1998; Miyamoto et al., 2003). The expectation of the state on family to play the key, and often solo, role of financing care and providing unpaid care was higher than the European counterparts. This expectation was addressed and embedded in the social policy frameworks through, for example, limited public spending on social care in all East Asian societies, and spousal tax deductions to encourage women to provide unpaid familial care in Japan (Yamashita et al., 2013). A developmental state and strong familialism in East Asia were two sides of the same coin. East Asian governments could concentrate on economic development because the family provided key welfare provisions and social protection (Yamashita et al., 2013). However, since the 1990s, along with the acute demographic trends of ageing populations and low fertility rates, there has been a policy shift for the government to take more financial responsibility for, and expand statutory roles in, the organisation of care for the elderly and children (e.g., Chan et al., 2011; Ochiai, 2013).

Several studies examined how these social policy reforms impacted the arrangement of care by adopting either a care regime or a 'care diamond' approach (Razavi, 2007; Ochiai, 2009; Soma et al., 2011; Ochiai, 2013). Both care regime and care diamond approaches capture how responsibility for financing and providing care is distributed by the state, the market, the family and the voluntary/community sector. This literature concluded that the care arrangements of East Asian societies have altered: from the concentration of family provision and finance of care to their distribution to other sectors (Ochiai, 2009; Chan et al., 2011; Yamashita et al., 2013). For example, Yamashita et al. (2013) state that, while other sectors have increased their contribution, the family is still the most important provider of care services and finance. Since 2000, family and long-term care policy reforms have further developed and diversified in East Asia: Korea, Taiwan and Japan have implemented generous care policy reforms in comparison to their European counterparts, but Hong

Kong sustained care responsibility as a private family responsibility and has continued the family-centred welfare regime. In terms of policy characteristics and outcomes, these care policy reforms implemented in the former societies are categorised as defamilialisation policies. An overview of these recent care policy reforms is provided below.

The Long-Term Care (LTC) insurance schemes that provide publicly funded elderly care services were implemented in 2000 in Japan and in 2008 in Korea. Taiwan implemented the Long-Term Care Services Act in 2017. The main aim of these LTC policies is to take the elderly care responsibilities from the family (defamilialisation), but also there are financial imperatives to control the health-care cost for older people (Yamashita, 2011; Kojima, 2018; Peng, 2018; Yamane, 2020). Since these policy implementations, the public spending per gross domestic product on long-term care has dramatically increased. According to Estévez-Abe and Naldini's (2016) calculation, between 2000 and 2013 Japan increased the coverage rate of publicly funded LTC ten times. Although the coverage rate is lower than the OECD average, Korea increased it 20 times. In Taiwan, with the new Long-Term Care Services Act 2017, the coverage of public care services has been dramatically increased (Kojima, 2021). However, in the regions where the average household income is higher than the national average, foreign domestic workers remain the most popular choice for families (Kojima, 2021), which is a distinctive difference between the Taiwan arrangement and that of Korea and Japan.

Childcare and support services have seen a drastic expansion in all these three East Asian societies to tackle the low fertility rate (Shimoebisu, 2015; Hong, 2020). In Japan, between 2000 and 2014, the enrolment rate of formal childcare increased from 5.5 to 11.4 per cent for children up to 12 months old and from 19.3 to 35.1 per cent for one–two year olds. Korea's formal childcare enrolment rate increased threefold between 2000 and 2010 and is well over the OECD average (Estévez-Abe and Naldini, 2016). In both Korea and Japan, preschool childcare has become publicly funded. Free public care provision is available for all preschool children in Korea. In Japan, although our data were generated before the major policy shift, it covers all three–five year olds and additionally for those in low-income households for zero–two year olds from October 2019. Taiwan also expanded childcare and support services, but the public/free childcare is limited to five year olds, and more focus is placed on offering community support services to mothers (Isobe et al., 2017). The use of domestic childcare workers, such as babysitters and childminders, is more common in Taiwan than in Korea and Japan. In short, the state responsibility of providing and financing both elderly and childcare has been expanded for Korea, Japan and Taiwan. The recent policy reforms on childcare have defamilialised a part of family dependence on financing and providing childcare. In contrast, Hong Kong firmly maintained elderly care as a private family responsibility. Instead of introducing public-funded social care, tax incentives and policy measures have been made to help families purchase care in the market, especially to hire migrant domestic workers (Peng, 2018). This private family responsibility also extends to childcare since little child benefit or parental leave is offered.

In sum, the care policy reforms in the last decade, both elderly care and child-care in Korea and Taiwan and childcare in Japan, significantly expanded the publicly funded care provision. Both policy aims and outcomes suggest that defamilialisation policies have been implemented in three former societies. We now look at how these defamilialisation policies have impacted women's experience and responsibility for providing multigenerational care.

Methodology

To illustrate the experience of multigenerational care that women have, we draw in the following sections on quantitative and qualitative data from our project 'Comparative Analysis of Care Regimes and Responsibility of Dual Care of Child Care and Elderly Care in East Asia' (Yamashita and Soma, 2016). This international and comparative project was designed to understand the contemporary practice and the experience of multigenerational care and how they are being shaped by and are shaping related social policy in the four East Asian societies of Hong Kong, Japan, Korea and Taiwan. The project was carried out using various research methods, including focus groups and semi-structured interviews, workshops, peer support sessions and both paper-based and online questionnaire surveys with purposive and random sampling between 2013 and 2018.

The analysis of this chapter is based on questionnaire surveys conducted during 2013 and 2014 in the above four societies.[1] The questionnaire contains the same questions for a comparative analysis and additional society-specific questions for each society written in Japanese, Korean or Chinese. The common questions include the frequency and kinds of care multigenerational carers provide, to whom they provide care, kinds of care service they use, their feelings about

---

[1]   Thus, the introduction of free childcare for three–five year olds and addition-ally for those in low-income households for zero–two year olds in Japan, and Taiwan's expansion of long-term care provision since 2017, are not reflected in these data.

providing multigenerational care, and familial and non-familial support they receive while providing this care. The questionnaire was distributed through childcare-related institutions, including nurseries, kindergartens, children's centres and community centres in Hong Kong, Japan and Taiwan. In Korea, the questionnaire was conducted via a website. Purposive sampling was carried out to collect the data from women who had at least one child under ten years old. The samples for the analysis of this chapter are only those participants who identified themselves as having provided or who are currently providing both childcare and elderly care, based on a broad definition of care introduced at the beginning of the questionnaire. It includes the physical side of care, the instrumental side of care (e.g., shopping and cleaning), the emotional side of care (e.g., regular visits or phone conversations) and the management side of care (communication with doctors and care professionals, arrangement of care services). The sample size of each society was as follows: Hong Kong (n = 588), Japan (n = 352), Korea (n = 556) and Taiwan (n = 306).

Results

To our knowledge, this is the first project to generate valuable data on multigenerational caring on such a scale. In this section, we mainly present the results of multigenerational carers' use of care services, and their feelings about providing care. We first provide the key descriptive result of multigenerational carers' profiles and their engagement with multigenerational care. More detailed results are presented by Soma et al. (2020). The discussion in the following section will focus on the theme of the sense of responsibility that multigenerational carers feel.

Age distributions: Multigenerational carers are likely to be in their 30s or 40s with a child/children aged between zero to five years old, and their parents and parents-in-law are in their 60s (and 70s in Japan) who require some level of support for their daily life.

Employment: on average, the two largest proportions of respondents were full-time employees (39.7 per cent) and housewives who are not employed (39.7 per cent), followed by part-time employees (14.4 per cent), self-employed (3.7 per cent) and others (2.4 per cent). Our data cannot tell if those respondents who are full-time housewives have left their job due to caring responsibilities or if they are on parental leave. For Korea, the regular employees (44.4 per cent) and full-time housewives (40.9 per cent) are the two majority groups. For Hong Kong, full-time housewives are the highest (47.3 per cent), followed by regular employees (36.2 per cent). Taiwan has the highest percentage of full-time employees (62.4 per cent) and significantly less full-time housewives (23.8 per cent). In Japan, the proportion of full-time housewives (40.1 per cent) is the highest, and that of non-regular workers is comparatively higher than in other societies and is the second-highest proportion.

Living arrangements: Around 10–15 per cent of multigenerational carers live with their parents across the societies. The figure is significantly higher for those who live with parents-in-law in Hong Kong and Taiwan and slightly higher in Japan than for those who live with their parents. In Korea, the proportions of co-residence with parents and parents-in-law are lower: around 10 per cent. Taiwan has the highest proportion of carers who live with their father-in-law (28.6 per cent) and mother-in-law (35 per cent).

Household income: The result indicates that the participants' household income is concentrated in the middle-income groups. In Korea and Japan, the participants' household monthly income centres around the national average annual household income. In Hong Kong, the household incomes range widely and in Taiwan, the participants are distributed relatively towards the lower household income groups than in other societies.

What multigenerational care do women provide?

Our samples consist of those who provide or have provided multigenerational care. Among them, 77.7 per cent are currently facing multigenerational care, and 22.3 per cent have provided multigenerational care in the past.

Looking at the levels and types of involvement with multigenerational caring, 'help parents and parents-in-law when they need help' and 'mental support such as listening to them' are the types of care that around half of multigenerational carers provide and for both parents and parents-in-law. In addition, across societies, higher percentages of women provide support or care to female parents than males. Apart from these two types, there are variations among societies in what care multigenerational carers provide. In Japan and Korea, being the primary carer for mothers and mothers-in-law is significantly higher than in other societies. A higher percentage of Korean multigenerational carers provide regular support to their older parents and parents-in-law. Financial assistance is high in Hong Kong and Korea, and only for mothers and mothers-in-law in Taiwan. Japan has a significantly lower proportion of multigenerational carers who provide financial support to their parents and parents-in-law. In Japan and Korea, because older people in need of care tend to use publicly funded care services available under the long-term care insurance system, the carers are often involved in care management, such as liaising with care providers and specialists. Also, a higher percentage of multi-generational carers are not involved with elderly care, apart from their mother, in both Japan and Korea.

Which care services do they use for multigenerational care?

We now look at the care services that multigenerational carers use, first elderly care and then childcare services (Table 9.1). Both in Hong Kong and Taiwan, domestic workers and domiciliary care services are the major services: in Hong Kong, domestic workers are used by 25.3 per cent, and domiciliary care services are used by 15.4 per cent, and in Taiwan 10.8 and 11.1 per cent, respectively.[2] On the other hand, in Korea and Japan, various services are used under the long-term care insurance schemes, including day-care services, domiciliary help services, leasing of welfare equipment and others.

Table 9.1   The usage of elderly care services

	Korea	Hong Kong	Taiwan	Japan
Domiciliary care services	11.2%	15.4%	11.1%	11.4%
Home-visit bathing care	3.9%			4.0%
Home nursing service	8.6%	1.9%	2.1%	5.1%
In-home rehabilitation	3.9%			2.8%
Day-care services	38.8%	3.0%	1.0%	12.2%
Day-care services (outpatient rehabilitation)	13.8%	0.9%		4.5%
Day-care services (nursing and medical care)			8.5%	
Short-term residential care/short stay	6.0%	0.3%		4.3%
Leasing of welfare equipment and purchase allowance	25.0%	4.5%	6.9%	7.1%
Instructional care services	6.9%	4.9%	6.2%˙	4.5%

---

[2]   As discussed earlier, Taiwan's expansion of long-term care provision since 2017 is not reflected in these data.

	Korea	Hong Kong	Taiwan	Japan
Domestic care workers	0%	25.3%	10.8%	0%
Other	16.4%	1.4%	0.7%	2.6%

Note: *The sum of Nursing homes (1.3%) and Long-term care centre (4.9%). The government now defines both centres as long-term care institutions.

The composition of childcare services usage differs from that of elderly care. Across all societies, most multigenerational carers use either or both nurseries and kindergartens (Table 9.2). Kindergartens usually provide a shorter time of childcare and are often more focused on children's education. In Japan and Hong Kong, children's centres are also accessed. In Hong Kong and Taiwan, similar to elderly care but in a much lower proportion, respondents have childcare provided by domestic workers. In Korea and Hong Kong, the percentage of grandparenting and nurseries at home are proportionally higher than in other societies.

Table 9.2 Usage of childcare services

	Korea	Hong Kong	Taiwan	Japan	Total
Nursery school	65.5%	40.0%	51.7%	33.1%	45.1%
Temporary nursery school care	1.7%	7.2%	0.0%	8.8%	5.2%
Kindergarten	31.5%	58.8%	60.7%	31.2%	48.6%
Local childcare support centre	5.2%	19.2%	0.0%	22.4%	13.6%
After-school care	0.0%	0.5%	1.3%	18.6%	4.7%
Care by mother without using services/help	6.9%	6.7%	2.3%	0.6%	4.5%
Grandparents' care	4.3%	3.1%	0.0%	0.3%	2.0%
Domestic worker	0.4%	6.0%	6.7%	0.0%	3.9%
Other	2.6%	3.1%	34.3%	7.3%	10.5%
Total (n)	232	582	300	317	1,431

How do women feel about providing multigenerational care?

Looking at the sense of burden caused by multigenerational care (Figure 9.1), 64.4 per cent of the respondents feel burdened ('burdened' and 'somewhat burdened') with providing multigenerational care. However, there is variation across societies: Japan has the highest percentage of carers who feel burdened (87.5 per cent), closely followed by Korea (75.4 per cent), while the numbers are relatively lower in Taiwan (56.9 per cent) and Hong Kong (56.7 per cent). In Hong Kong and Taiwan, just above 43 per cent do not feel too burdened ('not burdened' and 'somewhat not burdened').

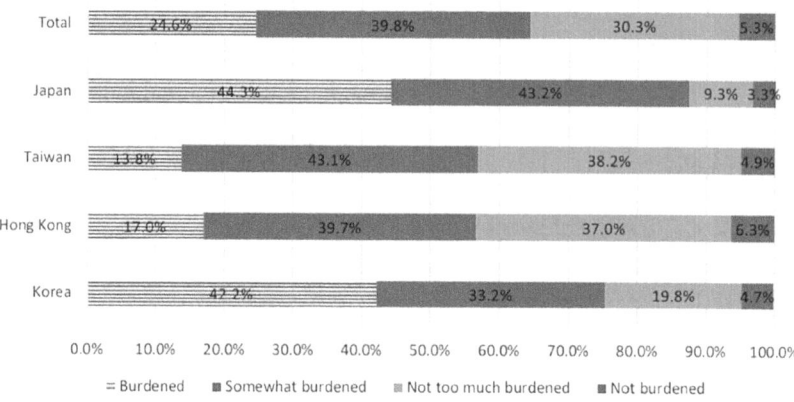

Figure 9.1   Feeling burdened from providing multigenerational care

Table 9.3 shows the specific burdens that multigenerational carers feel. Difficulties they face again vary. Cross-Societally, more than half of respondents feel mentally, physically and economically burdened and feel that they cannot provide sufficient care for their children. Looking at each society, carers in Hong Kong feel less physically burdened (46.4 per cent) than those in other societies. Korean carers feel the economic burdens most (69.2 per cent), as do carers in Taiwan (64.1 per cent) and Hong Kong (52.4 per cent), while Japanese carers feel less so (42.3 per cent), but they feel the most mentally burdened (73.5 per cent). Variations are observed in other areas too. Multigenerational carers in Korea feel less burdened about not being able to provide sufficient care to parents or parents-in-law (28 per cent), in comparison to 52.3 per cent in Taiwan, 49.6 per cent in Japan and 44.1 per cent in Hong Kong. Long-distance care was felt to be difficult by a relatively higher proportion of carers in Taiwan (28.8 per cent) and Hong Kong (28.4 per cent). Both in

Korea and Japan, carers feel a shortage of childcare facilities and services: 35.5 and 31.8 per cent, respectively, in comparison with 20.5 per cent in Hong Kong and 17.6 per cent in Taiwan. Korea rates significantly higher in the shortage of elderly care services, four times as much as Hong Kong: 25.6 per cent in Korea, 15.2 per cent in Japan, 10.5 per cent in Taiwan and 6.4 per cent in Hong Kong. These are especially interesting results, considering that Korea and Japan provide a more generous range and volume of publicly funded childcare and elderly care. At the same time, in Hong Kong, where publicly funded care is less available than in these two societies, the highest proportion of respondents (10.2 per cent) do not feel any burden.

Table 9.3   What multigenerational carers feel burdened about when providing care

	Korea	Hong Kong	Taiwan	Japan	Total
Cannot care for parents/ parents-in-law sufficiently	28.0%	44.1%	52.3%	49.6%	44.8%
Cannot care for children sufficiently	43.1%	50.9%	50.0%	55.7%	50.7%
Financially burdened	69.2%	52.4%	64.1%	42.3%	54.9%
Physically burdened	60.2%	46.4%	63.4%	62.7%	55.9%
Mentally burdened	65.4%	41.6%	62.7%	73.5%	57.2%
Long-distance care	17.1%	28.4%	28.8%	23.3%	25.6%
Gaps in the perception of care needs among siblings and relatives	25.1%	21.7%	21.6%	35.9%	25.6%
Lack of partner understanding	17.1%	16.0%	12.1%	21.6%	16.7%
Lack of childcare services	35.5%	20.5%	17.6%	31.8%	24.8%
Lack of long-term care services	25.6%	6.4%	10.5%	15.2%	12.2%
Don't feel any burden	2.8%	10.2%	6.2%	3.5%	6.7%
Others	2.4%	2.1%	2.6%	11.4%	4.4%
Total (n)	211	580	306	343	1,440

In addition, our project adjusted a care burden scale, Zarit Burden Interview (ZBI), to multigenerational care and used it to measure the stress and burden felt by multigenerational carers. ZBI is a widely applied instrument to measure the level of burden experienced by caregivers (see, for example, Bédard et al.,

2001). As shown in Figure 9.2, Korean carers' sense of burden is the highest in all questions. Japanese carers follow Koreans closely with the question regarding feeling stressed, having no time for oneself, feeling unable to control one's own life and experiencing a negative impact on relationships with family and friends. The levels of burden that carers in Hong Kong and Taiwan feel are similar to each other, and generally they feel less stressed or burdened about providing multigenerational care. They feel significantly less about being unable to control their own life, the negative impact of multigenerational caring on their family and friends' relationships. Adopting the defamilialisation approach, we will discuss these differences in carers' sense of burden and responsibilities when providing multigenerational care in the next concluding section.

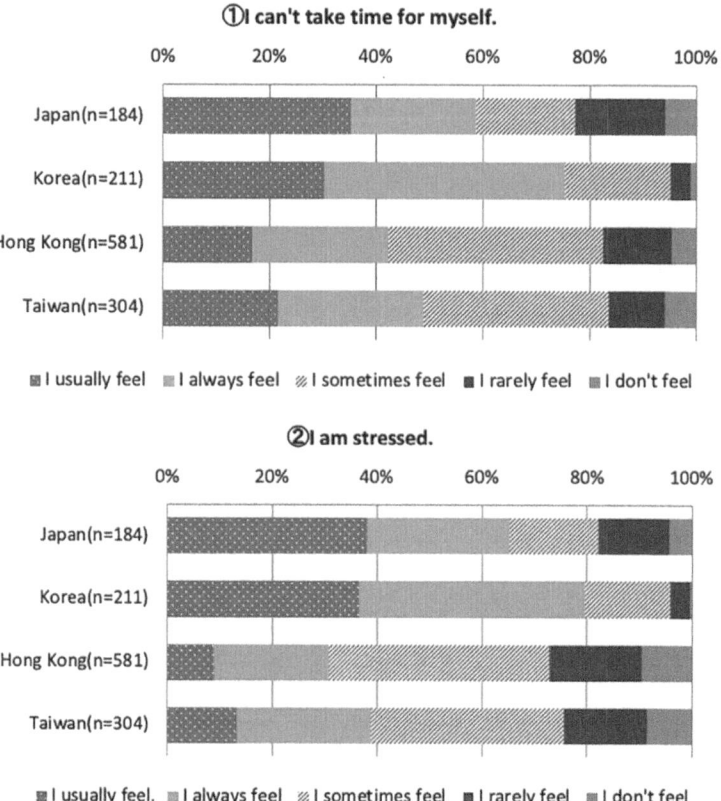

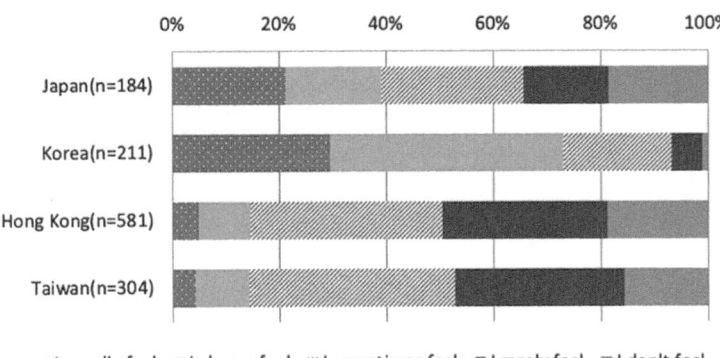

③Family and friendships are affected.

■ I usually feel   ■ I always feel   ▨ I sometimes feel   ■ I rarely feel   ■ I don't feel

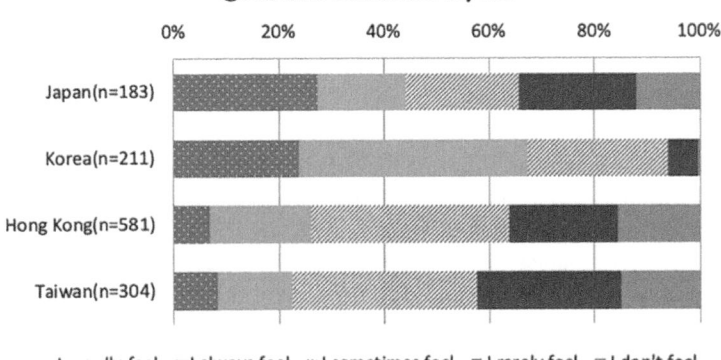

④I have no control over my life.

▨ I usually feel.   ■ I always feel   ▨ I sometimes feel   ■ I rarely feel   ■ I don't feel

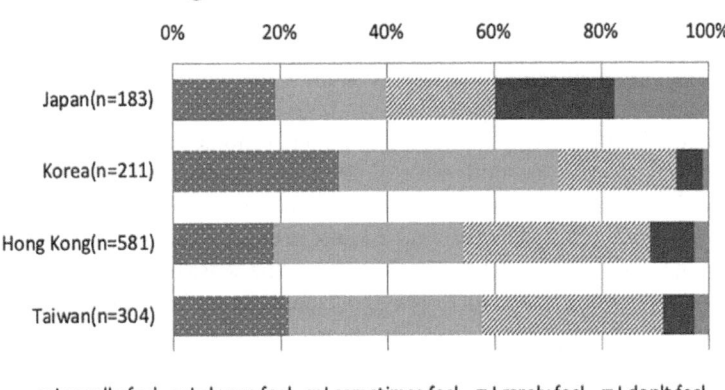

⑤We need to do more for our children.

■ I usually feel   ■ I always feel   ▨ I sometimes feel   ■ I rarely feel   ■ I don't feel

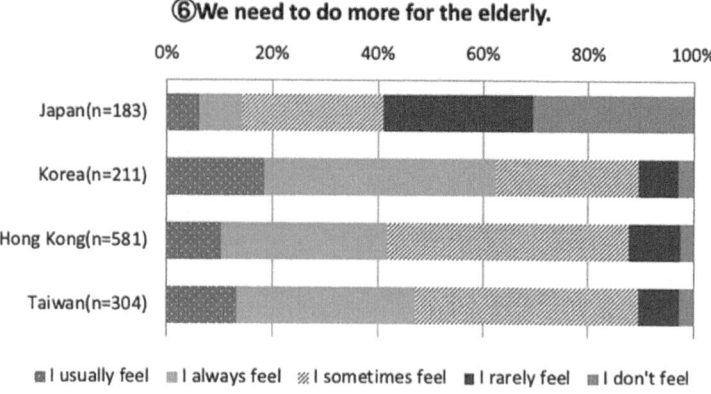

⑥We need to do more for the elderly.

■ I usually feel   ■ I always feel   ▨ I sometimes feel   ■ I rarely feel   ■ I don't feel

Figure 9.2   Types of stress that multigenerational carers feel

Concluding discussion

In this concluding section, adopting the defamilialisation approach, we analyse our key findings: why multigenerational carers in Japan and Korea feel a greater sense of burden than those in Hong Kong and Taiwan. We argue that defamilialisation policies in Japan and Korea sustained a family as the main provider of care services. It reduced some parts of the family responsibility of care, as apparent in the outcomes, but at the same time the implementation process of the defamilialisation policies sustained the family responsibility of care. The gendered care responsibilities in these societies have consequently been maintained even after the implementation of defamilialisation policies.

Our research reveals that care policy reforms based on defamilialisation in Korea and Japan appear not to have a positive impact on reducing women's sense of responsibility in providing multigenerational care. Overall, most women feel burdened with providing multigenerational care across four societies. However, there are noticeable differences in the proportions of women who feel burdened with providing the care: a higher group in Japan (87.5 per cent) and Korea (75.4 per cent) and a lower group in Taiwan (56.9 per cent) and Hong Kong (56.7 per cent). In other words, the sense of burden was shared more widely among those in Korea and Japan, where both publicly funded childcare and elderly care services have been expanded – the defamilialisation policies have been implemented – than in Hong Kong and Taiwan, where the private 'purchase' of domestic workers is one of the key care services. As discussed earlier, recent care policy reforms in Japan, Korea and Taiwan are categorised as defamilialisation policies in terms of both their policy aims and outcomes. However, our analysis shows that despite implementing defamilialisation policies in both child and elderly care, women's sense of responsibility for providing care has not reduced. Other studies point out the sustained gendered division of care in Japan and Korea (e.g., Hong, 2020; Kan et al., 2022). For example, Kan et al.'s (2022) comprehensive analysis of time use surveys reveals that, between 1986 and 2016, gender gaps in both paid and unpaid work were particularly large in Japan and Korea in comparison to all other countries in Esping-Andersen's (1990) three welfare regimes as well as Taiwan and China (Beijing). They argue that policies which rely on families as a key source of care provision, including those of Southern European countries, Japan and Korea, prevent women from increasing labour market work and reducing their share of domestic labour (Kan et al., 2022).

Reasons for women continuing to overwhelmingly take multigenerational care responsibilities centre around sustained familialism and gendered division of care even under the implementation of defamilialisation policies. In other words, defamilialisation policies were implemented along with keeping the normative position of the family, more precisely women, as the main provider of unpaid care. This paradoxical policy framework that promotes 'de-familialisation of care' with sustaining a gendered and family-centred approach to care has been discussed by other scholars. For example, Song (2020) argues that Korean care policy has rapidly expanded and developed towards defamilialisation since 2000, but they consistently emphasised family responsibility and forced women to carry out care roles through the formation and operation of social policies. For instance, even though publicly funded childcare was dramatically increased, the investment in childcare infrastructure was limited. Instead, the childcare was provided via the market, mainly by private companies without rigid regulations and systematic monitoring of care quality. The Korean government has failed to reform the private sector-centred care system itself (Soma, 2014). This has resulted in a substantial number of cases of child maltreatment in day nurseries which caused distrust of publicly funded childcare services among parents (Song and Baek, 2020). The low quality of childcare made parents take back their responsibility to finance and provide childcare. Parents' choices are either by mothers withdrawing from their job, hiring a domestic care worker or relying on their own mothers (Song and Baek, 2020). Our results also indicate that Korean multigenerational carers feel the shortage of childcare facilities and services (35.5 per cent): the highest among the four societies (Table 9.3). The public long-term care insurance services have also been dramatically expanded in Korea. However, the limited provision of public care services grew market options, such as hiring migrant co-ethnic care workers in the informal care service market (Estévez-Abe and Naldini, 2016; Hong and Han, 2017; Song, 2020). Consequently, family responsibility of care is sustained, and gendered division of care is reproduced with lower-class, migrant care workers or older women filling the unmet care needs.

Both Korea and Japan have rapidly increased publicly funded childcare due to the declining birth rate. However, in contrast to Korea, where defamilialising childcare has become the policy agenda by addressing the expansion of 'public childcare', it has never become so in Japan. In Japan, the government has never addressed the defamilialisation of childcare. Successive administrations have repeatedly discussed the importance of measures to tackle declining birth rates. Nonetheless, family policy has been politically positioned as a 'domain of women and children' and less prioritised than other main policy fields of pensions and medical care. In addition, under the unstable government and its family-oriented political ideology, the ruling party has lacked the will and ability to develop a systematic family policy (Soma and Yamashita, 2020b: 42). The development of the long-term care policy was different from the family policy, as the Japanese Long-Term Care Insurance Act clearly addresses its aim of taking family responsibility in financing and providing care for older family members; it was framed as a defamilialisation policy, what Japan terms 'social-isation of care'. However, due to the financial sustainability of the scheme, the coverage of care services has been narrowed, and the eligibility tightened, resulting in shifting the responsibility of care back to the family from the state (Fujisaki, 2013; Shimoebisu, 2015). For instance, the requirements for admission to a special nursing home include not only the person's circumstances but also the presence or absence of a carer and living conditions; if a family member living with the person can provide care, the person is considered to have a low level of care need (Shimoebisu, 2015).

Shire and Nemoto (2020) argue that in Japan, the family as the locus of care is sustained even when states finance market or public care services. They claim that family policy 'reinforced the family household as the locus of care, and reinforced the role of wives, mothers, and in eldercare, daughters, as those who provide for young and elderly family members' (Shire and Nemoto, 2020: 443). They define Japan among conservative gender regimes that 'constitute the domestic as a public sphere and transform through social and family policies, which reinforce a gendered division of labour' (Shire and Nemoto, 2020: 432). The centrality of domesticity in the process of implementing defamilialisation policies is also discussed by Yamane (2020), who examines the impact of the formalisation of elderly care work on gender relations in Japan. The defamil-ialisation of long-term care by the long-term care insurance implementation supported the increase of female employment, especially paid care work. However, Yamane (2020) argues that formal care work is regarded as an extension of informal care so that the formalisation of care work did not fully contribute to the shift in gender relations in Japan. Song and Baek (2020) argue that when defamilialisation policies are implemented without intervening in the injustice of gendered division of care work within the family household as well as men and companies' free riding of unpaid care, these policies do not take care responsibility from women. The maloperation of defamilialisation policies even contributes to reproducing the injustice and enlarging the disparity among women between those who can afford to purchase care services or rely on older family members' provision of care and those who cannot (Song and Baek, 2020).

The centrality of family and the gendered division of care in the policy and wider welfare regime in these societies can explain that the higher percentage of women in Korea and Japan find providing multigenerational care more difficult than those in Hong Kong and Taiwan. In addition, Korean and Japanese cases offer empirical evidence that defamilialisation policies without intervening in gendered distribution of care work will have the limited effect of taking care of familial responsibility of both child and elderly care and lessening the gendered division of care. Our findings also provide critical insight into the operationalisation of the defamilialisation concept. In addition to the analysis of the policy characteristics and outcomes, we argue that the comparative analysis of defamilialisation policy needs to integrate the socio-political contexts. Without such an approach, childcare and elderly care in Korea and Japan can be mistakenly considered as being defamilialised.

This chapter sheds light on women's experience of the emerging phenomenon of multigenerational care. Our research revealed that across four societies, multigenerational carers feel the burden of providing both elderly and childcare. However, there are notable differences across these societies. We developed our account on the difference between multigenerational carers' experience in Korea and Japan – where so-called defamilialisation policies are implemented – and those in Hong Kong and Taiwan – where the domestic worker is a key care service. We concluded that the position of gender in macro welfare and social systems reduces the effect of defamilialisation policies. Researching the sustaining normative roles of family in policy and the broader social and political regime remains key to understanding policy reforms on the gendered distribution of care work. This chapter is the first of these efforts to understand gendered policy impacts on care responsibility in East Asian societies. The analysis of multigenerational care enables researchers to explore the comprehensive picture of gendered care arrangements.

Acknowledgements

The authors would like to acknowledge the support of those who participated in our research and of our research project team, Song Dayoung, Raymond K.H. Chan, Han Songhua, Kate Yeong-Tsyr Wang, for providing the survey data.

This research was funded by the Japan Society for the Promotion of Science Grant-in-Aid for Scientific Research B, 'Comparative Analysis on Care Regime on Double Care Burden of Elderly and Child Care in East Asia' (24310192), 'Intergenerational Gender Comparative Analysis of Double Care Responsibility: towards Inclusive Community Care System' (16H03326), funded by the Center for Economic and Social Studies in Asia, Faculty of Economics, Yokohama National University.

References

Baek, K., Dayoung, S. and Jang, S. (2018) 'Unjust inter-generational re-distribution of care responsibility in the context of double care'. *Journal of Korean Women's Studies*, 34 (2): 33–69 (in Korean).

Bédard, M., William Molloy, D., Squire, L., Dubois, S., Leve, J.A. and O'Donnell, M. (2001) 'The Zarit Burden interview: A new short version and screening version'. *The Gerontologist*, 41 (5): 652–657.

Bettio, F. and Plantenga, J. (2004) 'Comparing care regimes in Europe'. *Feminist Economics*, 10 (1): 85–113.

Boyczuk, A.M. and Fletcher, P.C. (2016) 'The ebbs and flows: Stresses of sandwich generation caregivers'. *Journal of Adult Development*, 23 (1): 51–61.

Chan, R.K.H. and Wong, P.Y.K. (2018) 'The double burden of care in Hong Kong: Implications for care policies and arrangements'. In *Gender, Care and Migration in East Asia*, edited by R. Ogawa, R.K.H. Chan, A.S. Oishi and L.-R. Wang, 25–45. Singapore: Springer.

Chan, R.K.H., Soma, N. and Yamashita, J. (2011) 'Care regimes and responses: East Asian experiences compared'. *Journal of Comparative Social Welfare*, 27 (2): 175–186.

Chybalski, F. and Marcinkiewicz, E. (2021) 'Incorporating pro-family and pro-female components into empirical welfare state classification: Some new evidence for European countries'. *Innovation*, 34 (3): 399–421.

Ciccia, R. and Sainsbury, D. (2018) 'Gendering welfare state analysis: Tensions between care and paid work'. *European Journal of Politics and Gender*, 1: 93–109.

Daatland, S.O., Veenstra, M. and Lima, I.A. (2010) 'Norwegian sandwiches: On the prevalence and consequences of family and work role squeezes over the life course'. *European Journal of Ageing*, 7 (4): 271–281.

Esping-Andersen, G. (1990) *The Three Worlds of Welfare Capitalism*. Princeton, NJ: Princeton University Press.

Esping-Andersen, G. (1999) *Social Foundations of Postindustrial Economics*. Oxford: Oxford University Press.

Estévez-Abe, M. and Naldini, M. (2016) 'Politics of defamilialization: A comparison of Italy, Japan, Korea and Spain'. *Journal of European Social Policy*, 26 (4): 327–343.

Ferragina, E., Seeleib-Kaiser, M. and Tomlinson, M. (2013) 'Unemployment protection and family policy at the turn of the 21st century: A dynamic approach to welfare regime theory'. *Social Policy and Administration*, 47 (7): 783–805.

Fingerman, K.L., Pitzer, L.M., Wai, C., Birditt, K., Franks, M.M. and Zarit, S. (2010) 'Who gets what and why? Help middle-aged adults provide to parents and grows children'. *Journal of Gerontology: Social Sciences*, 66 (1): 87–98.

Fraser, N. (1994) 'After the family wage: Gender equity and the welfare state'. *Political Theory*, 22 (4): 591–618.

Fujisaki, H. (2013) 'Kea seisakuga zenteito suru kazoku moderu' (Family model presumed by care policies: Child-rearing and elderly care after the 1970s in Japan). *Japanese Sociological Review*, 64 (4): 604–624 (in Japanese).

Gillett, J.E. and Crisp, D.A. (2017) 'Examining coping style and the relationship between stress and subjective well-being in Australia's "sandwich generation"'. *Australasian Journal on Ageing*, 36 (3): 222–227.

Goodman, R., White, G. and Kwon, H.-j. (1998) *The East Asian Welfare Model*. London: Routledge.

Gornick, J.C. and Meyers, M.K. (2008) 'Creating gender egalitarian societies: An agenda for reform'. *Politics and Society*, 36 (3): 313–349.

Grundy, E. and Henretta, J.C. (2006) 'Between elderly parents and adult children: A new look at the intergenerational care provided by the "sandwich generation"'. *Ageing and Society*, 26 (5): 707–722.

Halinski, M., Duxbury, L. and Higgins, C. (2018) 'Working while caring for mom, dad, and junior too: Exploring the impact of employees' caregiving situation on demands, control, and perceived stress'. *Journal of Family Issues*, 39 (12): 3248–3275.

Hong, S.-A. (2020) 'Gendered politics of work–life balance in South Korea'. In *Routledge Handbook of East Asian Gender Studies*, edited by J. Liu and J. Yamashita, 185–196. Abingdon: Routledge.

Hong, S.-L. and Han, C.-K. (2017) 'A multi-dimensional analysis on care regime of foreign care workers in South Korea'. *Asia Pacific Journal of Social Work and Development*, 27 (3–4): 159–173.

Isobe, K., Goto, T. and Kikuchi, M. (2017) 'Taiwan ni okeru syoshika to kosodateshienseisaku' (Declining birthrate and family policy in Taiwan). *Osaka Sangyo University Journal of Economics*, 18 (2): 23–44 (in Japanese).

Kalmijn, M. and Saraceno, C. (2008) 'A comparative perspective on intergenerational support: Responsiveness to parental needs in individualistic and familialistic countries'. *European Societies*, 10 (3): 479–508.

Kan, M-Y., Zhou, M., Kolpashnikova, K., Hertog, E., Yoda, S. and Jun, J. (2022) 'Revisiting the gender revolution: Time on paid work, domestic work, and total work in East Asian and Western societies 1985–2016'. *Gender and Society*, 36 (3): 368–396.

Kojima, K. (2018) 'Taiwan no syakaihosyou (dai 3 kai) taiwan no koureisyakaigohoken nituite' (Social security in Taiwan (3) Taiwan long-term care system for the elderly). *Journal of Social Security Research*, 2 (4): 595–598 (in Japanese).

Kojima, K. (2021) 'Higashi ajia ni okeru kaigosya shien wo meguru jyokyo: taiwan wo reini' (Family caregiver support policy in East Asia: From Taiwan LTC policy). *Journal of Social Security Research*, 6 (1): 75–89 (in Japanese).

Kurowska, A. (2018) '(De)familialization and (de)genderization: Competing or complementary perspectives in comparative policy analysis?'. *Social Policy and Administration*, 52 (1): 29–49.

Leitner, S. (2003) 'Varieties of familialism: The caring function of the family in comparative perspective'. *European Societies*, 5 (4): 353–375.

Lewis, J. (1992) 'Gender and the development of welfare regimes'. *Journal of European Social Policy*, 2 (3): 159–173.

Lister, R. (1990) 'Women, economic dependency and citizenship'. *Journal of Social Policy*, 19 (4): 445–467.

Lohmann, H. and Zagel, H. (2016) 'Family policy in comparative perspective: The concepts and measurement of familization and defamilization'. *Journal of European Social Policy*, 26 (1): 48–65.

Mathieu, S. (2016) 'From the defamilialization to the "demotherization" of care work'. *Social Politics: International Studies in Gender, State and Society*, 23 (4): 576–591.

McLaughlin, E. and Glendinning, C. (1994) 'Principles and practice of social security payments for care'. *International Social Security Review*, 47 (3–4): 137–155.

Mitchell, B.A. (2014) 'Generational juggling acts in midlife families: Gendered and ethnocultural intersections'. *Journal of Women and Aging*, 26 (4): 332–350.

Miyamoto, T., Peng, I. and Uzuhashi, T. (2003) 'Nihongata fukushi kokka no ichi to dotai' (The position and dynamics of a Japan-type welfare state). In *Welfare States in Transition*, edited by G. Esping-Andersen, 295–336. Tokyo: Waseda University Press.

O'Sullivan, A. (2015) 'Pulled from all sides: The sandwich generation at work'. *Work*, 50 (3): 491–494.

Ochiai, E. (2009) 'Care diamonds and welfare regimes in East and South-East Asian societies: Bridging family and welfare sociology'. *International Journal of Japanese Sociology*, 1 (18): 60–78.

Ochiai, E. (2013) 'Introduction: Intimate work and the construction of Asian women'. In *Asian Women and Intimate Work*, edited by E. Ochiai and K. Aoyama, 1–34. Leiden: Brill.

OECD. (2021) Family database. www.oecd.org/els/family/database.htm

Orloff, A.S. (1993) 'Gender and the social rights of citizenship: The comparative analysis of gender relations and welfare states'. *American Sociological Review*, 58 (3): 303–328.

Orloff, A.S. (2009) 'Gendering the comparative analysis of welfare states: An unfinished agenda'. *Sociological Theory*, 27 (3): 317–343.

Peng, I. (2018) 'Shaping and reshaping care and migration in East and Southeast Asia'. *Critical Sociology*, 44 (7–8): 1117–1132.

Razavi, S. (2007) 'The political and social economy of care in a development context: Conceptual issues, research questions and policy options'. *Gender and Development Programme Paper*, 3 (June). Geneva: UNRISD.

Rubin, R.M. and White-Means, S.I. (2009) 'Informal caregiving: Dilemmas of sandwiched caregivers'. *Journal of Family and Economic Issues*, 30 (3): 252–267.

Saraceno, C. (2016) 'Varieties of familialism: Comparing four southern European and East Asian welfare regimes'. *Journal of European Social Policy*, 26 (4): 314–326.

Saraceno, C. and Keck, W. (2008) 'The institutional framework of intergenerational family obligations in Europe: A conceptual and methodological overview'. *Multilinks Project, WP1*. Berlin: WZB Social Science Research Center.

Saraceno, C. and Keck, W. (2010) 'Can we identify intergenerational policy regimes in Europe?', *European Societies*, 12 (5): 675–696.

Saxonberg, S. (2013) 'From defamilialization to degenderization: Toward a new welfare typology'. *Social Policy and Administration*, 47 (1): 26–49.

Shimoebisu, M. (2015) 'Kea seisaku ni okeru kazoku no ichi' (Position of the family in care policies). *Japanese Journal of Family Sociology*, 27 (1): 49–60 (in Japanese).

Shire, K.A. and Nemoto, K. (2020) 'The origins and transformations of conservative gender regimes in Germany and Japan'. *Social Politics*, 27 (3): 432–448.

Soma, N. (2014) 'Nikkan Hikaku kara Kangaeru Kosodate Hoiku Seisaku: Kankokuno Jirei wo Chushin ni' (Childcare policies from a comparative perspective of Japan and Korea: Focusing on the case of Korea). *Women's Labor Studies*, 58: 61–77 (in Japanese).

Soma, N. and Yamashita, J. (2020a) 'Double responsibilities and burdens of elderly care and grandchild care among middle–old-aged women in Japan from the perspective of institutional injustice', *Ohara Institute for Social Research*, 737: 1–16 (in Japanese).

Soma, N. and Yamashita J. (2020b) Don't manage it alone: Dual responsibility of child care and elderly care, Tokyo: Popurashinsho (in Japanese).

Soma, N., Yamashita, J. and Chan, R.K.H. (2011) 'Comparative framework for care regime in East Asia'. *Journal of Comparative Social Welfare*, 27 (2): 111–121.

Soma, N., Han, S., Yamashita, J., Chan, R.K.H., Song, D. and Wang, K.Y.T. (2020) 'Higashi Ajia niokeru Syakaiteki Risuku tositeno Daburu Kea' (Double responsibility of care as new social risk in East Asia). *Journal of Ohara Institute for Social Research*, 736: 3–41 (in Japanese).

Song, D. (2014) 'A study on double-care and multiplicity of caring experiences among women aged 30s to 40s in Korea'. *Korean Journal of Social Welfare*, 66 (3): 209–230 (in Korean).

Song, D. (2020) 'Family transitions and family policy in South Korea'. In *Routledge Handbook of East Asian Gender Studies*, edited by J. Liu and J. Yamashita, 236–252. Abingdon: Routledge.

Song, D. and Baek, K. (2020) 'Double burdens of elderly care and grandchild care among middle–old-aged women in Korea from the perspective of institutional injustice'. *Journal of Ohara Institute for Social Research*, 737: 17–32 (in Japanese).

Steiner, A.M. and Fletcher, P.C. (2017) 'Sandwich generation caregiving: A complex and dynamic role'. *Journal of Adult Development*, 24 (2): 133–143.

Suh, J. (2016) 'Measuring the "sandwich": Care for children and adults in the American time use survey 2003–2012'. *Journal of Family and Economic Issues*, 37 (2): 197–211.

Tan, P.L. (2018) 'Dual burdens of care: "Sandwiched couples" in East Asia'. *Journal of Aging and Health*, 30 (10): 1574–1594.

Ungerson, C. (1987) *Policy Is Personal: Sex, Gender, and Informal Care*. London: Tavistock Publications.

Yamane, S. (2020) 'Formal-care work under the Japanese quasi-market'. In *Routledge Handbook of East Asian Gender Studies*, edited by J. Liu and J. Yamashita, 169–184. Abingdon: Routledge.

Yamashita, J. (2011) 'Exploring the impact of the Japanese Long-Term Care Insurance Act on the gendered stratification of the care labour market through an analysis of the domiciliary care provided by welfare non-profit organisations'. *Social Policy and Society*, 10 (4): 433–443.

Yamashita, J. and Soma, N. (2015) 'The double responsibilities of care in Japan: Emerging new social risks for women providing both childcare and care for the elderly'. In *New Life Courses, Social Risks and Social Policy in East Asia*, edited by R.K.H. Chan, J. Zinn and L.-R. Wang, 95–112. London: Routledge.

Yamashita, J. and Soma, N. (2016) 'The dual responsibilities of care in Japan: Emerging new social risks for women providing both childcare and care for the elderly'. In *New Life Course, Social Risks and Social Policy in East Asia*, edited by K.H.C. Raymond, J. Zinn and L.-R. Wang, 95–111. London: Routledge.

Yamashita, J. and Soma, N. (2020) 'Daburu Kea to kouzouteki Anbibarensu' (Dual responsibility of care and structured ambivalence). *Ohara Institute for Social Research, Hosei University*, 737: 1–16 (in Japanese).

Yamashita, J., Soma, N. and Chan, R.K.H. (2013) 'Re-examining family-centred care arrangements in East Asia'. In *Handbook on East Asian Social Policy*, edited by M. Izuhara, 472–490. Cheltenham, UK and Northampton, MA, USA: Edward Elgar Publishing.

Zagel, H. and Lohmann, H. (2021) 'Conceptualising state–market–family relationships in comparative research: A conceptual goodness view on defamilization'. *Journal of Social Policy*, 50 (4): 852–870.

Zelezna, L. (2018) 'Care-giving to grandchildren and elderly parents: Role conflict or family solidarity?' *Ageing and Society*, 38 (5): 974–994.

10 Challenging the universal healthcare systems in Southeast Asia: COVID-19 crisis management in Indonesia and the Philippines

Huck-Ju Kwon, Ye Eun Ha, Kyungchul Yang, Seongyeon Park, and Sodam Yi

Introduction: the COVID-19 pandemic and public healthcare systems

Since cases of unusual illness with pneumonia-like symptoms were first recognized in Wuhan, China in late 2019, the infectious disease, now known as COVID-19, has spread around the world and caused one of the most serious pandemics in recent history. The COVID-19 pandemic has affected most countries in the world, both affluent and developing countries. The United States (US), France, Spain, and the United Kingdom (UK), as well as India, Brazil, and Russia are among the hardest-hit countries. By July 2021, more than 185 million people had contracted the coronavirus, resulting in 4 million deaths (WHO, 2021). While the US and UK began to resume normal life in summer 2021 with strong government drives for vaccination, many developing countries are still struggling to cope with the viral pandemic.

The aim of this chapter is to analyze contrasting policy responses to the health crisis caused by the COVID-19 pandemic in developing countries in Southeast Asia – Indonesia and the Philippines. In particular, it will examine the effectiveness of the public healthcare systems in the context of health crisis management in the two countries. The two countries have put universal health coverage into operation since the 2010s, which can be considered a great achievement. Indonesia and the Philippines, among other Southeast Asian countries, have responded to internal demands and international recommendations for universal health coverage (WHO, 2010). Despite the 1997 Asian Financial Crisis and the 2008 Global Financial Crisis, both societies, still considered as developing countries by the Organisation for Economic Co-operation and Development/Development Assistance Committee, were able to establish universal health coverage. It could also be seen as an important breakthrough in the development of the welfare systems in Southeast Asia since social policies in the region have been 'selective' and 'fragmented' in terms of protecting the population against social risks (Kwon and Kim, 2015; Ramesh, 2004), while East Asian societies such as South Korea and Taiwan have become more 'inclusive' with a series of reforms since the 1990s (Kwon, 2005).

Nevertheless, it is one thing to extend healthcare coverage to the whole population and it is another to deliver necessary healthcare to people in need (Bredenkamp et al., 2015). There has been a series of criticisms that the public healthcare systems in the two countries were not able to deliver health services that were affordable and accessible to everyone as expected under universal health coverage (Grundy et al., 2003; Rosser, 2012). For this reason, it is necessary to assess whether the healthcare system with universal coverage can deliver health services to people in need. The COVID-19 pandemic provides us with a unique opportunity to test the public healthcare systems in the two countries in terms of their capability of delivering services as well as the institutional structure of public healthcare systems including coverage and service package. In particular, an analysis of the healthcare system in the context of a crisis management system will enable us to identify the weaknesses as well as strengths of the public healthcare systems in a holistic manner, especially in the context of working with other public institutions such as local governments, emergency agencies, and private actors. Such analysis will also enable us to assess whether changes in the welfare systems such as universal health coverage have signified a genuine shift in the welfare regimes so that Indonesia and the Philippines have become more inclusive, moving closer to the welfare regimes in the more affluent societies in Northeast Asia (Kwon, 2005).

In order to examine the public healthcare systems in Indonesia and the Philippines in response to the COVID-19 pandemic, this chapter will adopt a perspective of crisis management, which considers a public healthcare system as part of the wider governance structure of crisis management. In the next section, the chapter will elaborate on the analytical framework of crisis management in which cognition, coordination, and capacity will be identified as core components of crisis management. In the following sections, it will analyze the public healthcare systems in Indonesia and the Philippines from the perspective of crisis management during the first year of the COVID-19 pandemic. It concludes with an attempt to identify the strengths and weaknesses of the public healthcare systems with universal coverage manifested in the context of the COVID-19 pandemic and elicit policy recommendations for strengthening universal health coverage. It will also discuss whether the universal health coverage in the two countries amounts to a significant shift in their welfare regimes and implications for the East and Southeast Asian welfare geography.

Crisis management system: cognition, coordination, and capacity

Despite measures to contain viral transmission, most developing countries have weak institutional capacities and insufficient resources to respond effectively to the spread of the virus. Weak public healthcare systems and a lack of medical experts, facilities, and equipment hinder effective responses to the spread of diseases and accessibility to medical treatment for those infected. It is not only a public healthcare system but also a crisis management system that should be mobilized together to deal with significant health contingencies like the COVID-19 pandemic.

In order to analyze crisis management systems, it is necessary to understand their components. What are the vital components of the crisis management system that enable public authorities and agencies to deal with national emergency situations? It is true that there have been different approaches of crisis management developed such as crisis leadership, crisis strategies and preparedness, and crisis governance (Comfort, 1988, 2007; Farazmand, 2007; Waugh, 2018). In this chapter, we take a crisis governance approach which enables us to examine how the public healthcare systems work with other public institutions (Farazmand, 2007). In their analysis of the emergency response to Hurricane Katrina in the US, Comfort and Haase (2006) point out that communication is critical to manage complex public responses to disaster situations. Hurricane Katrina destroyed the communication infrastructure in large local areas of New Orleans, Louisiana, and the public authorities were unable to coordinate their efforts due to a communication failure. In a crisis, many public authorities and agencies need to direct their efforts in a concerted manner since a whole range of emergency measures is deployed to cope with situations. Instead of isolated efforts, it is vital to coordinate those efforts to deal with a crisis. As in Hurricane Katrina, the COVID-19 pandemic affected large geographic areas of society, meaning that many different regional and local authorities had to be involved at the same time. Since communication is a means of coordination, coordination cannot be done without communication (Comfort, 2007; Peters, 2013). In this sense, coordination among public authorities and agencies would be the first component of effective crisis management. To facilitate such communication and therefore coordination, national coordination bodies have been established, such as the UK's Civil Contingencies Committee, commonly known as COBRA, to handle issues of national emergency. Its purpose is to coordinate different departments and agencies in response to national emergencies. In Korea, the Central Disaster and Safety Countermeasures Headquarters coordinates efforts of different government agencies. During the early spread of infection, a committee chaired by the prime minister met twice every week with a range of public agency participants attending.

Coordination among implementation agencies is equally important. Pressman and Wildavsky (1984) pointed out the importance of collaboration at a local level when they explained why development policies made at the federal level are often dashed at local levels. In crisis situations at the local level, different authorities and agencies need to work together. For instance, in a situation of large-scale traffic accidents, the police department and the fire department as well as paramedical emergency services are all required to act to deal with the complex demands of the situation. Effective collaboration between these agencies at the local level is crucial to responding to disasters and disruptions.

The second vital component of crisis management is capacity for implementation at the local level (Waugh, 1994). Although coordination of public efforts at the central level is critical, it is implementation at the local level that delivers necessary public measures and services. Regarding the coronavirus pandemic, some countries like Korea implemented test–track–treatment measures very effectively to contain the transmission of the virus. In these efforts, local governments, primary and secondary healthcare centers, and quarantine centers were involved in implementation and had relevant capacities. Each agency should have the necessary resources in terms of material and personnel. Public agencies should have stocks of resources in preparation for emergency situations (Ting, 2003). In the age of globalization with strong international competition, many private firms adopt a just-in-time operation system in which they only maintain the amount of stock necessary for short-term operation in order to prevent a waste of resources and time. Public agencies, due to budget constraints or efficiency reasons, often mimic such practices, maintaining just enough resources for routine daily operation. In the US, personal protective equipment and ventilators, which are regarded as simple primary medical material, were not readily available due to the fact that medical institutions did not have redundant stock for emergencies. To acquire the necessary equipment and facilities in times of crisis, an effective supply chain is necessary among public authorities and agencies. In the context of developing countries, public agencies are often not equipped with adequate resources due to budgetary constraints. Personnel with relevant skills are often lacking in public agencies in many developing countries. Such weak capacities lead to an inability to deal with crisis situations. In this context, it is necessary to assess whether the capacities required to deal with a crisis are in place in developing countries.

The third component of the crisis management system, which has been discussed in the literature, is the cognition of the crisis in advance (Comfort, 2007). In a crisis management system, cognition should come first. Hood (2006) uses the notion of detection to describe the process of information gathering. Cognition is the ability to understand the nature and size of emerging risks based on processing detected information (Comfort, 2007). Regarding natural hazards such as hurricanes, meteorological agencies can forecast such natural events in advance using state-of-the-art monitoring systems. Such forecasts as cognition of coming risks would give public agencies and ordinary citizens critical time for preparation in the wake of large tropical storms like Hurricane Katrina. As for other natural and social emergencies, we do not have sophisticated systems of cognition like the weather forecasting system. Nevertheless, the government needs to gather information in the form of quantitative and qualitative data and should be able to recognize signs of upcoming crisis. In her later work, Comfort proposed a notion of cognition to refer to the capacity to recognize the degree of emerging risk to which a community is exposed (Comfort, 2007). Regarding the spread of viruses such as COVID-19, the detection of viral infection at an earlier stage would provide an opportunity to recognize the coming pandemic and vital time to contain transmission to the wider community. One of the main reasons for Korea's control of the COVID-19 infection was the early detection of transmission at the end of January 2020.

In a nutshell, this chapter assumes that the three components (cognition, coordination, and capacity) are vital for a crisis management system to respond effectively to crisis situations such as the COVID-19 pandemic. Deficiency in these three components would prevent countries from launching effective responses to the crisis. The following sections will examine the crisis management system in Indonesia and the Philippines, respectively, paying special attention to these three components in the crisis management system, including the national crisis coordination bodies and national public healthcare systems.

The crisis management system and public healthcare in Indonesia

In Indonesia, the National Disaster Management Agency is responsible for coordinating national crisis management. The chief of the agency is the Secretary of National Defense, directly reporting to the President. Within the institutional structure, the Steering Committee coordinates efforts to respond to crisis and mobilize resources from the different departments of government. Nine government departments are members of the Steering Committee including the Departments of Finance, Health and Transportation as well as National Defense (OCHA, 2018). The public healthcare system is a crucial part of the national disaster management. As the Indonesia government triggered a national crisis management system after the first case was confirmed, the President issued the Presidential Decree No. 7 to establish a COVID-19 Response Acceleration Task Force (Irawati et al., 2020) which was focused on public health. The following sections will examine policy responses from the three dimensions of crisis management: cognition, coordination, and capacity.

Cognition and coordination

In Indonesia, the government confirmed the first case of COVID-19 on 2 March 2020, which was 10 days before the World Health Organization (WHO) declaration of the pandemic. Considering that the first case was confirmed in December 2019 in China and in late January 2020 in Thailand and Korea, it is not clear whether it was, in fact, the first infection or only the first detection in Indonesia. Considering the fact that most East and Southeast Asian countries have strong economic and social interactions with China, it is highly unlikely that the first detection was the first infection case in Indonesia (De Salazar et al., 2020). This suggests that the Indonesian government failed to recognize the emerging risks of the COVID-19 pandemic early.

Despite earlier decisions not allowing Chinese tourists to enter Indonesia without visas and stopping direct flights from China to Indonesia in February 2020, the Indonesian government did not implement rapid tests for COVID-19 such as polymerase chain reaction (PCR) until March 2020. According to the Global Health Security Index, real-time surveillance and reporting of risks related to the community health crisis were not well established in Indonesia (Global Health Security Index, 2019). It is fair to say that two vital months were lost to contain COVID-19 at an earlier stage (Massola, 2020). The Indonesia government began to implement a range of intervention measures from March 2020, including fast-response teams at airports and border points.

Health protocols to be followed by ordinary citizens were announced, including facial masks covering the nose and mouth. In April 2020, however, all 34 provinces in Indonesia reported confirmed cases of COVID-19 (Irawati et al., 2020). According to the data from the WHO, as of July 2021, the cumulative number of confirmed cases exceeded 2.4 million, and the cumulative death toll exceeded 60,000 (WHO, 2021). In addition, the number of new daily cases was reported as over 38,000 and the deaths per day reached over 1,000 as of July 2021.

In response to the WHO's declaration of the COVID-19 pandemic, the Indonesian government established the COVID-19 Response Acceleration Task Force by presidential decree on 13 March 2020. It was headed by the National Disaster Management Authority with senior officials participating from different ministries of the Indonesian government (Irawati et al., 2020). It was a rather small-scale task force team comprising senior bureaucrats to deal with natural hazards or disruptions on an ordinary scale, but it was not able to deal with an unprecedented scale of crisis like the COVID-19 pandemic. The task force did not have strong authority to coordinate different ministries, nor a wide range of expertise that could counter the challenges of COVID-19 transmission. After a short period of confusion and ineffectiveness, a large-scale COVID-19 Response Acceleration Task Force was relaunched with most government ministers, including the Ministers of Finance, Health, Home Affairs, and Defense, together with other relevant ministers. In the newly extended task force, all governors of provinces in Indonesia were also invited to participate.

The central government asked all provincial governments to establish regional COVID-19 handling task forces at the local level (Irawati et al., 2020: 213). Coordination of public responses to the COVID-19 pandemic was extended to private and business sectors. The COVID-19 Response Acceleration Task Force invited academics and health experts from universities to provide technical and educational support. Those academics and experts produced simulation models and scenarios of the pandemic's impact as a reference for policy planning and coordination (Fajarta, 2020). It is also worth noting that the media as a vehicle of mass communication played an important role in coordination. The media disseminated the guidelines issued by the task force and information related to the spread of COVID-19 to the community. Through a reinforced structure, the COVID-19 Response Acceleration Task Force was able to coordinate national and regional efforts to deal with the pandemic.

Nevertheless, due to the tepid attitude at the beginning of COVID-19 transmission, the vital period of time to contain transmission was lost. It was not only a mistake by the Indonesian government but also a serious mishandling of the pandemic by the WHO, which failed to give a clear warning to the world. Despite the efforts by the Indonesian Task Force, there were some bad decisions as well. For instance, the police department allowed two-wheeled vehicles to carry passengers during the early stage of the epidemic, but a number of experts criticized such a policy since it was presumed to spread coronavirus rapidly to the community. After controversies and confusion, the government decided to ban two-wheeled vehicles from carrying passengers (CNBC Indonesia, 2020). Decisions such as allowing homecoming for the Eid al-Fitr celebration and two-wheeled vehicles to carry passengers allowed COVID-19 to spread to wider communities. There were also several half-measures including (1) allowing religious activity in mosques and churches; (2) limiting operation hours for public transport but not limiting the capacity of the passengers; (3) allowing working in offices in some cities and provinces, when the average rate of infection is lower than the national average; and (4) opening borders and allowing cross-border travel with recent PCR test results (48 hours prior to departure) but without quarantine procedures. Further, citizens did not have full confidence in the government to comply with public protocols and come forward for testing (Massola, 2020). In a nutshell, the Indonesian government failed to detect the transmission of COVID-19 at the early stage and was unable to contain the crisis despite coordination efforts through the crisis management system due to ill-conceived containment measures.

Capacity to implement public healthcare in the crisis

Actual responses to COVID-19 were undertaken at the ground level through many different public authorities and agencies. At the center of collaboration, there are different public authorities and agencies with mandates for healthcare. In Indonesia, public healthcare falls into the category of concurrent government affairs, in which the authority for public healthcare is distributed at the different levels of central and local governments. In terms of healthcare provision, the Ministry of Health is responsible for the overall supervision and management of public healthcare as well as the tertiary and specialist hospitals. The management of primary and secondary public healthcare facilities is the responsibility of provincial and local governments with a greatly varying degree of capacity. In terms of public healthcare insurance, the Social Security Administration Body (BPJS) is responsible for public health insurance, with ASKES (civil service health insurance) and JAMSOSTEK (health insurance for formal sector workers) being parts of the BPJS structure. Given such a decentralized and fragmented structure of public healthcare in Indonesia, collaboration for implementation was more important than in an integrated system.

To understand policy responses to the COVID-19 pandemic, it is necessary to analyze the development of the public healthcare system up to the current system in operation in Indonesia. Law No. 24 of 2011 was a landmark decision in the development of healthcare policy in Indonesia (Aspinall, 2014). Based on the law, Indonesia began striving to establish a public healthcare insurance system that aims to provide universal healthcare coverage for the whole population.

Before Law No. 24 of 2011, public healthcare insurance was a fragmented system unevenly covering people in different job categories and across regions. Regarding public health insurance, formal sector workers, which accounted for about 15 percent of the workforce in Indonesia, were insured through JAMSOSTEK, which provided compensation for work-related injuries (Holmemo et al., 2020), while TASEN and ASABRI did the same for public officials and military personnel, respectively. For ordinary citizens, community health centers introduced by the Suharto government in the late 1960s were the primary public healthcare providers, with each center covering about 30,000 persons. The standard of medical care provided through public healthcare institutions was not high, and people with means visited private hospitals and clinics. The overall healthcare system was assessed as fragmented and unequal (ILO and JAMSOSTEK, 2008).

A major healthcare initiative was introduced after the Asian Financial Crisis in 1997, which also brought about democratization through the reform movement. The new constitutional amendment clearly stipulates the social rights of all Indonesian people, and the Presidential Advisory Council presented recommendations including the establishment of the national social security system (Suryahadi et al., 2014). Following such a recommendation, the Megawati government (2001–2004) brought about a healthcare program for poor people, which was part of the Jaringan Pengaman Sosial, social safety net programs to provide income support for low-income households. The following Yudhoyono government (2004–2009) turned it into a central government policy for healthcare in the form of the ASKESKIN program in 2004 and the JAMKESMAS (Suryahadi et al., 2014). With these initiatives, public healthcare policy in Indonesia had two major strands of public insurance based on earning-related contributions and public assistance programs based on subvention from the government. Together with these national programs, local governments introduced health insurance for residents in their regions. Despite the extension of public healthcare insurance throughout the 2000s, 35 percent of Indonesian people were left outside public health insurance or assistance programs.

Nevertheless, the Yudhoyono government did not strongly strive to estab-lish the national social security system as recommended by the Presidential Advisory Council. There was, however, a persistent group of people inside the government, along with outside experts, to achieve universal health coverage. In particular, the National Social Security Working Committee, established under the auspices of President Megawati in 2001, advocated the integration of social security programs into a single trust fund (Wisnu, 2007). Despite strong advocacy, it was not until 2011 that the Indonesian parliament passed the bill integrating different social security programs. Nevertheless, due to strong opposition to the bill, the final legislation included compromise provisions; the existing social security agencies would maintain their autonomy and the inte-gration would be completed in an incremental manner by 2029 (Ha, 2020: 35).

Based on the National Social Security Law, Indonesia established universal health coverage (see Table 10.1). While the national health insurance (Jaminan Kesehatan Nasional (JKN)) is managed by the BPJS, the Penerima Bantuan Iuran within the JKN is for poor households and is fully subsidized by the gov-ernment, a program developed from JAMKESMAS. Health insurance coverage has been expanded over the years since 2014. Nevertheless, 83 percent of the population was covered by 2019, and the government aimed to meet the goal of universal healthcare (Holmemo et al., 2020). Among 224 million insured, 60 percent were covered by a subsidized program for the poor through the Penerima Bantuan Iuran (Holmemo et al., 2020).

At the core of the collaboration for responding to COVID-19 were public healthcare institutions. It is important for healthcare institutions to have institutional capacity and resources to deal with the crisis. Apart from regu-lating people's daily lives to prevent the spread of the virus, implementing the 'three Ts' healthcare policy (test, trace, and treatment) was the main initial response to COVID-19. Public healthcare services increased testing using new innovations such as large-scale rapid diagnosis centers and drive-through tests (Cabinet Secretariat, 2020). Nevertheless, Indonesia was only able to carry out 76,000 tests per million people in March 2021, which ranks very low in global standings at 158th of 222 countries and territories. Among those who were tested, 15 to 25 percent were found to be positive depending on the test center, but these figures were very high compared to the WHO guidelines, which suggests that the Indonesian government could not effectively control the spread of the virus (De Salazar et al., 2020). One of the reasons for the low testing outcome was that the overall number of medical laboratories was small and the majority of them were in the private sector: 1,056 laboratories were in the private sector (81.7 percent), while 206 laboratories were under the district and/or city government (15.9 percent) and 27 under the provincial govern-

Table 10.1   Coverage and contribution of social insurance programs in Indonesia

Program		Targeted coverage	Coverage of the eligible	Amount of contribution	Implementing agency
National health insurance	JKN (national health insurance)	268 million people	223 million; 83% (2019)	5% of monthly income (salaried) or IDR42,000–IDR160,000 (non-salaried and non-workers)	BPJS Health
Employment insurance and pensions	JKK (work accident benefit)	120 million people	17.8 million; 15% (2017)	0.24–1.75% of monthly income	BPJS Employment
	JKM (death benefit)			0.3% of monthly income (salaried) or IDR 6,800 (non-salaried)	
	JHT (old-age savings)		15.4 million; 12% (2018)	5.7% of monthly income (salaried) or around 2% (non-salaried)	
	JP (pension)	45 million people	11.8 million; 26% (2018)	3% of monthly income	

Source: Modified from Holmemo et al. (2020).

ment (2.1 percent). These laboratories were also concentrated in DKI Jakarta, West Java, and Central Java. The other reason was that people tended to avoid going forward for testing since they were worried about social stigmatization once confirmed as infected with COVID-19 (Jakarta Post, 2021).

In terms of tracking, the Ministry of Information and Communication launched a mobile application to track movements of patients infected with COVID-19, but there were concerns that the application gathered too much personal information about the patients and possibilities that such personal information could be leaked or hacked (Jakarta Post, 2021). In terms of treatment, more than 200 hospitals were mobilized, including military, police, and state-run hospitals, in addition to the existing 132 official COVID-19 treatment hospitals as of 19 March 2020 (UNOCHA, 2020). With the coronavirus situation worsening, the government task force also converted the Jakarta Kemayoran Athlete's Village into an emergency center to accommodate 24,000 patients (Cabinet Secretariat, 2020). In order to secure medical equipment for treatment, the Ministry of Trade, Industry, and Energy collaborated with 35 private companies to promote mass production (Irawati et al., 2020). In the face of a shortage of oxygen cylinders for patients, the ministry demanded that private producers convert industrial oxygen to 100 percent medical use.

Despite the efforts from the Indonesian government, public authorities, and private actors, Indonesia was not able to control the spread of the COVID-19 (see Figure 10.1). The number of positive COVID-19 cases per day increased since March 2020. As of October 2020, all provinces in Indonesia reported positive cases of COVID-19. The largest infection took place in DKI Jakarta and East Java. On 8 January 2021, the number of daily confirmed cases reached 10,617 (WHO, 2021). In response, the government implemented another social distancing policy, the so-called Enforcement of Restrictions on Community Activities (PPKM), focusing on the local level, and gradually lowered the number of confirmed cases starting from February 2021, but there were still about 5,000 confirmed cases (Cabinet Secretariat, 2021).

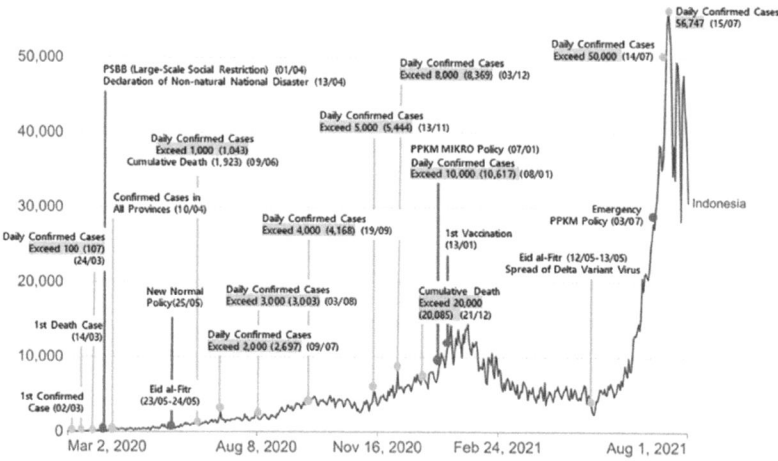

Source: CSSE (2021); Our World in Data (2021).

Figure 10.1   Number of infections in Indonesia in 2020–2021

On 13 January 2021, the vaccination process started in earnest in Indonesia. The first phase of COVID-19 vaccination targeted health workers in February, but was delayed. In May, the number of confirmed cases broke new records every day due to the aftermath of the holidays and the Delta Plus variant virus (Al Jazeera, 2021). On 15 July, the daily confirmed rate reached its peak at 56,757. According to data from the Ministry of Health, as of 29 July 2021, the cumulative number of confirmed cases had exceeded 3.2 million, and the cumulative number of deaths had exceeded 85,000 (WHO, 2021). Due to the number of cases rapidly increasing, Indonesia had the problem of insufficient hospital beds, oxygen, and medicine, as well as low vaccination rates. To make matters worse, as the government conducted emergency PPKM, which was a stricter regulation than before, demonstrations continued against the implementation of the regulation, while some companies in the private sector kept on working, violating government regulations.

The crisis management system and public healthcare in the Philippines

In the Philippines, the National Disaster Risk Reduction and Management Council (NDRRMC) is responsible for coordinating crisis management. It is situated under the Secretary of National Defense with other secretaries of departments participating in the Council, including the Secretaries of the Department of Interior and Local Government and Secretary of the Department of Social Welfare and Development. Since primary healthcare belongs to the local government units, and public healthcare is managed by the Department of Social Welfare and Development, the public healthcare system is a crucial part of crisis management. At the beginning of the COVID-19 crisis, President Duterte declared a State of Public Health Emergency across the Philippines and established the Inter-Agency Task Force for the Management of Infectious Disease (IATF), instead of using the NDRRMC. This was because the COVID-19 pandemic required health-specific responses rather than national disaster cases in which the Department of Defense often takes a spearhead role.

Cognition and coordination

The first detection of COVID-19 in the Philippines was a case of a foreign tourist on 30 January 2020. At the beginning of February 2020, the Philippine government began to implement measures to prevent the spread of COVID-19, such as travel restrictions for people from countries with high numbers of infections such as China and South Korea (Mendoza et al., 2020). These measures were initiated by the IATF. The infection of the local population was only detected on 9 March 2020. Like Indonesia, the first detection of COVID-19 in the Philippines was late compared to Thailand and Korea. It is unlikely that this first detection was in fact the first infection, and it was highly probable that COVID-19 had spread to local communities from mid-January to early March 2020 (De Salazar et al., 2020). Such late detection led to a failure in cognition of the emerging crisis, and also it made the scale of the epidemic much bigger and policy responses much more difficult than otherwise.

On the same day as the first detection of local population infection, President Duterte declared a State of Public Health Emergency across the entire archipelago of the Philippines, and Congress passed the Act of Bayanihan to Heal as One, which granted the President temporary power to exercise necessary measures. The IATF set up a National Action Plan against the COVID-19 pandemic, which outlined four phases of emergency actions (Mendoza et al., 2020: 327). The four phases were set according to calendar months rather than degree of transmission of infection, and Phase 1 was set from March to June 2020. Although the IATF designed the National Action Plan against COVID-19, it was not only the ministries and agencies of the central government but also the local government that implemented planned actions such as prevent–detect–isolate–treatment–reintegrate (Mendoza et al., 2020). However, such measures implemented by local government units turned out to be largely ineffective due to fiscal and technical limitations that local government units had in the Philippines.

In late March 2020, the IATF was extended to other departments of the government such as the Departments of Defense, Education, and Trade and Industry. Following government resolution 15 of 2020, the National Task Force was also established together with a number of technical advisory working groups, including those on Social Amelioration, Data Analytics, the Management of Repatriated Oversea Filipino Workers, and Anticipatory and Forward Planning.

As it became apparent that the COVID-19 pandemic posed a serious national health challenge, the Philippine government assembled the NDRRMC chaired by the Secretary of Defense with the Secretary of the Interior and Local Government as vice-chair. These responses showed that the Philippine government was very serious about the threat of COVID-19. While it was understandable that the Philippine government raised the levels of policy coordination as threats from the COVID-19 pandemic intensified, it was much more of a command-and-control style than coordination. President

Duterte, wearing a military uniform, issued orders to be followed not only by the uniformed service but also civilian personnel (Lasco, 2020). Some restrictions and regulations imposed on citizens were seen as rather draconian such as measures of complete community-wide lockdown. President Duterte exercised power like an authoritarian dictator during the massive lockdown period. Lasco criticizes Duterte's government policy responses to COVID-19 as medical populism (Lasco, 2020).

Capacity to implement public healthcare in the crisis

Despite the increasing number of national task forces and technical working groups, the actual responses were carried out by local government units. They had to carry out operational responses such as enforcing community health protocols, quarantine rules, and detections. More importantly, local government units were responsible for providing necessary healthcare services, especially emergency medical treatment, while the Department of Health was responsible for overall policy decisions and management of the health system.

Here, it is necessary to examine the public healthcare system in the Philippines in order to analyze its capacity to implement public healthcare policies against the COVID-19 pandemic. In terms of provision of public healthcare, local government units are major providers of primary and secondary healthcare through public health centers and hospitals. Local government units are autonomous in managing healthcare in their own locality and are regarded as independent entities under the guidance of the Department of Health. After decentralization reform based on the Local Government Code (RA 7160) in 1991, local government units have tried to improve healthcare facilities and the quality of medical services. Due to the financial and human resource constraints, there is significant variation in healthcare services among the local government units. Two-thirds of hospital beds are located on the islands of Luzon, which include the metropolitan area of the National Capital Region. There is similar disparity in healthcare workers among localities. Remote areas in geographical terms are worse off not only in economic terms but also in terms of healthcare. Over 90 percent of doctors and nearly 70 percent of nurses were stationed in metropolitan areas and large cities. The distribution of healthcare resources and facilities has been a difficult challenge for local government units as well as the national government. In terms of service quality, there was also a large variation between localities. Although the government tried to reduce such gaps, it did not produce positive results (Liwanag and Wyss, 2018).

Compared to public healthcare, private healthcare institutions, both for-profit and non-profit organizations, are much larger in terms of human resources and financial ability. Private healthcare organizations provide about 30 percent of healthcare and are required to follow Department of Health guidelines (Philstar Global, 2021). They are also required to submit necessary documents to the National Health Insurance Administration for certification. All hospital-level medical institutions should be certified by and registered with the Health Insurance Administration. Private-sector hospitals and clinics are focused on specialized medical services, while local government units are responsible for primary public healthcare.

The Philippines established the National Health Insurance System in 1995, which is based on the National Health Insurance Act. At the time, universal health coverage remained an aspiration rather than a reality. It is managed by the Philippine Health Insurance Corporation (PhilHealth), which is financed by health insurance contributions, expenditure from the central government, and local government units (Obermann et al., 2018). In 1999, the Philippine government under President Estrada initiated the Health Sector Reform Agenda, which aimed to strengthen healthcare capacities of local government units. In particular, it tried to facilitate collaboration between local government units in order to maximize healthcare resources and facilities managed by different local government units (Grundy et al., 2003). The Arroyo government (2001–2010) implemented the FOURmular One program in order to increase financial investment in the healthcare sector in the Philippines. It was the Aquino government (2010–2016) that set out to put universal healthcare coverage into practice (the *Kalusugan Pangkalahatan*). The government introduced the Sin Tax Law in 2013, which involved taxes on alcohol and cigarettes, and fiscal space created by the Sin Tax was utilized for universal healthcare coverage (Obermann et al., 2018). Together with government revenue, which has fluctuated over the years, the main PhilHealth budget comes from health insurance contributions (Oxford Business Group, 2021). It covers 92 percent of the population, and figures indicate that universal healthcare coverage had been achieved in the Philippines in 2019. Contributions are earnings-related so that high income earners pay higher contributions, but the ceiling of contributions to health insurance is set too low (the contribution rate is 3.5 percent of monthly basic income with a ceiling of contribution of PHP3,220, equivalent to USD64) (PhilHealth, 2020). Poor households in the bottom quintiles are subsidized by the government to participate in PhilHealth.

Nevertheless, it is another matter whether universal healthcare coverage can be translated into effective healthcare services for the whole population in times of healthcare need. First, healthcare access remains very unequal. Table 10.2

Table 10.2   Distribution of hospital beds by region in the Philippines

Region	Hospitals	Hospital beds	Beds/10,000 population
National Capital Region	163	29,723	23.1
Rest of Luzon	627	36,676	8.2
Visayas	167	15,196	7.8
Mindanao	267	20,093	8.3
Philippines	1224	101,688	10.1

Source: WHO (2018: 131).

shows the distribution of hospital beds by region. Hospitals and hospital beds are concentrated in the National Capital Region and the rest of Luzon. The number of beds per 10,000 people in the National Capital Region is about three times that in other regions.

Second, despite universal healthcare, Filipinos are required to spend a large amount of out-of-pocket money for healthcare. The proportion of out-of-pocket payments has been very high in the Philippines, at the level of more than 50 percent (and it was recorded at 55.8 percent in 2014), compared to other Southeast Asian countries such as Vietnam (46.95 percent) and Indonesia (35.3 percent) (WHO, 2018: 116). Because of such a high proportion of out-of-pocket payments, social protection for ordinary people remains very weak. Third, healthcare is focused on in-patient treatment rather than out-patient treatment and preventative public healthcare.

As discussed above, the Philippine government triggered the crisis management system on 8 March 2020 and imposed large-scale lockdown measures to prevent the spread of COVID-19. Despite such strong regulations, the number of COVID-19 infections increased every day. One of the underlying reasons was related to the very late detection of the first infection among the local population on 7 March 2020. The spread of the virus to the local community was probably unnoticed during the month of February 2020.

The direct reason was the inadequacy in diagnostic testing. In 2020, the Philippine government required local government units to establish at least one biosafety laboratory with real-time PCR testing capacity per region as well as dedicated laboratory and support staff. Nevertheless, it turned out that testing capacity fell far short of demand at the start of the pandemic.

The country had to transfer swab samples to laboratories in Australia and Japan for COVID-19 confirmation. It inevitably took a long time to confirm test results, and a large number of infection cases went undetected. As of September 2020, the total number of confirmed cases of COVID-19 was more than 276,000. This is equivalent to 2.6 percent of the total population and was the second-largest number of cases in Southeast Asia, next to only Indonesia. The Philippine government argued that the high number of infection cases was due to active testing, which averaged 30,000 per day. By September 2020, the number of people tested was more than 3,293,000, which was equivalent of 3 percent of the total population.

In terms of treatment of patients with COVID-19, the public healthcare system in the Philippines felt a severe strain under the initial surge of infections. In May 2020, the Philippine government issued an administrative order requiring public and private hospitals to make 30 percent of their beds available to COVID-19 patients. Later, the government reduced the number to 20 percent for private hospitals (Philstar Global, 2021). In September 2020, 1,857 intensive care unit beds were made available in secondary and tertiary hospitals (Mendoza et al., 2020: 352), along with 13,769 isolation beds for COVID-19 patients. In order to meet the surging need for treatment the government set up COVID-19 temporary treatment and monitoring facilities with a capacity of 3,568 beds, but more than 50 percent of them were quickly occupied by patients, and more than 70 percent of beds were occupied in some facilities. In terms of payment for the treatment of COVID-19 patients, the government announced first that PhilHealth would cover the whole cost of treatment, but patients had to pay the co-payments for their treatment according to the degree of illness. The daily number of people infected by COVID-19 increased, and the Philippine government and people struggled with the pandemic.

Figure 10.2 shows the trend of COVID-19 patient numbers in the Philippines, and despite policy efforts the COVID-19 pandemic was not under control. Due to new variants such as the Delta variant the prevention of viral transmission became an elusive task. Given such difficulties, the Philippine healthcare system did not have the necessary capacity to deal with a health crisis such as the COVID-19 pandemic.

Conclusion

This chapter examined the dynamics of the public healthcare systems with universal coverage in Indonesia and the Philippines in the context of the

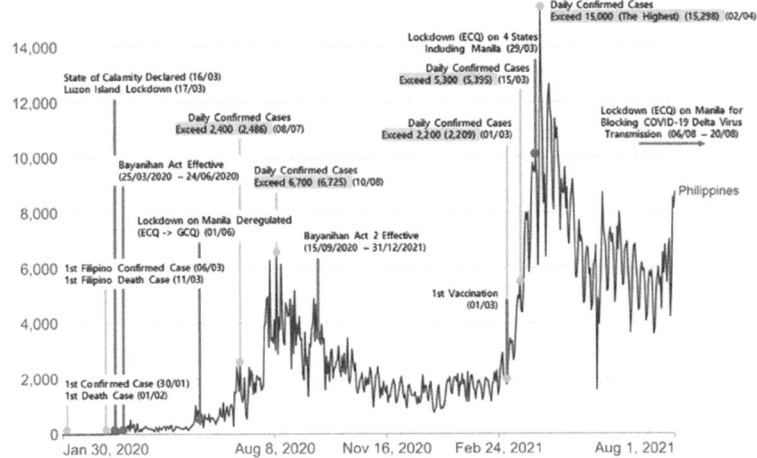

Source: CSSE (2021); Our World in Data (2021).

Figure 10.2   Number of COVID-19 patients in the Philippines

COVID-19 pandemic. In particular, it analyzed from a perspective of crisis management, because such analysis enabled us to see the public health systems in practice and assess them in a dynamic way. The analysis was focused on three components of crisis management systems for effective responses: cognition, coordination, and capacity.

Overall, the crisis management to contain COVID-19 in both Indonesia and the Philippines was very disappointing, if not a complete failure. There are several reasons for inadequate responses. Both governments were slow to recognize the speed of viral transmission and the scale of the COVID-19 pandemic at the early stage. In terms of coordination, the governments of Indonesia and the Philippines struggled to coordinate various government agencies and authorities including local government units. In the Philippines the restriction measures were very strict and somewhat draconian, and emergency power was concentrated in the central government. Concentration of power does not guarantee effective coordination. In contrast, Indonesia began with small-scale crisis management. After some confusion and mistakes, Indonesia extended the scale of its crisis management system as local transmission of COVID-19 turned out to be serious. Both countries heavily relied on restrictions and regulations, which imposed a burden on ordinary citizens to control the transmission of the virus.

This chapter also highlighted that the inadequate capacity of the public health-care systems in both countries were the main reason that the crisis caused by COVID-19 was not well managed: there was a lack of necessary facilities, resources, and skilled personnel. In particular, both countries were unable to implement testing as required by the WHO guidelines due to a lack of facilities and resources. In terms of treatment for COVID-19 patients, local hospitals struggled to cope with increased numbers of patients. Because of the decentral-ization reform undertaken since the 2010s together with universal healthcare coverage, local government authorities were responsible for primary and secondary healthcare provisions, and these hospitals were not equipped with facilities and resources to deal with the COVID-19 pandemic. These expe-riences show that the major reforms in public healthcare systems in the two countries, in particular universal health coverage, were not combined with necessary capacities to deal with a public healthcare crisis. Public healthcare systems did not have the necessary resources, facilities, and personnel to meet healthcare needs. There were also too many public authorities and agencies to collaborate due to the decentralization of public healthcare.

In the context of the development of welfare regimes in Southeast Asia, the achievement of universal health coverage in Indonesia and the Philippines has signaled an important shift since the welfare systems were characterized as fragmented and selective. Nevertheless, the institutionalization of universal health coverage does not guarantee effective delivery of healthcare to people in need, and the COVID-19 pandemic put the public healthcare systems in a severe test as to whether they could deliver healthcare in a universal manner in a time of crisis. Overall, there were critical weaknesses in terms of the capacity of the public healthcare systems in Indonesia and the Philippines. Universal coverage in public healthcare systems has not brought about real changes in their welfare regimes. In order to make universal health coverage more effective, it is critical to have necessary capacity in healthcare systems: medical resources, facilities, and skilled personnel should be strengthened and distributed in an even manner throughout the countries. Otherwise, universal healthcare coverage will ring very hollow in the future as well as at present.

Acknowledgements

This research is part of a larger study on 'Comparative Analysis of Policy Responses to COVID-19 in Asian Developing Countries: Focusing on Indonesia and the Philippines', Asia Development Institute, Seoul National University (0777-20210009).

References

Al Jazeera (2021) '"It will get very bad": Experts warn on Indonesia COVID surge', www .aljazeera.com/news/2021/6/18/indonesia-covid

Aspinall, E. (2014) 'Health care and democratization in Indonesia', *Democratization*, 21 (5), 803–823.

Bredenkamp, C., Evans, T., Lagrada, L., Langenbrunner, J., Nachuk, S. and Palu, T. (2015) 'Emerging challenges in implementing universal health coverage in Asia', *Social Science and Medicine*, 145, 243–248.

Cabinet Secretariat (2020) *COVID-19 Handling Strategy*, DKI Jakarta: Cabinet Secretariat, Indonesia.

Cabinet Secretariat (2021) 'Gov't to extend PPKM implementation in 7 provinces', https://setkab.go.id/en/govt-to-extend-ppkm-implementation-in-7-provinces/

CNBC Indonesia (2020) 'Ojol rules bring passengers confused and harvest criticism', www.cnbcindonesia.com/news/20200412174515-4-151342/aturan-ojol-bawa -penumpang-bikin-bingung-dan-panen-kritik

Comfort, L.K. (1988) *Managing Disaster: Strategies and Policy Perspectives*, Durham, NC: Duke University Press.

Comfort, L.K. (2007) 'Crisis management in hindsight: Cognition, communication, coordination, and control', *Public Administration Review*, 67 (s1), 189–197.

Comfort, L.K. and Haase, T. (2006) 'Communication, coherence, and collective action: The impact of Hurricane Katrina on communications infrastructure', *Public Works Management and Policy*, 10 (4), 328–343.

CSSE (2021) 'COVID-19 dashboard', https://coronavirus.jhu.edu/map.html

De Salazar, P.M., Niehus, R., Taylor, A., Buckee, C. and Lipsitch, M. (2020) 'Using predicted imports of 2019-nCoV cases to determine locations that may not be identifying all imported cases', *medRxiv*, 2020.02.04.20020495.

Fajarta, C.R. (2020) 'Create standard aviation health protocol, Ministry of Transportation collaborates with academic world', www .beritasatu .com/ ekonomi/ 678381/ buat -standard-protokol-kesehatan-penerbangan-kemhub-gandeng-dunia-akademik

Farazmand, A. (2007) 'Learning from the Katrina crisis: A global and international perspective with implications for future crisis management', *Public Administration Review*, 67 (s1), 149–159.

Global Health Security Index (2019) '2019 GHS Index country profile for Indonesia'.

Grundy, J., Healy, V., Gorgolon, L. and Sandig, E. (2003) 'Overview of devolution of health services in the Philippines', *Rural and Remote Health*, 3, 1–10.

Ha, Y.E. (2020) 'A study of the social security developments in Indonesia: Implications for a policy paradigm change', MA thesis, Seoul National University.

Holmemo, C., Acosta, P., George, T., Palacios, R., Pinxten, J., Sen, S. and Tiwari, S. (2020) *Investing in People: Social Protection for Indonesia's 2045 Vision*, Jakarta: World Bank.

Hood, C. (2006) 'The tools of government in information age', in M. Moran, M. Rein and R.E. Goodin (eds), *The Oxford Handbook of Public Policy*, Oxford: Oxford University Press, 469–481.

ILO and JAMSOSTEK (2008) *Social Security in Indonesia: Advancing the Development Agenda*, Geneva and Jakarta: ILO and JAMSOSTEK, 85.

Irawati, E., Fitria, R. and Adwiyah, R. (2020) 'COVID-19 in Indonesia', in S. Kim (ed.), *COVID-19 Response Systems and International Cooperation: Focusing on*

Korea, Thailand, Indonesia and the Philippines, Seoul: Korea Insitute of Public Administration, 203–296.

Jakarta Post (2021) 'Robust personal data protection critical in COVID-19 fight', 20 July.

Kwon, H.J. (2005) 'Transforming the developmental welfare state in East Asia', *Development and Change*, 36 (3), 477–497.

Kwon, H.J. and Kim, W. (2015) 'The evolution of cash transfers in Indonesia: Policy transfer and national adaptation', *Asia and the Pacific Policy Studies*, 2 (2), 425–440.

Lasco, G. (2020) 'Medical populism and the COVID-19 pandemic', *Global Public Health*, 15 (10), 1417–1429.

Liwanag, H. and Wyss, K. (2018) 'What conditions enable decentralization to improve the health system? Qualitative analysis of perspectives on decision space after 25 years of devolution in the Philippines', *PLoS ONE*, 13 (11), e0206809.

Massola, J. (2020) 'Why are there no cases of coronavirus in Indonesia?', *Sydney Morning Herald*, www .smh .com .au/ world/ asia/ why -are -there -are -no -cases -of -coronavirus-in-indonesia-20200213-p540o1.html

Mendoza, M., Caliso, R., Boy-Navarro, D. and Lumntao, G. (2020) 'COVID-19 in the Philippines', in S. Kim (ed.), *COVID-19 Response Systems and International Cooperation: Focusing on Korea, Thailand, Indonesia and the Philippines*, Seoul: Korea Institute of Public Administration, 297–408.

Obermann, K., Jowett, M. and Kwon, S. (2018) 'The role of national health insurance for achieving UHC in the Philippines: A mixed methods analysis', *Global Health Action*, 11, 1–16.

OCHA (2018) *Indonesia: Disaster Management Reference Handbook*, https://reliefweb .int/ report/ indonesia/ indonesia -disaster -management -reference -handbook -june -2018

Our World in Data (2021) 'Coronavirus (COVID-19) cases', https:// ourworldindata .org/covid-cases

Oxford Business Group (2021) 'A look at the Philippines health sector during and after COVID-19', 20 July.

Peters, B.G. (2013) 'Toward policy coordination: Alternatives to hierarchy', *Policy and Politics*, 41 (4), 569–584.

PhilHealth (2020) *Premium Contribution Schedule in the National Health Insurance Program and All Others Concerned*, Pangasinan: PhilHealth, 5.

Philstar Global (2021) 'Private hospitals' COVID-19 bed capacity allocation cut to 20%', www.philstar.com/headlines/2020/07/23/2029977/private-hospitals-covid-19 -bed-capacity-allocation-cut-20

Pressman, J.L. and Wildavsky, A. (1984) *Implementation*, Berkeley, CA: University of California Press.

Ramesh, M. (2004) *Social Policy in East and South East Asia: Education, Health, Housing and Income Maintenance*, London: Routledge.

Rosser, A. (2012) 'Realising free health care for the poor in Indonesia: The politics of illegal fees', *Journal of Contemporary Asia*, 42 (2), 255–275.

Suryahadi, A., Febriany, V. and Yumna, A. (2014) 'Expanding social security in Indonesia: The processes and challenges', UNRISD working paper 2014-14.

Ting, M.M. (2003) 'A strategic theory of bureaucratic redundancy', *American Journal of Political Science*, 47 (2), 274–292.

UNOCHA (2020) 'Countries: COVID-19 country dashboard', https://roap.data.unocha .org/country-page.html

Waugh, W.L. (1994) 'Regionalizing emergency management: Counties as state and local government', *Public Administration Review*, 54 (3), 253–258.

Waugh, W.L. (2018) 'Leadership and emergency management', in A. Farazmand (ed.), *Global Encyclopedia of Public Administration, Public Policy, and Governance*, Cham: Springer International Publishing, 3601–3606.

WHO (2010) *The World Health Report: Health Systems Financing: The Path to Universal Coverage*, Geneva: World Health Organization.

WHO (2018) 'The Philippines health system review', *Health Systems in Transition*, 8.

WHO (2021) 'WHO corona virus dash board', https://covid19.who.int/

Wisnu, D. (2007) 'Governing social security: Economic crisis and reform in Indonesia, the Philippines and Singapore', PhD thesis, Ohio State University.

Index